Kant's Humorous Writings

ALSO AVAILABLE FROM BLOOMSBURY

Antigone, Slavoj Žižek
Venice Saved, Simone Weil
Alienation and Freedom, Frantz Fanon

Kant's Humorous Writings

An Illustrated Guide

Robert R. Clewis

BLOOMSBURY ACADEMIC
LONDON • NEW YORK • OXFORD • NEW DELHI • SYDNEY

BLOOMSBURY ACADEMIC
Bloomsbury Publishing Plc
50 Bedford Square, London, WC1B 3DP, UK
1385 Broadway, New York, NY 10018, USA

BLOOMSBURY, BLOOMSBURY ACADEMIC and the Diana logo are trademarks of Bloomsbury Publishing Plc

First published in Great Britain 2021

Copyright © Robert R. Clewis, 2021

Robert R. Clewis has asserted his right under the Copyright, Designs and Patents Act, 1988, to be identified as Author of this work.

For legal purposes the Acknowledgements on p. xxi constitute an extension of this copyright page.

Cover design by Charlotte Daniels
Cover image: Nicholas Ilic

All rights reserved. No part of this publication may be reproduced or transmitted in any form or by any means, electronic or mechanical, including photocopying, recording, or any information storage or retrieval system, without prior permission in writing from the publishers.

Bloomsbury Publishing Plc does not have any control over, or responsibility for, any third-party websites referred to or in this book. All internet addresses given in this book were correct at the time of going to press. The author and publisher regret any inconvenience caused if addresses have changed or sites have ceased to exist, but can accept no responsibility for any such changes.

A catalogue record for this book is available from the British Library.

A catalog record for this book is available from the Library of Congress.

ISBN: HB: 978-1-3501-1278-0
PB: 978-1-3501-1279-7
ePDF: 978-1-3501-1277-3
eBook: 978-1-3501-1280-3

Typeset by RefineCatch Limited, Bungay, Suffolk

To find out more about our authors and books visit www.bloomsbury.com and sign up for our newsletters.

To **Richard Martin Clewis, Jr.** and **Chester McConnell Thompson**

Contents

List of Figures   ix
Preface   x
Foreword by Noël Carroll   xvi
Acknowledgments   xxi
Note on Text and Sources   xxii
Abbreviations   xxiii

Part One Kant's Theory of Humor   1

1 The Secret Soul of Kant's Joke   3

2 Three Questions about Laughter at Humor   44

3 Kant and the Ethics of Humor   66

Part Two Jokes   103

Incongruity Jokes   105
    1. The Merchant's Wig   107
    2. Happy Funeral Mourners   109
    3. Swift Wit   111
    4. Dying of Good Health   113
    5. £200   115
    6. Of Juice and Justice   117
    7. King Louis' Gate   121

8. Thinking with One's Body   123
9. The Happy Cuckold   125
10. Full of Bull   127
11. With Friends Like These   131

Ethnic and Sexist Jokes and Quips   133

12. Foam in a Bottle   135
13. German Fools   137
14. The Bearded Woman   139
15. Samuel Johnson's Wife   143

Jokes with a Point   145

16. Abelard's Flying Ox   147
17. Which Way the Wind Blows   149
18. Philosophy Detox   151
19. The Voltaire Bros   153
20. The Life You Save May Be Your Own   155

Part Three Sayings with a Message   157

21. Ragout, with Wit on the Side   159
22. Hooped Skirts and Pruned Trees   161
23. Heidegger as a Woman   163
24. There Are No Ugly Noses   165
25. A Whale Barrel   167
26. To Each his Own   169
27. Pyrrho's Pig: That's What I'm Talking about   171
28. Hobson's Choice   175
29. Sex and Death   177
30. An Honest Man Is Hard to Find   179

Appendix: Chapter Summaries   181
Notes   183
Bibliography   232
Index   245

Figures

1 The Aesthetic Arts   26

30 Illustrations, all by Nicholas Ilic

Preface

When I first read one of Kant's major works, *Critique of the Power of Judgment* (1790), I was surprised to find that it included his reflections on laughter and humor. What was humor doing here? This was after all a work of Critical philosophy offered by the transcendental philosopher. I was even more surprised to find no fewer than three jokes in that *Critique*. Later, when studying Kant's university lectures on anthropology,[1] I realized that there were many more references to jest and joking. Humor seemed to be important to Kant. Could he have had a sense of humor?

This is certainly not the traditional view of Kant. Nietzsche, a lover of laughter, writes: "I should actually risk an order of rank among philosophers depending on the rank of their laughter—all the way up to those capable of *golden* laughter."[2] Surely Nietzsche would place Kant near the bottom of his list. "Even in good old Kant," he claims, there is a "certain odor of blood and torture." Kant's "categorical imperative smells of cruelty."[3] Nietzsche could have hardly imagined a jovial Kant.

People who knew Kant personally had a different impression. Johann Gottfried Herder—an important poet-theologian-critic in his own right—attended Kant's courses between 1762 and 1764. Decades after his student years, Herder penned this: "I have had the good fortune of knowing a philosopher who was my teacher. . . . Talk rich in ideas issued from his lips, joking, humor and wit were at his disposal, and his teaching lectures were the most amusing entertainment. . . . This man whom I name . . . is Immanuel Kant."[4] About three years before his death—even after a bitter dispute with Kant—Herder admitted that he "marveled over the teacher's dialectical wit . . . and his eloquence."[5] Johann Bernoulli (1744–1807) wrote something similar about Kant too. "This famous philosopher is so lively and charming in conversation and so refined in manners, that one would not easily guess the probing depth of his intellect. His eyes and his facial features instantly reveal great wit. . . . Various stories and anecdotes from all kinds of people and countries spice up his lectures, and make them all the more instructive and popular."[6] Kant's wit apparently extended beyond the classroom. He was known to be an enlivening conversationalist and raconteur, and he was reported to have been a valued guest at soirées and dinner parties.[7]

Nevertheless, stereotypes of boring old Kant linger on. The philosopher is known for taking daily walks, rigid maxims and rule-following, being "Prussian" and a hypochondriac to boot. This caricature does not go away easily. A prominent scholar of humor once stated that Kant, despite his remarks on laughter, "seems pretty dour."[8] More recently, a popular book on humor claimed: "The great German philosopher pioneered the incongruity theory of humor, but instead of telling jokes to his friends he preferred to share with them his bodily complaints, which included headaches and chronic constipation."[9] True, Kant did openly talk about his health concerns, but he also loved to tell jokes to friends and students.

Is it possible to imagine a laughing Kant? This collection of Kant's humorous writings might help.

This book is not a joke. Unlike *The Sexual Life of Immanuel Kant*, it is not a literary hoax.[10] According to Norman Malcolm, the Austrian philosopher Ludwig Wittgenstein once said that a "serious and good philosophical work could be written that would consist entirely of jokes (without being facetious)."[11] But the jokes and anecdotes collected in Parts Two and Three amount to no such philosophical work. Kant's stories often have an intellectual or moral point, but this does not mean that they make for a serious philosophical oeuvre.

Kant's jokes and anecdotes—here translated rather freely so as to improve the set-up and conclusion—are classified under several headings. Based on their content, Kant's *jokes* can be classified into the following kinds: jokes of general incongruity (including wordplay), ethnic/sexist jokes or quips, and jokes with a message.[12] In addition, he tells vivid *anecdotes* to make a philosophical point. While not exactly jokes, these anecdotes display a kind of wit. (This taxonomy is rough-and-ready and should not be insisted on too much, but I hope it is helpful.)

This book is an "illustrated guide," and in several senses. First, before I present Kant's jokes and anecdotes in Parts Two and Three, I discuss Kant's theory of humor in three chapters in Part One. These chapters are meant to guide the reader to a better appreciation of Kant's jokes. Second, Kant used many of the jokes and quips to clarify and explain his thoughts about humor. His witticisms help us understand—they illustrate—what Kant found humorous. They reveal what sources and writers helped him formulate his ideas about humor. In addition, I have provided commentary on each of the jokes or anecdotes. Finally, in a third sense of "illustrate," this book contains pictorial illustrations. The stories and jokes are accompanied by these images in order to breathe life into the material. To be sure, other books by or about Kant contain pictures or illustrations. Kant's third *Critique*, the *Critique of the Power of Judgment*, has been published with illustrations and photos.[13] There is even a noteworthy graphic novel about Kant and his relationship with his servant Lampe.[14] Unlike these, however, the present guide takes thirty jokes or anecdotes told by Kant, and pairs each of them with a specially commissioned illustration wonderfully carried out by Nicholas Ilic.

This collection of "humorous writings" reveals what Kant considered amusing. To come up with his ideas about humor, he needed some material, and it is interesting to see whom he admired and quoted. We see that Kant took from Samuel Butler, Jonathan Swift, Laurence Sterne, Edward Young, and Voltaire. The sayings and jokes become interesting not merely on their own, but as they contribute to a deeper understanding of Kant as a writer and philosopher of humor and as a lecturer at the Albertina University of Königsberg.[15] (After the Second World War, his city Königsberg, East Prussia, became Kaliningrad, Russia. Today it's a Russian exclave between Poland and Lithuania, not far from the Baltic Sea.)

This book is not intended to be an introduction to Kant's philosophy in general—even if I am happy if the reader learns something about freedom, society, or dinner parties. It is not a textbook on the philosophy of humor, and it doesn't tell you how to be funny. Nor is it a comprehensive survey of theories of humor. I mention some theories, old and new, but my discussion does not amount to a comprehensive survey. Rather, this guide is intended for both students and scholars of Kant, eighteenth-century aesthetics, and/or the philosophy of humor, and, more broadly, the interested public. I realize that this is quite an array of audiences, but I hope each reader will find something of interest.

And while I quote extensively from writings and lectures deriving from various periods and recognize that Kant's ideas developed over decades, I should point out that my main concern is not to examine for its own sake the *development* of Kant's ideas about humor, wit, or prudence in joking.[16]

Long ago, *Lives of Eminent Philosophers* by Diogenes Laertius reported anecdotes and sayings associated with various philosophers of western antiquity and also summarized their teachings and biographies.[17] Although I can imagine a decent compilation of wisecracks from several philosophers from the history of western philosophy — e.g., Schopenhauer's jokes, Nietzsche's witticisms (how about Hegel?) — this book focuses on Kant.[18] Parts Two and Three bring together only Kant's jokes and anecdotes. In this respect it is similar to recent collections of humorous sayings by individuals such as the nineteenth-century Danish writer, Søren Kierkegaard, and the contemporary Slovenian author, Slavoj Žižek.[19] But, as should be clear by now, this book does more than just throw together some of Kant's sayings or excerpts, without providing either commentary on those excerpts or extensive chapters on the underlying philosophy of humor.[20] Finally, I should clarify that my aim is not to make Kant look ridiculous, which is the effect (intentional or not) of Eugen Skasa-Weiss's rather bizarre book, *Kant's Grosse Völkerschau*, which contains twenty-one illustrations and excerpts of Kant's views on geography and related matters.[21] Not all of Kant's jokes are amusing, but my aim is not to lampoon him.

Before concluding, I should offer a quick summary of Kant's thoughts on humor, especially if the reader wishes to skip my three chapters and jump straight to the jokes.[22] We find something comically amusing, Kant thinks, when we enjoy an incongruity or mismatch between the way things are and the way we expect them to be. His view is not that we are comically amused by *all* incongruities. Instead, the claim is that when we are comically amused, it is (typically) because we are responding to some perceived incongruity that is enjoyed in itself, that is, without any discomfort or real concern about what we hear or perceive. (In other words, we take the joke as just a joke.) Furthermore, Kant recognizes both the physical and the intellectual elements in humor. Kant thinks that laughter at a joke releases the tension that was built up as we created expectations about what we were hearing or reading. This physical release is agreeable. Laughing at humor involves a workout for both body and mind. When the mind "playfully" considers the content of the joke or gag (the humor), the body responds with the pleasurable physical release. Since his account of humor refers to a "play with thoughts" and a play with "aesthetic ideas," humor could potentially have an important role in his philosophical system, perhaps even more than he realized. Finally, there is an important ethical and socio-anthropological dimension to humor. Humor can bring us together, and Kant thinks that there is a place for wholesome, amicable teasing. Joshing and ribbing need not always be cruel or inappropriate. It is okay sometimes to laugh at others—a comic or even our friends—especially if they are in a position to tease us back. Humor offers an important way for us to have fun together, to laugh *with* (not just at) others, and to exercise our abilities for socialization.

Finally, I offer two caveats. First, the humorous "writings" do not all come from Kant's published works. Kant shared a version of some of them in his university lectures, and these jokes are found in student notes that were jotted down by transcribers rather than in his published writings. Second, not everything here is humorous. (I was once tempted to call the book *Kant's Humorous Writings: I Wish They Existed*.) Readers may find the jokes to be boring or even offensive. No promise is being made that the reader will find the jokes amusing. (Then again, not everything collected here was intended by Kant to be sidesplitting. Part Three collects stories and anecdotes.) Kant cribbed some of the jokes off other authors, even if he did offer his take on them. So, you are not expected to guffaw, chuckle, or even smile at each joke. (I'm setting the bar as low as possible here.) Kant is no Mark Twain or Oscar Wilde. Having said that, we can hope to have some fun as we examine Kant's views of humor.

There is some truth to the widely repeated saying, "Analyzing a joke is like dissecting a frog: no one is really interested, and the frog dies from it."[23] (Incidentally, the eighteenth-century philosopher Francis Hutcheson made this point long ago.[24]) To put it another way: "Comedy dies quickly under a microscope."[25] Thus, if you're convinced that the best way to kill a joke is to explain it, you might skip my chapters and the commentaries accompanying each joke/story, and just read Kant's quips. On the other hand, if you are interested in understanding Kant's views, you can read Noël Carroll's Foreword and my chapters.

I'll leave you with this. If and when a joke or aphorism fails to be amusing, keep in mind this maxim from Baruch Spinoza:

Do not complain, do not rejoice, try to understand.[26]

Foreword
by Noël Carroll

Kant's Humorous Writings: An Illustrated Guide by Robert Clewis might just as readily be entitled *Everything You Ever Wanted to Know about Kant and Humor*. The comprehensive coverage includes a catalogue of all of the jokes Kant mentions plus witticisms accompanied by insightful commentaries and delightful pictorial illustrations, all informed by the author's impressive grasp of historical and contemporary comic philosophizing, along with a sustained section on Kant's theory of humor which canvasses Kant's categorization of humor as an agreeable rather than a fine art in terms of wit, naiveté, and caprice and which also addresses Kant's position on the ethics of humor and much more, such as the place of comic amusement in Kant's systematic account of judgment. Whew! Who could ask for anything more?

One topic that I find especially intriguing in the author's discussion of Kant's theory of humor is his suggestion that Kant's view has elements of all three of the major comic theories: the release theory, the incongruity theory, and the superiority theory.

Of course, the association of Kant with the release (or relief) theory of comic amusement comes as no surprise. Kant is generally regarded as a proponent of that approach. His most frequently quoted observation on the matter of humor is probably: "Laughter is an affect that arises if a tense expectation is transformed into nothing."[1]

Here it is helpful to think of a joke as a prime example of what Kant is getting at. Whether a puzzle, like a moron joke, or a narrative, a joke comes to a conclusion—what is typically called a punch line. This punch line is the answer to a question—an explicit question in a puzzle joke or a typically implicit, closure-inducing one in a narrative-joke.

The fact that the listener is confronted with a question produces an expectation—an expectation of an answer to the question—which is tense insofar as its obscurity is a cognitive challenge. But then when the punch line arrives that tension disappears—turns into nothing—because it is silly. The theory is a release theory because the tension of being put-on-the-spot to come up with the answer putatively proposed by the set-up of the joke dissipates—that is, is released.

Whereas the most famous release theory of humor—that of Sigmund Freud[2]—spoke of the release of pent-up, gradually amassing over time, repressed psychic energies of various sorts, Kant's theory situates the release locally in the moment of the comic exchange. The set-up of the joke puts the listener in a state of mental preparedness by means of a question, whether explicit or implicit, to which she anticipates and may even feel beholden to answer. Then the tension of that already cognitive high-alert heightens momentarily as the curiously absurd punch line arrives, only to almost immediately evaporate upon the recognition that it possesses no real cognitive challenge or threat (that it's nothing, in yet another sense).

The psychic tension in Kant's theory of humor is self-generated—that is, generated within the comic context in contrast to the psychic tensions presupposed in the Freudian system which gather in the course of everyday life, mounting as if in an enclosed pipeline, only to be hydraulically evacuated by the punch line of the joke. Kant's theory differs from psychoanalytic theories by locating the tension in the question as produced within the joke situation itself, rather than identifying the joke situation as an instrument for releasing tension originating elsewhere.

The jest itself creates the tension—the pressure to find a cognitive resolution—but the absurdity of the proposed solution, the punch line, loosens or lightens the pressure, resulting in a feeling of relief or what we may call levity. The presentation of the joke perturbs the listener's equilibrium which is restored when she recognizes the perturbation is inconsequential nonsense—a scenario Kant himself suggests by means of his outmoded biological speculations.

However, Kant's departure from the approach of the psychoanalytic release theories is not a deficiency. Quite the contrary, it saves him from the standard objections to psychoanalytic theories, like Freud's, namely that the repressed psychic energies and hydraulic mechanisms they posit are scientifically suspect. Thus, Kant's proposal is all the more plausible insofar as, once it is divorced from its own speculative biology, all that it requires is recognition of the common phenomenological state of being taken aback by a frustrated expectation—a deviation from one's sense of how things are or should be—only to discover the deviation is not a challenge but rather calls for no response, allowing the listener to, cognitively speaking, stand down.

Thus, it has always been unobjectionable to classify Kant as a release (or relief) theorist of humor. But it should be clear from the preceding account that he is also an incongruity theorist. Why? Because the object of comic amusement—that which dissolves the tension into "nothing"—is a perceived incongruity.

Admittedly, Kant does not use the notion of incongruity. He speaks of "something absurd." But clearly Kant has in mind what contemporary comic theorists have in mind by "incongruity." Kant says: "Whatever is to arouse lively, convulsive laughter must contain something absurd (hence something that the understanding cannot like for its own sake)."[3]

Here, by "absurd" Kant means nonsense. "How do crazy people find their way through the forest? They take the psychopath." The pun here is a non sequitur; it has nothing to do with ascertaining one's direction. It is an incongruous answer to the question—a deviation from what the answer should be—because it is strictly speaking irrelevant.[4] So, after mobilizing one's mental resources to discover an answer to the question, the recognition of the absurdity of the answer turns off the cognitive alarms and restores, as Kant would say, our psychic equilibrium. The perception of incongruity triggers the release—the phenomenological experience of lightening, or lightness or levity otherwise known as the feeling of comic amusement.

So, Kant unquestionably combines elements of the release theories and incongruity theories in his account of comic amusement. But what of the oldest of comic theories—the superiority theory? Professor Clewis cites examples of superiority jokes in Kant and he argues that Kant accepts superiority humor within certain moral constraints.

Of course, it should come as no surprise that Kant can accommodate superiority humor within his framework insofar as the incongruity theory, which he appears to endorse, can encompass a great many superiority jokes. What is the infamous moron's behavior if it is not a deviation of the ways in which people do and/or should behave?

Nevertheless, I am tempted to speculate that an even closer association of Kant and the superiority theory of humor can be conjectured. To see what I have in mind, recall the structure of jokes.

Jokes involve a set-up—either a question or a narrative—and a punch line. The punch line itself, although it may initially *appear* to answer an implicit or explicit question set forth by the set-up turns out, upon almost immediate reflection, to be nonsense. The initial appearance of sense (of an intelligible answer) tricks the listener who momentarily gives way to the perception of harmless incongruity and, hence, mirth. In this way, the listener of the joke becomes a butt of the joke. Verbal jokes, in a manner of speaking, are a subspecies of practical jokes. We audience members come out of the jest transaction with "egg on our faces." The teller of the joke has tricked us. Perhaps this is the grain of truth in the superiority theory of humor.

But even if this is the grain of truth in the superiority theory of comic amusement, is there any reason to suppose that Kant accepts it? Kant says, "It is noteworthy that in all such cases the joke must contain something that can deceive us for a moment. That is why, when the illusion vanishes, transformed into nothing, the mind looks at the illusion once more in order to give it another try and so by rapid succession of tension and relaxation is bounced back and made to sway."[5]

In this passage, I think that Kant is describing phenomenologically the experience of the aftermath of the delivery of the punch line of the joke, as we mull over the play between the feigned appearance of sense (Kant's "illusion") and our recognition of nonsense. With a good joke especially, we take pleasure in rehearsing that trajectory, running it over in our mind, savoring it, so to speak, for its wit. But in addition to this phenomenological observation, Kant also notices a structural requirement of the joke transaction, namely that it involve deception, at least for a moment. That is, the joke must trick us, albeit trick us in way that becomes transparent almost (but not quite) immediately.

Moreover, Kant's awareness of the role of deception aligns him with what I have called the grain of truth in the superiority theory of comic amusement, at least with respect to jokes. The superiority in these cases is not cruel or contemptuous, but amicable. In most situations, it is a matter of just kidding. Indeed, the joke-exchange is rarely vicious, since it is typically introduced with the admission that it is a joke ("Have you heard the one about *x*?").

Yet, in momentarily reducing our listeners to the butts of our nonsense we are nevertheless assuming a superior role. After all, we have gulled them into taking nonsense seriously, if only for a split second. And this would seem to fit with Kant's account insofar as he maintains that deception is a necessary ingredient in a joke.

This is not a criticism of Prof. Clewis's view. It is an attempt to push a bit further on his claim that Kant's theory of humor is compatible with elements of all the traditional philosophical approaches to humor. His account has inspired me to additional speculation as I am sure many others will be inspired in so many different directions by Prof. Clewis's seminal and fecund exploration of the field.

Acknowledgments

My sincere thanks to Noël Carroll for writing the Foreword, at once generous and astute.

I am very grateful to Nicholas Ilic for skillfully bringing to life the jokes and anecdotes through his illustrations.

For sharing their comments and suggestions or in various ways shaping this book, I thank Uygar Abaci, Peter Adamson, Stefano Bacin, Steven Benko, Kimberly Blessing, Henny Blomme, Jane Boddy, Javier Burdman, John Carvalho, Cecilia Durojaye, Janis Chakars, Loraine Clewis, Rick Clewis, Michael Clinton, Karin de Boer, Wiebke Deimling, Don Duclow, Richard Eldridge, Susan Feagin, Serena Feloj, Gabriele Gava, Paul Guyer, Espen Hammer, Jamie Hebbeler, Thomas Hilgers, Gerfried Horst, Abigail Kennedy, David Kim, Robert Louden, Matthew McAndrew, Michael McBeath, Lisa McGarry, Patrick McGrain, Bennett McNulty, Colin McQuillan, Steffen Mehlich, Mikhail Melnik, Patrick Messina, Jennifer Mensch, Stefano Micali, Marianne Motherby, Michael Olson, Lara Ostaric, Amanda Pirrone, Otheus, Gisela Schlüter, Elisa Schwab, Susan Shell, Andrew Valins, Bob Valins, Bart Vandenabeele, Achim Vesper, Mary van Brunt, Jennifer Wade, Joseph Westfall, Marcus Willaschek, Reed Winegar, Mary Wiseman, and David Wood. I also thank the anonymous reviewers as well as Lisa Goodrum, Lucy Russell, and Liza Thompson at Bloomsbury.

This project was in part made possible by the support of the Max Planck Institute for Empirical Aesthetics in Frankfurt am Main. I am grateful to my host, Winfried Menninghaus, and the group of scholars and researchers in Frankfurt with whom I discussed this project. I would likewise like to thank the members of the audiences at the Goethe University of Frankfurt (the philosophy department as well as the research cluster *Normative Orders*) and at the Institute of Philosophy at KU Leuven, as well as the Berlin-based society, Friends of Kant and Königsberg.

Responsibility for the finished work is my own. If there are errors, I am to blame. (But the jokes are Kant's.)

Note on Text and Sources

Page references to Kant's writings are to the Academy Edition or *Akademie-Ausgabe* (AA) of Kant's writings, *Kant's gesammelte Schriften* (*Kant's Collected Writings*), cited by volume and, separated by a colon, followed by the page number. References to Kant's *Critique of Pure Reason* follow the convention of citing the A edition (1781) followed by the B edition (1787).

The English translations of jokes and anecdotes in Parts Two and Three were undertaken by me (Clewis). The translations tend to be on the freer side and were carried out while bearing in mind readability and—ideally—humor. To improve Kant's set-up and delivery, I took some liberties with punctuation, italics, pronouns, verb tense, sentence length and order, word order, listing first and last names, and the like. When helpful, I used more accessible language and aimed for clearer sentences.[1]

If you are looking for translations that are more literal than the translations of jokes and anecdotes found here, you can consult the volumes in the series, *The Cambridge Edition of the Works of Immanuel Kant* (Cambridge: Cambridge University Press, 1992–).

In commentary and the chapters, Kant's text that was not translated by me was taken from the volumes in *The Cambridge Edition*, with occasional modifications. These volumes include the volume and page number of *Kant's gesammelte Schriften*, so it is easy to make cross-references between the English and German editions.

In preparing the commentaries on the jokes and anecdotes in Parts Two and Three, the footnotes in both *The Cambridge Edition* and the Academy Edition provided useful information concerning the sources and background of Kant's writings.

Abbreviations

AA	Akademie-Ausgabe (*Kant's gesammelte Schriften*)
Anthropology	*Anthropology from a Pragmatic Point of View*
CPJ	*Critique of the Power of Judgment*
Observations	*Observations on the Feeling of the Beautiful and Sublime*
"Remarks"	"Remarks" in the *Observations on the Feeling of the Beautiful and Sublime*

PART ONE

Kant's Theory of Humor

Chapter 1
The Secret Soul of Kant's Joke

Any useful guide to Kant's humorous writings should, I would imagine, characterize Kant's theory of humor. In the present case, in order to understand the jokes and anecdotes gathered in Parts Two and Three of this book, it seems prudent to address the topic at the outset. So, with a nod to Nietzsche let us ask: What is the secret soul of Kant's joke?[1]

As I noted in the Preface, Kant is not generally known for his wit or sense of humor. He *is* renowned for his philosophical writings, in particular the three *Critiques*: *Critique of Pure Reason* (1781/87), the *Critique of Practical Reason* (1788), and the *Critique of the Power of Judgment* (1790). These works have been profoundly influential in aesthetic theory, the philosophy of nature, ethics, epistemology, and metaphysics. About half a century after these works appeared, the German poet Heinrich Heine claimed that Kant initiated an intellectual revolution in Germany that was analogous to the political Revolution in France.[2] At the same time, Heine asserted that Kant "lived a mechanically ordered, almost abstract bachelor existence."[3] Due to such characterizations, Kant is usually considered to be boring, overly punctual, and methodical—allegedly fitting for a philosopher whose ethical theory was based on maxims and principles. These views persist even today. One author recently claimed that Kant "was not a particularly funny guy."[4]

But the image of Kant as dour and humorless is misleading. When Kant was a younger man, decades before he became famous for his three *Critiques*, he was known in social circles as the gallant or elegant *Magister* (maestro).[5] Kant's presence is reported to have animated balls and dinner parties, and he would tell stories and jokes to his classes at the University of Königsberg.

Kant admired humorists from Rabelais and Cervantes to Butler, Swift, and Voltaire.[6] He esteemed Laurence Sterne's *Tristram Shandy*, Edward Young's *The Universal Passion* and *Night-Thoughts*, Henry Fielding's *Tom Jones*, and Pope's *Peri Bathous, or the Art of Sinking in Poetry*. He also appreciated Hogarth's satirical engravings.[7]

Kant's views on humor were also probably informed by his personal friends and acquaintances. Kant spent time with intellectuals in Königsberg such as Johann Georg Hamann (1730–88), a literary critic and Christian theologian who wrote in a witty, idiosyncratic style, and Theodore Hippel (1741–96), who authored plays such as *The Man of the Clock*. (This play was reportedly based on Kant's close friend Joseph Green, who pedantically lived by the clock,[8] a stereotype later associated with Kant, rather unfortunately.) It is likely that Hamann, Hippel, and Kant and other friends had lively conversations about jest and comedy and that these exchanges shaped the formation of Kant's ideas about humor.

As he developed this account, Kant engaged with the dominant theories of humor of his day. In order to understand Kant's theory, we need to discuss three main theories of humor: superiority theory, incongruity theory, and relief theory.

In this introductory chapter, I explain these theories of humor, providing some historical context (section 1). I then characterize Kant's account as a combination of these three theories, with elements of Kant's own contribution, mental play theory (section 2). I describe his views of the "agreeable arts" and the three "arts" of laughter (wit, naiveté, caprice) (section 3). Finally, I bring together and give shape to Kant's somewhat scattered reflections on theatrical comedy (section 4).

1. Superiority, Incongruity, and Release Theories

Before proceeding, however, we need to clarify some terms. These are not intended to be once-and-for-all definitions, but merely guides for the subsequent discussion.[9]

Humor is what comic amusement is directed at, in other words, the object of our attention when we find something comically amusing or feel comic merriment.[10] Of course, not every instance of humor is thought to be funny or results in laughter.[11] Even if not all instances of humor elicit comic amusement, comic amusement is paradigmatically a response to an instance of humor. It admits of degrees, ranging from mild amusement to the paroxysms of mirth.[12] Humor can be *found*, as when one stumbles on a funny mistake or ambiguity in a dinner menu or newspaper headline. Or, it can be invented and crafted, as jokes are.

Wit can be thought of as a person's capacity to create or generate humor, that is, to elicit comic amusement. (Kant sometimes uses the term in a broader sense than this, however, as I will explain in this chapter.)

Laughter is a bodily response involving the expulsion of air from the lungs, accompanying sounds, characteristic facial distortions, and even the shaking of the whole body.[13] Laughter can be caused by a number of things besides comic amusement, including tickling, intoxication, a sense of inclusion or exclusion, stress, embarrassment, and nervousness. There are cultural differences in how and why we laugh, and there are many different kinds of laughter.

Jokes can be told for all sorts of reasons—to break the ice, to relate bad news, to impress your peers, and so on. Yet a joke's ability to serve in these functions or capacities is, in my view, parasitic upon the joke's realizing its quintessential and primary aim, which is to elicit comic amusement.

There are many kinds of jokes. Some are formula jokes ("An elephant walks into a bar . . .") and some are fiction or story jokes, that is, have a narrative structure.[14] Most narrative jokes take longer to tell than quips, wisecracks, witticisms, witty sayings, and bon mots.[15] The line between jokes and quips (etc.) is fuzzy; indeed, such lack of clear demarcation can be seen in the excerpts collected in this book. Some of Kant's "jokes" are so short that they are perhaps best seen as only quips or bon mots. Quips, wisecracks, witticisms, witty sayings, and bon mots are closely related, often overlapping, forms of expression that are usually but not always intended to elicit comic amusement. In addition to jokes, quips, wisecracks (etc.), there are many other kinds of humor, most of which are not addressed in this guide to Kant on humor for the simple reason that Kant did not discuss them: situational humor, prop comedy, parody, impersonation, and so on.[16]

Finally, it should be noted that not all forms of amusement are comic. Soap operas and crossword puzzles amuse those who watch or complete them, but they are not comic.[17]

Humor has several functions: to create social bonds, to ostracize, to let off steam, to deal with life's trials, just to name a few. We joke about the problems and absurdities of life. If we face a difficult situation, we might use humor to cope or rebel.[18] Humans can make jest even in the darkest of times. In the opening scene of the autobiographical novel, *The Sunflower* (1969), God's absence becomes the object of a joke (amusing or not).[19]

Jokes come in many forms. Some jokes contain a visual element and work better when written.

Question: What do you call bears with no ears?
Answer: B

Meanwhile, other jokes work better when heard rather than read.

Question: According to Freud, what comes between fear and sex?
Answer: *Fünf.*[20]

The Freud joke requires more background knowledge to get it than the previous joke does; you need to know how to count in German. Likewise, the following joke requires awareness of the British and Australian use of the term "bloody" as a mild expletive and intensifier.

What do you call a Kant scholar who gets a paper cut?
Another bloody Kantian.[21]

Again, not all jokes, even amusing ones, issue in laughter.

Sometimes we just lose it and find everything funny and cannot stop laughing. That kind of laughter has little claim on anyone else. In this book, I (following Kant) instead focus on laughter that can in principle be shared. As the author of a 1937 essay on Kant and humor put it, "we are not concerned with such phenomena as the laughter resulting from tickling, the giggling of school-girls, or the cachinnations of the jackass, whether quadruped or biped."[22]

With these brief (and surely unsatisfactory) clarifications in place, we can now turn to the first of the theories of humor to be discussed.

Superiority theory   We feel comic amusement because we feel we are better than the object of our laughter or ridicule.

In a narrative joke, something is said, something is done, and, occasionally, someone or something is the butt of the story. Superiority theory (sometimes called "disparagement" theory) picks up on this. According to the theory, we are amused by people's failings or their inabilities to realize their aims. Or, we laugh at our former selves (as if, for a moment, the present self were laughing at the past self). Instead of laughing *with*, the theory emphasizes, we laugh at. For instance, viewers of Larry Charles's 2006 film *Borat: Cultural Learnings of America for Make Benefit Glorious Nation of Kazakhstan* might find themselves laughing at some of the Americans that Borat is revealing to be ignorant, sexist, or racist.[23] According to the theory, a joke establishes a hierarchy in which the teller of the joke is elevated above the butt of the joke or object of the laughter.[24] Test it out with this joke:

> A Texan and a graduate from a "top-ranked" graduate program meet.
>
> **Texan** (with accent):   Hi, where're you from?
>
> **Graduate**:   I come from a place where we do not end sentences with prepositions.
>
> **Texan** (slowly):   Okay, where are you from, Asshole?[25]

There is a sense of justice underlying the joke: we feel good that the Texan one-upped the graduate. We feel a sense of superiority over the graduate.

Superiority theory has its roots going back to ancient Greece. Until it was widely criticized in the eighteenth century, it was the dominant way of thinking about comedy, humor, and laughter. In *Philebus*, Plato discusses malicious (*phthonic*) laughter, a kind of rejoicing at the misfortunes of others, even our friends.[26] In *Rhetoric*, Aristotle offers reflections that are consonant with superiority theory. He characterizes wit as a kind of *insolence*, even if an educated or well-bred kind.[27] Likewise, in the *Poetics* he maintains that comedy is an imitation (*mimesis*) of characters of an "inferior" or "lower" type.[28] Aristotle had planned to explain this idea in the second book of the *Poetics*, but since it has been lost, we don't know for sure what he had in mind.

The theory was also prevalent during the early modern period. In *Human Nature*, English philosopher Thomas Hobbes denied that laughter was response to jest alone. Rather,

> the passion of laughter is nothing else but sudden glory arising from a sudden conception of some eminency in ourselves, by comparison with the infirmity of others, or with our own formerly: for men laugh at the follies of themselves past.[29]

In *The Passions of the Soul*, Descartes analyzed laughter as an expression of scorn, a mixture of joy and mild hatred. Although he provided physiological explanations of laughter (similar to release theory, as we will see) and held that laughter involves surprise or wonder at the novel or unexpected (like incongruity theory), Descartes tended to focus on laughter's function in *ridicule*.[30] In the eighteenth century, superiority theory slowly faded in popularity as writers such as Francis Hutcheson mounted compelling criticisms against it. But even in the nineteenth and twentieth centuries, it still had its defenders. Nietzsche is an example, though, as usual, his account is multi-faceted and complex. Although Nietzsche pays attention to the physiological and physical aspects of humor in that he discusses bodily or "intestinal" laughter,[31] he at the same time endorses a kind of superiority theory. "Laughter means: being *schadenfroh*, but with a good conscience."[32] Laughter is a mocking response to the solemn and serious. "Supposing that gods, too, philosophize . . . I should not doubt that they also know how to laugh the while in a superhuman and new way—and at the expense of all serious things." In short, "gods enjoy mockery."[33]

More recently (1982), Roger Scruton made some claims that some readers have interpreted as affirming a version of superiority theory.[34] But Scruton does not accept the label. He denies that he is committed to the traditional (Hobbesian) superiority theory, on the grounds that "to lower the object" of one's amusement is "not necessarily to raise the subject."[35] Instead, he says, laughter at humor can lower both subject and object together, creating a kind of "kinship" with the person or thing at which one laughs.[36]

Even if there is insufficient space for a complete evaluation of each of the theories, we can still sneak in a brief assessment. One of the strengths of superiority theory is that it accounts for various forms of ridicule—scoffing, mocking, joshing, roasting, pranking, telling "yo Mamma" jokes, as well as comebacks, put-downs, comedic insults, and ripostes. It seems to account for why a pair of guys laughed when I once tripped on a sidewalk crack.

But it has some drawbacks. First, a sense of superiority is neither sufficient nor necessary for comic amusement. We can feel scorn or feel contempt without feeling comic amusement. It is easy to think of examples of this; I leave it to the reader to come up with their own. And a feeling of superiority is not necessary either: we can feel comic amusement without feeling we are better than or above anyone. We laugh at the comedian with bananas on his head and in his pockets, or at a good pun, without feeling superiority to them or to the pun. If anything, we *admire* the wit of the person who made a clever pun. (And as for my tripping on the crack, perhaps that was an instance of the unexpected, or of a human acting in an atypical, even mechanical, fashion? In fact, that's precisely how Kant, like Henri Bergson after him, understands such cases.[37]) This leads to the second theory.

Incongruity theory We are amused by humor because we enjoy a mismatch between what we perceive and our ordinary expectations, norms, or concepts.

"Incongruity" here refers to a violation of mental patterns, categories, or norms, or our expectations about them. Incongruities can be generated by mistakes or errors of all kinds, from category mistakes to spelling errors. The theory turns on the fact that we have expectations about the structure of reality and the patterns of language. When patterns, properties, categories or the like are transgressed, we can enjoy such transgressions in themselves.

Jay Leno, a former host of the American late night TV show *The Tonight Show*, used to go through headlines, menus, and classified ads containing real but unintentional mistakes. They were funny because of some incongruity, usually created by a semantic ambiguity. These instances of humor count as *found* (or "inadvertent") humor, not intentional joking. Here are two examples of this kind: "Farmer Bill Dies in House," and "Drunk Gets Nine Months in Violin Case."[38] Here's my own example. There is a photography studio in Sulzano, Italy—not far from Milan—owned by a family named Gotti, a perfectly normal Italian last name. The shop sign shows the name of the shop, *Foto Ottica Gotti*. But it displays the ordinary words *foto ottica gotti* written together and lower case: it says *fotootticagotti* for all to see. It thus unwittingly pairs an (almost identically spelled) version of the explicative, "screwed over" (*fottuti*, which could be translated with the F-word) with the word "diarrheas" (*cagotti*). Read this way, it becomes a rather bizarre shop sign. Finally, one sometimes used to see on public garbage cans, "REFUSE TO BE PUT IN THIS BASKET."[39] On account of the two-fold meaning of "refuse," the official notice, like the Italian shop sign, momentarily loses its authority.

According to the theory, when finding something comically amusing, it is necessary to contemplate, or attend to, an incongruity in fun. The mismatch should not be a source of distress or concern to us. If I'm the owner of the Gotti shop, say signora Gotti herself, I may just become upset when I realize my unintentional mistake, not find it amusing. The confrontation with the incongruous, if we are to find it funny, cannot at the same time be the cause of serious or painful concerns.[40] In situations in which we are distressed by the event/story, or confused, we will not find the incongruity amusing or enjoy it in itself, but will simply become upset or frustrated. To express a similar point about distance, Bergson claimed that in responding to the comic we have a "momentary anesthesia of the heart."[41]

To be most charitable to incongruity theory, it seems best to interpret the perceived incongruity as a *necessary*, but not sufficient, condition of comic amusement.[42] On this reading, to achieve the result (comic amusement), some kind of incongruity must be perceived. But the perception of an incongruity is not sufficient to produce the amusement. If a tree suddenly falls through the roof, we are likely to be shocked and upset, not comically amused.

Although Kant is sometimes incorrectly identified as the "pioneer" of the incongruity theory,[43] he was definitely not the first to propose the theory in the modern period. There were important precedents in the British and German traditions. For instance, in *Reflections on Laughter* (1725) Hutcheson presented a version of incongruity theory while criticizing (Hobbesian) superiority theory. It is possible (but not certain) that Hutcheson's incongruity theory influenced Kant's thoughts about humor, for Kant was familiar with some of his other moral and aesthetic writings.[44]

In 1764 James Beattie wrote, "Laughter seems to arise from the view of things incongruous united in the same assemblage."[45] A few years earlier, Alexander Gerard had claimed that "wit, humour, and ridicule are skillful imitations of odd and incongruous originals." The object of the sense for the ludicrous, for Gerard, is "in general incongruity, or a surprising and uncommon mixture of relation and contrariety in things."[46] Here it seems best to read incongruity theory as claiming that *surprise* may, but need not, arise when we perceive an incongruity. In other words, the point is not that we are startled or surprised by the incongruity—we may have heard the joke or seen the comedy before. Rather, the point is that the enjoyment of the incongruity is the cause of our amused response.

In nearly all discussions of incongruity theory, Moses Mendelssohn is ignored, yet his *Rhapsody* (1761) contains reflections on laughter that should be classified as an incongruity theory—before Kant. According to Mendelssohn, laughter is founded "on a contrast between a perfection and an imperfection."[47] Mendelssohn's thought was formed in part by the Wolffian intellectual tradition, and for Christian Wolff, too, laughter was a response to an absurdity.[48] In addition to Mendelssohn, some of Kant's near contemporaries supported the idea that contrast or incongruity underlies humor. Lessing's *Hamburg Dramaturgy* and Goethe's *Elective Affinities* described the laughable or ridiculous (*lächerlich*) as originating in a contrast.[49]

After Kant, Schopenhauer defined the ludicrous in general as an incongruity between a perception and the concept under which we subsume it.[50] Søren Kierkegaard, too, with his theory of irony and contradiction, developed a version of incongruity theory.[51] And there are many, many other proponents of the theory, from William Hazlitt in the early nineteenth century to contemporary social scientists who adopt a version of incongruity theory as they conduct empirical research.

Indeed, the theory, in some form or other, is the dominant paradigm in empirical humor research. According to one article, "The incongruity theory is widely accepted today and is taking on a dominant role in humor research."[52] Most psycholinguistic theories agree that the resolution of "puzzling incongruities" between levels of meaning is pivotal for humor processing.[53]

Incongruity theory is also well received in the humanities. According to literary critic Terry Eagleton, the theory "remains the most plausible account of why we laugh."[54] Philosopher Noël Carroll views the theory as a useful heuristic that, while slippery, is not vacuous. He thinks it should be provisionally embraced as the best way to advance the discussion, even if the concept of incongruity can and should be made more precise.[55]

Still, there are at least two potential problems with the theory. First, it may be possible to come up with examples of humor that do not in any conspicuous sense involve incongruities.[56] If that turns out to be the case, we might simply say that *most*, not all, comic amusement consists in the enjoyment of a mismatch or incongruity. Cicero seems to have made precisely this move, even if he was thinking of jokes in particular rather than of comic amusement in general.[57] Second, one might worry that the concept of incongruity is too broad or elastic, that it can be made to cover so many cases as to become no longer useful or meaningful.[58] This seems to be a legitimate worry, and the concept should be made more precise if possible.

The third and final theory that I wish to introduce is *release theory*, sometimes called relief theory.

Release theory We laugh at humor in order to release pent-up psychological energy or forces.

Aristotle, equipped with his notion of catharsis in response to tragedy, may have described a parallel release in response to comedy, but since his full treatment on comedy did not survive, we cannot know for sure. Adopting the science of his day, Shaftesbury (1709) suggested that the comical releases constrained "animal spirits."

> The natural free spirits of ingenious men, if imprisoned and controlled, will find out other ways of motion to relieve themselves in their constraint; and whether it be in burlesque, mimicry, or buffoonery, they will be glad at any rate to vent themselves, and be revenged upon their constrainers.[59]

Since Kant was familiar with and mentions Shaftesbury in some of his writings,[60] it is possible that he was also acquainted with Shaftesbury's theory of wit and humor.

Relief theory became more popular after Kant, however, emerging prominently in the work of Herbert Spencer. In a short essay on the physiology of laughter, the Victorian philosopher claimed that when we perceive an unexpected "incongruity," excess "nervous energy" builds up. The excess energy must discharge itself, and there "results an efflux through the motor nerves to various classes of the muscles, producing the half convulsive actions we term laughter."[61] Spencer's theory is couched in language that may sound foreign to us today. For Spencer, the physiological outbreak of laughter is equivalent to the nerve "force" that is liberated by the stopping, or slowing down, of a thought process that was previously animated. The process is governed by the law of the conservation of energy.[62]

The most celebrated version of relief theory comes from a 1905 work by the founder of psychoanalysis, Sigmund Freud. According to *Jokes and Their Relation to the Unconscious*, laughter provides pleasure because it economizes on the energy that would ordinarily be used to contain or repress a disturbing emotional activity. A joke transforms a serious conflict into a trivial one, thereby releasing emotional tension.[63] Freud held that the energy relieved in laughter is agreeable and satisfying because it discharges energy that would ordinarily be used to contain or repress the psychic activity or emotions involving sexual desire or hostility.[64] Here is how Freud put it in *The Interpretation of Dreams*:

> Evidence, finally, of the increase in activity which becomes necessary when these primary modes of functioning are inhibited is to be found in the fact that we produce a comic effect, that is, a surplus of energy which has to be discharged in laughter, if we allow these modes of thinking to force their way through into consciousness.[65]

Even Nietzsche offers elements of a relief theory. "Everything *sudden* pleases if it does no *harm*; hence wit. . . . For a tension is thus released."[66] The American pragmatist John Dewey, too, espoused a kind of relief theory.[67]

On the positive side, release theory seems to account for nervous laughter and laughing in response to awkward moments. The approach, especially if updated in light of more recent science, might also appeal to people looking for a mechanistic or physiological account of laughter.[68]

But, in general, few scholars or researchers defend it today. First, it seems too susceptible to counterexamples: relief seems neither sufficient nor necessary for comic amusement. It is easy to see that it is not sufficient: the relief of nervous energy when we realize that our loved one has—narrowly—avoided being hit by a bus, rarely produces a response of either comic amusement or laughter. Relief is not necessary for comic amusement either, for we might simply crack a smile at a word play or pun, without laughing and without releasing nervous energy. This gets at a more general worry: the theory seems to be more about laughter than comic amusement. While the theory might explain the physiological mechanism underlying laughter, it does not explain why we laugh in response to comic amusement, which is presumably what a theory of humor is (or should be) after.[69] Finally, it seems too wedded to scientifically questionable ideas such as nervous energy and the release of forces. The nature of the energy used to repress emotions remains unclear.

These, then, are three of the principal theories of humor. There are other ones—inferiority theory, dispositional theory, and more—and even these three theories sometimes contain their own variations and subsets.[70] But this should suffice as an overview and historical background.[71]

Although I've presented these theorists in a straightforward way, in reality many of them combined parts of different theories. Schopenhauer added elements of superiority theory to his incongruity theory. Spencer and Freud both added aspects of incongruity theory to their release theories.[72] Kant, I want to show in the next section, also unites distinct theoretical elements.

2. Kant's Theory of Humor: A Combination

Although there is clear textual support for calling Kant an incongruity theorist, his account also contains parts of a release theory and even some elements of superiority theory. Moreover, since the third *Critique* refers to a "mere play of representations" and a "play of thoughts" (*Gedankenspiel*), I would like to suggest that Kant offers his own unique version of a "play" theory, where the mind playfully reflects on an incongruity.[73] I will explain this below.

The **incongruity** aspects of Kant's theory are easy to identify. For instance, he claims that comic laughter is an "affect" resulting from the "sudden transformation of a heightened expectation into nothing." We laugh "because our expectation was heightened and suddenly disappeared into nothing."[74] What causes this change of expectation is precisely the incongruity in the humor, something "nonsensical."

> In everything that is to provoke a lively, uproarious laughter, there must be something nonsensical (in which, therefore, the understanding in itself can take no satisfaction). **Laughter is an affect resulting from the sudden transformation of a heightened expectation into nothing.** This very transformation, which is certainly nothing enjoyable for the understanding, is nevertheless indirectly enjoyable and, for a moment, very lively. The cause must thus consist in the influence of the representation on the body and its reciprocal effect on the mind; certainly not insofar as the representation is objectively an object of gratification (for how can a disappointed expectation be gratifying?), but rather solely through the fact that as a mere play of representations it produces an equilibrium of the vital forces in the body.[75]

Thus, laughter in response to comic jest is pleasant ("indirectly enjoyable"). It is disinterested (it is not "objectively an object of gratification").[76] And it involves a disappearance of an expectation[77] into nothing, as we perceive the humorous incongruity. (As examples of how this works, consider Kant's jokes Happy Funeral Mourners and Foam in a Bottle, Nos. 2 and 12.) The notion of an expectation disappearing into nothing is not immediately clear, so here is a way to understand it. Once we get into the mindset that we are listening to a joke, we listen to it with certain expectations that are based on how we think the world is or should be.[78] (No. 2: most folks are happy when they are paid. No. 12: most people know about beer foam and bottles.) We begin processing a joke with our normal default assumptions intact. That mode of interpretation is disrupted and then overthrown by the punch line, calling forth a more compelling, though fantastical, interpretation.[79] (The funeral mourners are paid to look sad, not happy; the Indian guest seems to think that the beer froth has to be forced *into* a bottle.) In this way, when the story or narrative describes an incongruity relative to that framework, our expectation is not fulfilled. This lack of fulfillment counts, loosely speaking, as a kind of "nothing." In a more basic sense, it is of course something.[80] The mind is playing with some content after all.

There are other texts where Kant claims that amused laughter is a response to a perceived mismatch or leap (*Absprung*). We read in one of the anthropology lectures (1775/76):

> All laughing matter is always a leap. First my nerves are led to a certain prospect; the mind now tries to follow after a rational thing. If now a leap from the prospect suddenly follows, and before the mind realizes what is happening, it is on the other side, then it bursts into laughter.[81]

This is fully consonant with the account in the *Critique* of 1790:

> It is noteworthy that in all such cases the joke must always contain something that can deceive for a moment: hence, when the illusion disappears into nothing, the mind looks back again in order to try it once more, and thus is hurried this way and that by rapidly succeeding increases and decreases of tension and set into oscillation: which, because that which as it were struck the string bounces back suddenly (not through a gradual slackening), is bound to cause a movement of the mind and an internal bodily movement in harmony with it, which continues involuntarily, and produces weariness, but at the same time also cheerfulness (the effects of a motion that is beneficial to health).[82]

This brings us to the **relief** component: both passages describe a kind of release in the response to humor. In listening to a joke or viewing a comic situation, a sort of tension builds, and upon hearing the punch line or resolution, we let it out. We "burst" into laughter. When we hear the punch line in a joke, there is a sudden relaxation or letting-out that starts an oscillating movement in the diaphragm and intestines.

> The play begins with thoughts which . . . insofar as they are to be expressed sensibly, also occupy the body; and since the understanding, in this presentation in which it does not find what was expected, suddenly relaxes, one feels the effect of this relaxation in the body through the oscillation of the organs.[83]

The reaction to the humorous, the third *Critique* states, "produces the successive movement of the mind in two opposite directions, which at the same time gives the body a healthy shake."[84] The movement in the mind ("the play begins with thoughts") is expressed through the body, namely, as oscillations of the viscera. The bodily vibration harmoniously corresponds to the mind's bouncing back and forth, its play of thoughts as it goes from initial expectation, to illusion or misconception, to a possible momentary explanation, and back again to the illusion. Now we can see how Kant could write that it is both an "expectation" and an "illusion" that disappears into nothing—an otherwise puzzling claim. These descriptions refer to distinct moments in the process of mental play. Our ordinary expectations disappear when the illusion is generated. When the illusion disappears, there is an apparent resolution, and on and on. The visceral oscillation corresponds to this mental play.

Kant provided a mechanistic explanation of laughter relatively early on. In marginal notes from around 1765, we read, "What is mechanical in laughter is the vibration of the diaphragm and the lungs as well as the contorted facial expression, for the mouth is pulled from another place."[85] The note continues:

> It seems that the cause of laughter consists in the vibrating of quickly pinched nerves, which propagates through the entire system; other pleasures come from uniform movements of the nerve fluid. Thus, if I hear something that has the appearance of a prudent and purposive relation, but which entirely cancels itself out [*aufhebt*] in trifles, then the nerve that is bent towards one side is, as it were, repelled and quivers.[86]

This cancellation of an expectation regarding what initially seems "prudent and purposive" sounds strikingly close to the expectation's "disappearance into nothing" described in the third *Critique*.

The release element can also be seen in a key passage from the *Anthropology* (1798), published toward the end of Kant's life. It is from a section revealingly called "On the affects by which nature promotes health mechanically."

> Laughter's jerky (nearly convulsive) exhaling of air . . . strengthens the feeling of vital force through the wholesome exercise of the

diaphragm. It may be a hired jester (harlequin) who makes us laugh or a sly wit belonging to our circle of friends, a "wag" who seems to have no mischief in mind and does not join in the laughter, but with seeming simplicity suddenly releases a tense anticipation (like a taut string). The resulting laughter is always a shaking of the muscles involved in digestion, which promotes it far better than the physician's wisdom would do. Even a great absurdity [*Albernheit*] of a mistaken power of judgment [*einer fehlgreifenden Urtheilskraft*] can produce exactly the same effect.[87]

Several commentators have noticed the release element in Kant's theory, from Carroll to a contributor to a recent handbook on linguistics and humor.[88] Critchley comments on Kant's theory thus: "In hearing the punch-line, the tension disappears and we experience comic relief."[89] Eagleton also points out that Kant "combines the release theory with the concept of incongruity." Eagleton adds, "Physical and psychological motions are directly coupled, in a way that links the incongruity theory to the release thesis."[90] Marmysz likewise recognizes that Kant identifies an explosive release in laughter. "It feels good to laugh, claims Kant, because in laughter we experience a sort of catharsis that purges the painful unease of our encounter with incongruity."[91] Finally, Swift claims that, like Nietzsche after him, Kant recognizes a kind of physiological laughter that is "capable of providing a release of tension in the body."[92]

The release elements in Kant's account should not be taken to mean that his account focuses exclusively on humor's bodily effects, however. Some scholars emphasize more the body, some more the mind, but in fact Kant holds that there are both bodily and intellectual elements in our response to humor. The mind is the "source" of laughter, and the effect (convulsion) is in the body. We read in an anthropology lecture: "Laughter is aroused in the mind by thoughts, by the livening up of life, or also mechanically. Laughter comes from the mind and convulses the body."[93] The bodily reaction results from the intellectual play in response to an incongruous content, including a great "absurdity" (*Albernheit*) that, while arising from our mistaken judgment, at the same time does not trouble or puzzle us. The mind perceives the incongruity, enjoys it as such or by itself, and we laugh heartily in response to it. Thus, the mind makes the diaphragm shake.[94] According to the third *Critique*, in laughter one "can get at the body even through the soul," and we can use the soul as a doctor for the body.[95]

Let us now turn to Kant's rather complex relation to **superiority theory**. Kant seems to have been familiar with superiority theory, and in fact in the third *Critique* he appears to reject it. On the joke, Foam in a Bottle (No. 12), he comments, "We do not laugh . . . because we find ourselves cleverer than this unknowing person [*Unwissenden*]."[96] Thus, it is easy to miss the fact that Kant finds a place for harmless ridicule and teasing. In fact, it is even in his definition of a joke (*Scherz*): "Joke: a teasing that leads to laughter."[97] Let us look at additional textual evidence for attributing a superiority element to Kant's account of humor.

Kant distinguishes between *wholesome* and *malicious* laughter, that is, the phthonic kind examined by Plato. Kant does this in several passages, but the basic point is the same. An ethics lecture reads: "A habitual scoffer shows that he has little respect for others, and does not judge things at their true value."[98] In *Anthropology*, he distinguishes "good-natured laughing" from "malicious laughing combined with bitterness."[99] In a longer passage from that work, Kant even *recommends* poking fun at someone as long as one does not actually offend the person.

> A good-natured and at the same time cultivated way of stimulating a social gathering is to have someone in it as the butt of our wit (to pull his leg) without being caustic (ridicule [*Spott*] without being offensive), provided that he is prepared to reply in kind with his own wit, thus bringing a cheerful laughter into the group.[100]

Note that the person is allowed to provide their own comebacks and ripostes. Moreover, the ridicule should never reach the point of gloating (*Schadenfreude*).

> But if this happens at the expense of a simpleton [*Einfaltspinsels*] whom one tosses to another like a ball, then this laughter as a kind of gloating [*Lachen als schadenfroh*] is unrefined at the very least.[101]

Here the blame lies firmly on the side of the gloaters. But it can also happen that one lets oneself be used as an object of mockery.

> If it happens to a suck-up who, just to be center stage, abandons himself to the mischievous game or allows himself to be made a fool of, then it is a proof of bad taste as well as obtuse moral feeling on the part of those who can burst out laughing about this.[102]

Here laughter shows not only a moral deficiency on the part of those who laugh, it also shows a lack of self-respect on the part of the freeloader or suck-up (*Schmarotzer*) who lets himself be used in that way. This is important, since it implies that in laughing matters, Kant thinks that we have duties both to others and *ourselves*, a point we will return to in chapter three. In fact, in another passage from *Anthropology*, Kant comes close to saying just that.

> If we call someone who harms [*schadet*] himself (temporarily or permanently) a buffoon [*Narren*] ... then we must think of his behavior as an offense to humanity in general and consequently as an offense committed against someone else.[103]

We also find the distinction between innocent and harmful ridicule in Kant's practical philosophy. In *The Doctrine of Virtue* part of *The Metaphysics of Morals*, Kant distinguishes between "wanton faultfinding and mockery" and light banter. The former is "the propensity to expose others to laughter" in order to make their faults "the immediate object of one's amusement." This malicious kind is not permissible since it does not respect the other person.

> Holding up to ridicule a person's real faults, or supposed faults as if they were real, in order to deprive him of the respect he deserves, . . . a mania for *caustic* mockery . . ., has something of fiendish joy in it. And this makes it an even more serious violation of one's duty of respect for other human beings.[104]

Caustic mockery fails to contain an accurate estimate of value, especially moral value. Light banter, on the other hand, is acceptable, as when we make fun of our friend's quirks or peculiarities (when they depart from the "rule of fashion").[105] Yet again there are limits. If someone writes a mocking, negative review of your book, you should be careful about how much wit you use should you choose to respond to them. When reason necessarily takes a moral interest, then no matter how much ridicule the adversary may have uttered and thereby left himself open to laughter, it is more befitting the dignity of the object and respect for humanity either to put up no defense against the attack or to conduct it with dignity and seriousness.[106]

Sometimes, it is better just to refrain from unleashing a biting riposte.[107]

Kant comes close to endorsing a kind of superiority-based laughter when he reviews and judges the rival systems that compete with his philosophy. He thinks that because his philosophical system is superior, he will have the last laugh.

But if it is true, as Shaftesbury asserts, that a doctrine's ability to withstand being laughed at [*Belachen*] is not a ludicrous touchstone of its truth (especially in the case of a practical doctrine), then the Critical philosophy's turn must finally come to laugh last and so laugh best when it sees the systems of those who have talked big for such a long time collapse like houses of cards one after another and their adherents scatter, a fate they cannot avoid.[108]

Although this laughter might seem to border on being malicious and spiteful, perhaps Kant thinks that such superiority-based laughter is defensible because it is grounded in the truth of his (practical) teachings and the superiority of his philosophical system. Laughter could, in that case, arguably be justified and remain within the moral limits he places on laughter.

In short, it is tempting to assert that Kant rejects all elements of superiority in laughter, but as the foregoing passages show, the matter is not so simple. Within moral limits, there is a place for harmless ridicule and wholesome teasing. Likewise, Kant thinks that literary satire has important socio-cultural functions, and that in many instances these uses redeem it. Of course, Kant thinks we should avoid outright contempt for others. "Good-natured laughter" is ethically permissible, but real "contempt" for others or humanity is impermissible.[109] Kant takes a middle position, allowing a great deal of room for satirical jest but ultimately setting ethical bounds on ridicule.

The fourth element in Kant's account of humor to be discussed is **free play**. Kant states that laughter in response to a humorous joke is a kind of "play of sensations." But it is a play of sensations that is generated by a "play of thoughts" or "a mere play of representations."[110] Although he never really explains how a play of thoughts can produce a play of sensations, presumably the latter occurs because in laughter at humor the movements of the body reflect those of the mind as it judges the content of the joke or object of humor. In other words, the oscillation in laughter at humor harmoniously corresponds to the mind's bouncing back and forth, as we have seen.

The remarks by one commentator can help us understand the mental free play in Kant's account. Laughter occurs, Canivet says, "after the violation of the norm of the harmonious proportion between the imagination and understanding."[111] Since the mind cannot simultaneously retain both this violation and its resolution, it moves to-and-fro. This results in a mental play. As noted, there is an initial expectation, followed by a misconception or illusion. We seek an explanation for the latter, settle on a potential candidate, then return to the misconception to test its fit, contemplate the illusion again, and so on. (The process is similar to trying to keep in mind both sides of a logical paradox such as a liar's paradox or Russell's Paradox.) Recall Kant's passage: "For a while we toss back and forth like a ball our own misconception about an object that is otherwise indifferent to us, or rather our own idea that we've been chasing, while we were merely trying to grasp and hold it firm."[112] In the response to the humorous joke, the imagination and understanding are set into a harmonious play with the misconception or illusion and its resolution (or, as Kant also puts it, with aesthetic ideas, to be explained below).

There is some controversy regarding the timing of the mental play. Does the play come before the bodily response, after, or are they perhaps simultaneous? To me, it is quite clear that a previously cited passage implies that the mental play is prior ("the play begins with thoughts").[113] Yet one commentator, Stephen Nichols, does not opt for this reading. He instead holds that in Kant's account, the bodily response—laughter—comes first. "The body, rather than the mind, engages the process much earlier than he recognizes. . . . The mental process that Kant sees as the cause of laughter . . . is really a subsequent analysis devised by the mind to explain what the body has already expressed risibly."[114] But as far as Kant interpretation goes, this can't be right, since Kant denies that, in nature, an effect can precede its cause.

Effects, for Kant, do not precede causes.[115] Thus, given Nichols own admission that the "mental process" is the "cause of laughter," the laughter cannot precede the mental process. Still, if we are being charitable, we can admit that there seems to be an experience-based reason for Nichols's reading. Even if laughter (if any) is subsequent to the mental play in response to humor, in actual experience the laughter appears so quickly as to strike us as being *simultaneous* with the mental play. Apparent simultaneity is not the same as preceding the mental play, but it is at least close to it.

When we respond to humor, the imagination (the ability to form images) and understanding (the ability to use concepts) are in play with each other. Since it is not immediately clear what exactly is supposed to be at play, we should try to clarify this. There appear to be two candidates; both enjoy textual support.

The first candidate for what is at play in the free play, as we have seen, is misunderstanding or mistaken judgment. Following Godfrey, we can say that the free play is an imaginative play with some misapprehension.[116] If the response to humor involves a "representation in understanding,"[117] as the third *Critique* states, it is precisely a *mis*understanding. Godfrey is worth quoting here.

> We see that the laughable consists in some paradox or incongruity, by which the understanding is entrapped and its concepts and train of thought spoilt, but the mind, leaving the ordinary standpoint of the understanding, preserves its poise through the imagination dwelling on the possibility of the absurdity; this mental exercise is accompanied by pleasure, for it is free harmonious activity of the mental powers; the imagination, which is usually the faithful slave of the understanding, now takes the lead, and the understanding merely develops the consequences of the suggestions of the imagination.[118]

Part Two of this guide contains some jokes that illustrate misapprehension of this kind. The best example Kant gives of a humorous misunderstanding is The Stuffed Aunt (quoted in No. 6).

The second candidate for the object of the play is what Kant calls an "aesthetic idea." The material for laughter, Kant writes, is a kind of "play with aesthetic ideas."[119] Aesthetic ideas are representations of the imagination that are so rich that the understanding cannot bring them under a concept or rule.[120] They are infinitely abundant in meaning, unable to be fully captured by a concept; they are conceptually indeterminate. That is why Kant says that in a joke ultimately "nothing is thought": aesthetic ideas are never brought to concepts.[121]

> Music and material for laughter are two kinds of *play with aesthetic ideas or even representations of the understanding* [*Verstandesvorstellungen*], by which in the end *nothing is thought* and which can gratify merely through their change, and nevertheless do so in a lively fashion; by which they make it fairly evident that the animation in both cases is merely bodily, although it is aroused by *ideas of the mind*, and that the feeling of health resulting from a movement of the intestines corresponding to that play constitutes the whole gratification in a lively party, which is extolled as so refined and spirited.[122]

A virtue of this option is that, if the thought content is a play with aesthetic ideas, it makes it clear how the imagination can be involved in the play. (Finding a role for the imagination was also a virtue of the first option, as the block quote from Godfrey made clear.) Aesthetic ideas are produced by the imagination; they give sensible expression to ideas of reason.

Like the first option, this one enjoys solid textual support, and the role of aesthetic ideas in laughter has been aptly noted in the literature on Kant.[123] Nonetheless, this reading has to address a potential objection, namely, that since a joke, once it is told, becomes determinate, it does not meet a crucial requirement of aesthetic ideas: conceptual indeterminacy.[124] An aesthetic object (here, the joke), for Kant, cannot be fully determined by concepts. Upon hearing the punch line, the objection goes, there is a resolution, not indeterminacy. So in a joke there cannot really be a play with aesthetic ideas.

However, a joke is not resolved in a determinate way, or at least a *good* one is not. (Presumably Kant wishes to analyze good or funny jokes, just as the artworks he discusses are beautiful and full of "spirit.") First, according to Kant's account, the response to a joke incites an ongoing movement in the mind. The mind moves back and forth continuously. Bringing with its initial expectations, the mind encounters an illusion or misconception, looks for an answer, thinks it finds one, and returns to the initial misapprehension or illusion to check the fit; and the process starts over again. Second, there is a sense in which (good) jokes are inexhaustible and boundless. Just as we repeatedly engage with "spirited" artworks, people tell their favorite jokes over and over. A good joke keeps on giving. It continues to be amusing, or at least rich with meaning. As Kant put it in one of his notes from around 1765, "Being reminded of something funny is really amusing," and—more to our point—it "also does not wear off as easily as other agreeable anecdotes."[125] Even if people don't respond to the joke the same way every time (which is after all true in the case of repeated interaction with artworks), it continues to offer food for thought, with its play of images, meanings, and concepts. For instance, word plays and puns that hinge on ambiguities require a simultaneous retention of more than one sense or meaning.[126] Like liar's paradoxes and other logical paradoxes (or No. 10, Full of Bull, and No. 11, With Friends Like These), a good play on words can lead to a mental process that goes on and on. Perhaps this is why Kant sometimes characterizes jokes in terms of paradox. If these two reasons are compelling, then the conceptual indeterminacy found in aesthetic ideas can also be found in jokes.[127]

To be sure, there are physiological and mechanistic aspects to the third *Critique*'s account of laughter at humor. At the same time, there are intellectualist aspects in that Kant centers his account around the notion of a free play "with thoughts." Like Joseph Addison, Kant assigns to reason a governing role in laughter at humor.[128] Kant's emphasis on the intellectual component in laughter at humor goes at least as far back as the 1760s.[129] In a marginal note from the 1780s, too, he attributes an "ideal" component to comic amusement. "The cause of laughter starts out as ideal," he writes, "yet only through bodily movement does it please."[130]

Due to such intellectualist aspects, it is tempting to conclude that the account found in the third *Critique* commits Kant to the view that the ability to provoke comic laughter is (or should be) one of the *fine* arts. (This is not as strange as it may at first appear. Contemporary standup comedy, for instance, could plausibly be considered an art form. One philosopher of art, Peter Kivy, recently proposed that fiction or narrative jokes are "miniature works of art," though he conceded that they are only "folk" or popular art rather than "high" art.[131]) Thus, according to another commentator (Hounsokou), the Kantian arts of laughter do not just affect the body, but also "please intellectually."[132] Yet the status of the arts of laughter in Kant's account is hardly straightforward. It is as if there were two sides to the account, the intellectualist and the physiological. Technically, Kant called laughter only one of the *agreeable* arts, since he focused more on the bodily effects of laughter. I turn to this issue in the next section.

3. Agreeable Arts, and Three Arts of Laughter (Wit, Naiveté, Caprice)

Kant calls humor an art (*Kunst*). But he does not thereby mean that it is a fine (*schön*) art, a class that would include poetry, painting, music,[133] theater, sculpture, and dance. If the ability to elicit laughter is an art, it is an art of the "agreeable." Due to laughter's bodily effects and his physiological, mechanistic understanding thereof, Kant calls the ability to elicit laughter (humor) an art of the agreeable rather than one of the fine arts.

The agreeable arts and the fine arts fall under a larger class, the aesthetic arts. But in its general sense, "aesthetic" (from *aesthetikos*) just means related to sensation or perception: there are aesthetic judgments of "sense" as well as judgments of beauty and sublimity. An aesthetic art is intended to arouse pleasure. Since this pleasure can be either agreeable or intellectual, the aesthetic arts are either agreeable or fine. It is *agreeable* art if the pleasure comes from mere sensations or a play of sensations. It is *fine* art if the pleasure comes from ways of cognizing (*Erkenntnisarten*) or a play of cognitions.[134] (See Fig. 1.)

The Aesthetic Arts

Agreeable arts
(play of sensations)

laughter (wit, naiveté, caprice), background music, dinnerware, the three table arts, games

Fine (*schön*) arts
(play of cognitions)

poetry, painting, sculpture, theater, music, dance

Figure 1 The Aesthetic Arts

There are three table arts: recounting interesting stories, conducting an unrestrained and lively conversation, and creating a light and merry atmosphere.

Agreeable arts are those which are aimed merely at enjoyment; of this kind are all those charms that can gratify the company at a table, such as telling entertaining stories, getting the company talking in an open and lively manner, creating by means of jokes and laughter a certain tone of merriment, in which, as is said, much can be chattered about and nobody will be held responsible for what he says, because it is only intended as momentary entertainment, not as some enduring material for later reflection or discussion.[135]

The agreeable arts do not stop there, however. There is the agreeable art of dinnerware or table setting. Then there is table music: large banquets should have background music. Finally, there are those games that involve no further interest than that of making time go by unnoticed, along the lines Kant recommended in No. 25 (A Whale Barrel).[136] Table talk and dinnerware, table music, gaming, and the arts of laughter are all agreeable arts because they are diversions aimed at creating pleasant sensations or enjoyment.

Under the concept of the arts of laughter, or arts of making people laugh via humor, there are three species. These are three ways of eliciting laughter, understood as the response to something comically amusing. They are wit (*Witz*), naiveté (*Naivität*), and caprice (*Laune*).[137]

Let us begin with **wit**, starting with its historical context. The term (*ingenium*, *Witz*) was already widely used in Kant's intellectual tradition, which stems from the work of Leibniz and includes Wolff,[138] Baumgarten,[139] and Meier.[140] For them, "wit" is an ability to connect diverse ideas—not a (narrower) ability to be funny or evoke comic amusement. For Wolff, for instance, *Witz* (*ingenium*) is the ease of perceiving similarities among different things.[141] Baumgarten, who discusses wit or ingenuity (*ingenium*) in several sections of *Metaphysica*, defines wit as "proficiency in observing the correspondences of things."[142] In §576 of *Metaphysica*, Baumgarten refers to the "play" (*lusus*) and "fruit" of ingenuity (*ingenii*), and Kant likewise takes up the notion of wit as play and even "free" play.[143] Analyses of wit were not confined to Germany and continental Europe, however, and we find a similar understanding of "wit" in the British tradition. Writers with whom Kant was familiar, in particular, Locke[144] and Addison,[145] discuss wit as a power to connect ideas.

Even in his relatively early writings, Kant appropriates this sense of wit as a far-reaching mental gift or talent, the ability to connect ideas easily. In *Essay on the Maladies of the Head* (1764) Kant writes, "The agility in grasping something and remembering it, likewise the facility in expressing it properly, very much depend on wit."[146] Kant later develops this idea that wit is ease in grasping something. In the anthropology lectures and in *Anthropology*, Kant uses the German *Witz* and the Latin *ingenium* to capture this notion.[147] According to *Anthropology*, "It is a peculiar faculty of assimilating, which belongs to the understanding (as the faculty of cognizing the universal), insofar as it brings objects under genera."[148]

In *Anthropology*, Kant makes two broad distinctions within the concept of "productive" wit.

The first distinction employs some jargon. The distinction is between comparative wit (*ingenium comparans*), a talent for comparing and assimilating things that are superficially different, and argumentative wit (*ingenium argutans*), a talent for making subtle distinctions. Unfortunately, this distinction is actually misleading, since it turns out that wit is basically the *ingenium comparans*. This can be seen in the general definition of wit as a "faculty of assimilating,"[149] which is exactly how Kant describes the *ingenium comparans*. *Ingenium argutans*, it turns out, is something close to what Kant calls the *determining* power of judgment.

To see this, we need to get even more technical. In *Anthropology*, Kant says that the *power of judgment* limits (comparative) wit. Wit

> needs the power of judgment to determine the particular under the universal and in order to apply the faculty of thought toward cognition. . . . The activity of comparative wit is more like play; but that of the power of judgment is more like business. . . . Wit snatches at sudden inspiration; the power of judgment strives for insight.[150]

The meaning here is not immediately clear, but it is worth recalling the third *Critique*'s distinction between the reflecting and determining power of judgment.[151] In its merely reflecting function, the power of judgment finds the universal (rule, law, principle) for a given particular. Examples would be when the power of judgment abstracts from particulars to form empirical concepts, finding similarities among different things, or when it searches for empirical laws. It also includes, Kant maintains, judging—by way of feeling—something to be beautiful or sublime. In its *determining* function, in contrast, the power of judgment applies the universal (concept, principle) to the particular. Of these two functions, the power of judgment that curbs and restrains wit would clearly be the power of judgment in its determining function.

Finding the universal, or searching for similarities and ways to subsume particulars under more general concepts, sounds similar to what comparative wit does. If that is right, then the reflecting power of judgment performs many of the same functions as comparative wit.[152] In fact, a short note on anthropology from around 1770 suggests just this. "Wit: for provisional judgments. Power of judgment: for determining judgments."[153] This assumes that we can read "provisional" judgments as a precursor to reflecting judgments. This is a fair assumption. As Claudio La Rocca notes, "The difference between provisional and determining judgments prefigures the distinction between the reflecting and determining power of judgment."[154]

Indeed, in *Anthropology* (§44) we find a confirmation that wit is very similar to what the third *Critique* calls the reflecting power of judgment. The *Anthropology* reads:

> Just as the faculty of discovering the particular for the universal (the rule) is the *power of judgment*, so the faculty of thinking up the universal for the particular is *wit* (*ingenium*). The power of judgment is a matter of noting the differences in a manifold that is identical in part; wit is a matter of noting the identity of a manifold that is different in part.[155]

Reinhard Brandt correctly observes that this contrast between the power of judgment and wit "is similar to the distinction between the determining and the reflecting power of judgment."[156] Gottfried Gabriel agrees: this distinction between the power of judgment and wit "corresponds" to the contrast Kant makes between the determining and reflecting power of judgment in the third *Critique*.[157] In fact, Gabriel goes further and adds that one could even suppose an "identity" between wit and reflecting power of judgment.[158] And even a third commentator

(Rodríguez) who adopts a more cautious interpretation still admits: "The concepts of 'reflecting power of judgment' and 'determining power of judgment' in the third *Critique* correspond to the concepts 'wit' and 'power of judgment' in the *Anthropology*."[159] It seems correct to agree with these scholars and arrive at a similar conclusion concerning the strong similarities between wit and the reflecting power of judgment.

How was it possible for Kant to make such a comparison (if not identity) between the two concepts in the rather late publication, *Anthropology from a Pragmatic Point of View* (1798)? Rather surprisingly, the concept of the reflecting power of judgment is, among all of Kant's publications, found only in the third *Critique*.[160] In short, it is Kant's substitute, within the framework of transcendental philosophy, of the (scholastic and empirical-psychological) concept of wit (*Witz*).[161] That explains how we can find a *reverse* substitution of wit and reflecting power of judgment in the *Anthropology*. When Kant finally published a version of his anthropology lectures in 1798 (based, significantly, on his own handwritten manuscript rather than student transcriptions), he was able to substitute a concept that he had presented in the *Critique* of 1790 (reflecting power of judgment) with his *earlier* concept (wit). In appealing to the concept of wit in the published *Anthropology*, Kant appealed to a traditional, empirical-psychological concept that he had already been lecturing on for years but which itself was substituted in the Critical system by the concept of reflecting power of judgment.

OK, this may be fine as far as Kant's intellectual development goes, but what does wit (in this broader sense of making comparisons and seeing similarities) have to do with humor? In the anthropological writings and the third *Critique*, Kant does not explicitly connect incongruity to "wit" as a capacity for identifying or generating *humor*. But it is easy to see how he might do so. A person of wit perceives connections between disparate or unlike things and ideas. Making such connections can reveal incongruities, and these can sometimes strike us as humorous. Ease and quickness in comparing sometimes exposes incongruities that evoke comic amusement.

Let us turn to the second distinction, namely, the one between two kinds of wit: superficial and profound.

It is true that profundity is not a matter of wit; but insofar as wit, through the imagery [*das Bildliche*] that it adds to thought, can be a vehicle or garb for reason and its management of morally practical ideas, it can be thought of as profound wit (as distinguished from superficial wit).[162]

Examples of such profound wit would be the anecdotes and thought experiments classified in this book as "Sayings with a Message" (e.g., Nos. 28, 29, 30). But the three jokes in the third *Critique* (Nos. 1, 2, and 12) show light, rather than profound, wit. Indeed, the majority of Kant's jokes collected in this book are not profound but lighthearted, most of them playing with some incongruity.

Whereas superficial wit makes use of incongruity, profound wit is more enduring because it appeals to reason. Pope, Butler, and Voltaire exhibit superficial wit and are amusing. Young, in contrast, has profound wit and evokes admiration.

However, it is an easy wit (like that of Voltaire's), and always only a *play* [*Spiel*]. On the other hand, the person who presents true and important principles in clothing (like Edward Young in his satires)[163] can be called a very difficult [*centnerschwerer*] wit, because it is a *serious business* and arouses more admiration than amusement.[164]

Like comedic satirists today, Pope and Butler (even if using only superficial wit) make the contemptible look even worse. They do it in a way that can be both comically amusing and useful for socio-political or ethical reform.[165] But profound wit dresses up reason's ideas, presenting them in concrete examples and stories.

There is a risk posed by light and humorous wit: it can become too cute. Jokes that merely make use of word play are guilty here. Kant faults two authors in this respect: the French abbot Nicolas Trublet (1697–1770) and the British lexicographer Samuel Johnson. Light wit can become nauseating. Just as engaging with beauty for too long can lead to feelings of saturation and disgust, exposure to too much light wit can cause a sense of weariness.[166] In the *Observations*, Kant writes, "Nothing is so disgusting as pure sweetness."[167] This idea is repeated even in the second *Critique* ("joking [*Scherzen*] easily becomes insipid")[168] as well as in *Anthropology*, where even mental pleasure involving the communication of thoughts can become nauseating.

But if it [mental pleasure] is forced on us and still as mental nutrition is not beneficial to us, the mind finds it repulsive (as in, e.g., the constant repetition of would-be flashes of wit or humor, whose sameness can be unwholesome to us), and thus the natural instinct to be free of it is also called disgust by analogy.[169]

In Kant's view, Trublet's "Essay on Several Subjects of Literature and Morality" (1735) contains more cheap linguistic tricks than substance and insight. (Kant may here be following one of his favorite satirists, Voltaire, who engaged in a literary dispute with Trublet.) "When one reads the abbot Trublet's gags [*Einfälle*], one becomes so weary and tired of the excessive *bons mots*" that one prefers something that is ordinary and without taste.[170]

> Wit goes more for the *sauce*. Judgment goes for the *sustenance*. The hunt for *witty sayings* (*bons mots*), as the Abbot Trublet does so well, thereby putting wit on the rack, makes for shallow minds, or eventually disgusts well-grounded ones.[171]

Wit, as the capacity to find similarities, should remain subordinate to the understanding.[172] If we are not to become satiated or disgusted, a witticism needs content supplied by reason in the form of "ideas." In that case, the imagination can play with thoughts and/or ideas. *Anthropology* states:

> We can also be disgusted [*verekeln*] by it [i.e., wit], since its effect leaves nothing permanent. If all of these things and persons [i.e., texts, speeches] are to be called spirited, then they must arouse an interest by means of ideas. For this sets the power of imagination in motion, which sees before it a great play area [*Spielraum*] for concepts of this kind.[173]

Kant does not consider all bad jokes to be *morally* disgusting. Some jokes become nauseating because they involve just cheap wordplay, puns, or contrasts, with little to no connection to "ideas" at all. But they do not all oppose moral ideas.

Kant finds Trublet's weaknesses to be typical of the French cast of mind, for he thinks that the French "very much like to be witty" and are happy to sacrifice truth to wit.[174] The French incline toward lighthearted jest and triviality. "The fault which is closest to this national character is the ridiculous or, in a more polite expression, the lighthearted. Important things are treated like jokes, and trivialities serve for serious occupation."[175] These passages from the *Observations* reveal that Kant's assertions go beyond a distaste for Trublet. There is a philosophically interesting point underlying Kant's attempts at cultural anthropology and sociology. Kant holds that, if there is a conflict between light wit and reason, the former should be subordinated to reason. Ideally, he thinks, wit should be combined with reason, thoroughness, and truth.

In any case, the English too, not just the French, are sometimes guilty of indulging in insubstantial wit. It is after claiming that profound wit serves reason that Kant offers quip No. 15 (Samuel Johnson's Wife). ("As one of the *so-called* admirable sayings of Samuel Johnson about women goes . . .")[176] Despite containing a playful antithesis, Johnson's saying is not in fact admirable because it does not support reason. (One might also add that the implicit sexism in Johnson's remark makes it morally repugnant or disgusting, but Kant does not state this.)

We can now turn to the second art of laughter.[177] **Naiveté** is an eruption of the sincerity, originally natural to us, which is opposed to the dissimulation that has become habitual. According to one translation, it is "the resistance of the uprightness that is originally natural to humanity against the art of pretense that has become second nature."[178] It is called "naive" when, in manners (*Manieren*), nature looks like art and art looks like nature.[179]

Whereas a joke teller tells jokes that are constructed, the naive person is unintentionally funny. The humor is found, we might say, not created. For instance, the humor in Art Linkletter's American variety TV show *House Party* segment, "Kids Say the Darndest Things," was based on honest statements made by children who were "naive" in this sense. Here is another example. A father, standing beside his seven-year-old daughter, admires his shiny, clean car in his driveway. His neighbor comes out and compliments him on taking the time to wash the car. The child suddenly blurts out, "But Dad, we just took it to the *car wash*." Derailing innocence can strike us as funny. Marmysz comments on Kant, "The naive individual fails to disguise innocent intentions, and we laugh for this very reason."[180]

The naive can be fitted into Kant's general account of humor as involving a disappearance of an expectation into nothing. When we encounter the naive person, our expectation that we will have to figure out the person's (hidden) true intentions suddenly disappears.[181] Naiveté is the simplicity that characterizes the absence of corruption by society's customs and manners. The naive person comes across as innocent. The contrast between what we are used to or expect, and how the naive person appears, can seem funny or amusing. We are surprised at the naive person's words or behavior, and our expectation of artifice is transformed into nothing.[182] When we are shown this innocence, Kant writes, "the joker in ourselves is exposed, and this produces the successive movement of the mind in two opposite directions, which at the same time gives the body a healthy shake."[183] In laughing at naiveté, we are ultimately laughing at ourselves. We see that, like nearly everyone else, we usually follow artifices that require us sometimes to dissemble, or hold our tongues, or, worse, may even encourage us to be dishonest or lie.

Humor's use for morality is never far from Kant's account. We see this in his view of naiveté. In the end, the uprightness revealed in naiveté is a *moral* phenomenon that happens at times to evoke laughter.[184] This explains why in such cases we are not actually laughing *at* or mocking the naive person, and thus why such laughter does not imply our feeling superior to them. The naive person has a moral innocence. In Kant's account, we cannot be superior to morality. We are instead constrained by morality—even as it springs, autonomously, from reason—and we have a duty to strive to be morally upright. When we encounter naiveté, we chance upon what seems to be an agreement of nature with freedom. We stumble upon a person in which simplicity takes on the look of morality.

Thus, there can be no "art" of being naive. Naiveté cannot be placed among the fine arts, since naiveté is found rather than crafted. Still, naiveté can be *represented* in fictional works. Kant writes, "An art for being naive is thus a contradiction; but it is certainly possible to represent naiveté in a fictional person, and this is a beautiful although also rare art."[185]

Caprice is the third and final "art" of laughter. "Caprice" is a decent translation of *Laune*, but it could also be translated as "whimsicality" or even as "humor" (in the more traditional sense associated with temperament and mood).[186] Like the naive, *Laune* is discussed by Kant in just a single paragraph.

The capricious person sees life in a different way or discloses the world in a new light. Here it is not so much a matter of joke telling, as of a quirky, eccentric outlook or style. The person of caprice takes some event, even a painful one, and makes us laugh about it. The third *Critique* reads:

> Caprice in the good sense signifies the talent of being able to transpose oneself at will into a certain mental disposition in which everything is judged quite differently from what is usual (even completely reversed), and yet in accordance with certain principles of reason in such a mental disposition.[187]

The adoption of a different perspective, this reversal, leads to the amusing situation. In an anthropology lecture from 1784/85, Kant attributes originality to caprice. "A wit is called capricious [*launigt*] when an uncommon mental disposition underlies it. . . . The capricious wit rests upon an original disposition of mind [*Gemüths*]."[188] At the same time, the person of caprice, Kant thinks, is not completely nonsensical but adopts "certain principles of reason."

People with caprice detach themselves from situations in such a way that they become comical. Kant has satirists in mind, but we could also expand this to include today's standup comedians who recount an awkward or painful moment in an amusing way. Using observational humor, they see the world from a novel vantage point.

At one point Kant associated *Laune* with genius.[189] In the early 1770s, the connection was very close. The genius, he said, has *Laune*.[190] In the 1770s, Kant wrote (in a marginal note) that "genius depends on *Laune*."[191] But in the third *Critique*, Kant more strictly separates caprice and genius. Caprice is "part of the originality of spirit," though it is "not on that account part of the talent for beautiful art."[192] In other words, *Laune* is not the original force creating artwork; genius is. Genius is the ability to create a unique kind of "sense" which, when tamed by taste, becomes the infinite, boundless sense expressed in works of art.[193] Kant never clarifies the source of the "aesthetic ideas" that are in play in a joke. Perhaps, to conjecture, caprice's connection with genius offers a clue: the play with aesthetic ideas is made possible by *Laune* as part of the originality of spirit. Just as genius produces artworks, perhaps *Laune* creates jokes. Of course, Kant never puts it this way and the claim would apply only to jokes stemming from *Laune*, but it is one way to explain the source of some aesthetic ideas in humor.

One scholar (Hounsokou) regrets that Kant did not provide examples of what he meant by *Laune*.[194] In fact there is an abundance of textual material on caprice, it is just not in the third *Critique*. In a lecture from 1775/76 Kant is reported to have said:

> Writings that contrast comically are the most capricious [*launigsten*], and they please greatly. . . . This way vice can be represented as revolting and incongruous [*ungereimt*]. The question is, what is better, to make vice look worthy of revulsion and anger, or, in a *Laune*, to make it look incongruous, silly, and laughable. The latter is to be preferred. Humans are set straight more by being laughed at than from irate rebuke. The mind's state and situation is better when one ridicules vice than when one regards it with anger and revulsion.[195]

Kant then gives Henry Fielding[196] as an example of an appropriate satirist or ridiculer.

> Fielding writes so capriciously, he portrays the miser in the most laughable form, that he becomes more contemptible than he would have been had I portrayed his evil side. This kind of contrasting is the best way, as it sharpens the mind and at the same time makes the vicious person laughable.[197]

So, as we have seen, not only is there room for ridicule using caprice to create incongruities or absurdities, sometimes it is the best response to vice.

> But one can also make a comical contrast and express an apparent contradiction in the tone of truth, or express something obviously contemptible in the language of praise, in order to make the incongruity/absurdity [*Ungereimtheit*] still more palpable—like Fielding in his *Jonathan Wild*.[198]

Like superficial wit, *Laune* can go too far. An "eccentric" wit can sometimes dominate practical judgment.

> Having no character yet being fickle [*wetterwendisch*], capricious [*launisch*], and (without malice) unreliable; willfully making enemies

for oneself but without even hating anyone; and ridiculing one's friend bitingly but without wanting to hurt him [*wehe thun*]: this lies in a partly innate predisposition of eccentric [*verschrobenen*] wit ruling over the practical power of judgment.[199]

Although Kant makes conceptual distinctions among wit (as the capacity to use incongruity to evoke comic amusement), naiveté, and *Laune*, they are often found in the same person or author. Moreover, there is even a connection to *superiority*. Using ridicule or "persiflage" (i.e., light teasing) without hurting is actually a mark of the *launichten* wit.[200] According to a rich passage from *Anthropology*,

> Capricious [*launichter*] wit means one that comes from a mind disposed to paradox, where the (cunning) jokester peers from behind the trusting sound of simplicity in order to expose someone (or his opinion) to laughter by exalting, with apparent eulogy (persiflage), the opposite of what is worthy of approval—for example, [Pope's][201] *Art of Sinking in Poetry*, or Butler's *Hudibras*. Such a wit, which uses contrast to make what is contemptible even more contemptible, is very stimulating through the surprise of the unexpected.[202]

We thus find in the *Anthropology* all three elements from section §54 of the third *Critique*.[203] The 1) *launichter* 2) wit uses 3) naiveté ("trusting sound of simplicity") to expose someone to ridicule through the use of incongruity ("paradox," "the unexpected"). And, as we have already seen, *Anthropology* contains another example of a combination of these elements: the capricious and witty "wag" who appears to have no mischief in mind, yet (naive like) does not join in the laughter but "with seeming simplicity" is able to cause a release of tension in us, as our expectations are not fulfilled.[204] In a marginal note, Kant characterizes the natural talent for wit ("motherwit") as "naive."[205] So, while Kant draws conceptual distinctions among the three arts of laughter, in reality they are often found together.

4. Kant's Thoughts on Comedy

To round out this chapter, I would like to give some form to Kant's somewhat scattered remarks on theatrical comedy.

Kant adopted the traditional distinction between tragedy and comedy, contrasting the two literary genres in *Observations on the Feeling of the Beautiful and Sublime* (1764).[206] Throughout his writings and lectures, Kant writes surprising little about tragedy, and he says even less about comedy. In the third *Critique*, he refers to comedy (*Lustspiel*) not even once. Even if he does not develop a theory of tragic plays in the third *Critique*, he twice mentions tragedy (*Trauerspiel*); moreover, if one also looks to his other writings and lectures, there is enough material to construct a Kantian theory of tragedy.[207] It is for systematic reasons that Kant chooses not to examine either comedy or tragedy in the third *Critique*, for he is interested in pure aesthetic judgments insofar as they constitute synthetic judgments *a priori*, not in pursuing theories of literary genres.[208] Whereas G. W. F. Hegel, in his lectures on aesthetics, analyzes the distinctive features of tragedy and comedy, discussing classical Greek and modern dramatists such as Aeschylus, Sophocles, Aristophanes, Shakespeare, Schiller, and Molière, Kant nowhere offers an extended, philosophical analysis of comedy as a literary genre. Thus, if we are to learn anything about Kant's views of comedy, we have to be content with weaving together some of the claims that are found in his unpublished notes, lectures, and minor writings.

To understand his thoughts on comedy, let's first consider how Kant would have been acquainted with theater and the dramatic arts. Unfortunately, it is difficult to be very detailed about which Kant literary sources shaped his ideas here, or what plays he appreciated and admired, and why he did so. We do know that he not only watched plays but read some of them as well. He criticizes the plays of Lessing such as *Nathan the Wise* (1779), a dramatic play, for being entertaining in certain parts only rather than on the whole.[209] He made this comment in a lecture of 1781/82. Since the play was not performed until 1783 in Berlin, it is clear Kant made this claim on the basis of reading the work. Indeed, he contrasts watching a comedy with reading it, so we can assume that Kant became familiar with comedic plays by reading and viewing them, and sometimes both.[210]

He considered Shakespeare's tragedies (and, I assume, comedies) to be potential sources of knowledge about human beings.[211] It appears that Kant's ideas about theater were in agreement with the pro-theater views of Voltaire and Diderot (whether or not he read their accounts of theater), and opposed to the anti-theatrical views of Plato and Rousseau.[212] Since Kant saw comedies with friends such as Hamann and Hippel (himself a playwright), it seems safe to assume that his thoughts on comedy were shaped by discussing popular comedies and other plays with them. It is likely they watched the tragedies of Voltaire, Weiße, and Lessing, and comedies such as Lessing's *Freethinker*,[213] Goldoni's *The Gentleman and the Lady*, Molière's *Miser*, and Hippel's *Man of the Clock*.[214]

Given this context, what did Kant think about comedy? His description in the *Observations* is unfortunately not very original. "Comedy represents intrigues, marvelous entanglements and clever people who know how to wriggle out of them, fools who let themselves be deceived, jests and ridiculous characters. Here love is not so grave, it is merry and intimate."[215]

Like other writers of the day (Du Bos, Hume, Lessing), Kant seems most interested in describing our *responses* to a play. Thus, more than offering a definition of comedy, Kant describes how the comedy affects us. "Through capricious/whimsical [*launigte*] and interesting comedies, the mind becomes aroused and the heart braver."[216] While distinct from tragedy, comedy can contain elements normally associated with tragedy, such as the terrifying and the sublime. A comedy can contain the "magnanimous" and "sublime." Since "the sublime has something in common with the frightful," it can evoke something like fear.[217] Kant thinks that comedy generally elicits a feeling of beauty more than of sublimity. But he qualifies this by adding that in comedy a noble (sublime) feeling can nonetheless be partly combined with the beautiful.[218]

Like a poem and a novel, a comic play is "capable of furnishing ideal delights in us." These "arise from the way that the mind produces cognitions for itself from all kinds of representations of the senses."[219] Moreover, Kant's response-based approach can be seen in his drawing attention to the fact that in German a tragedy (*Trauerspiel*) and a comedy (*Lustspiel*) are a kind of pleasing play (*Spiel*).[220] Comedies and tragedies promote a feeling of life through a disinterested "play of opposing affects." The disinterestedness in such a play of emotions can be contrasted with the interest in games of chance that are played "especially for money."[221]

Another kind of response to a comedy, of course, is our evaluation of it. Kant states in a marginal note, "In a comedy we are perhaps often *entertained* by understanding and sense, but not satisfied.

The entertainment happens during the play, the *satisfaction* at its conclusion."[222] According to *Anthropology*, at the conclusion of a drama, as at the end of the dinner party, "one's mind inevitably occupies itself with recalling the various phases" of what happened.[223] And according to an anthropology lecture, we assess the whole comedy according to its aftertaste (*Nachschmack*).

Likewise one has enjoyment in aftertaste due to a comedy that ends well; one gets an idea and in the end realizes that it was well conceived [*überlegt*], and then it delights. This way a comedy can please in its plot, even if in the end one does not get what one was looking to get a hold of. . . . Enjoyment in pleasure [*Vergnügen im Genuß*] discloses the measure of sensation. Enjoyment in aftertaste arises from reflection about the sensation of what preceded. For example, when the comedy lets out, everyone does a recapitulation.[224]

Kant is not necessarily implying that the ability for such taste need not be cultivated or that it is not the result of education and practice. The ability to formulate such a "recapitulation" seems to require more training than the ability to taste food. What is required is "reflection," after all, not mere sensation. The activity that consists in the discrimination of unity, timing, and wit, and the determination of whether a play is "well conceived," generating a particular "aftertaste," seems best viewed as an achievement on the part of the spectator, rather than as an immediate perception.[225] This may be why Kant thinks that the play produces "ideal" pleasures, and that the mind produces, from out of the perceived representations on stage, "cognitions for itself."

Like Hume, Kant thinks that our evaluations of comedy vary with age.[226] Kant associates a taste for comedy with old age, and a taste for tragic plays with youth. He expressed such a view as early as around 1765,[227] and as late as the *Anthropology* of 1798, so he appears to have held the view for well over three decades. Why does he think that older people prefer comedies, even the burlesque (*Burlesken*), while youth prefer tragedies? The first reason is that the young have an instinct to test their powers. It is not exactly clear what Kant means by testing their powers, however. Which powers does he have in mind, and how are they tested? Perhaps he means that the youth probe their capacities to feel strong emotions (affects) and sensations. They see just how thrilled or moved they can be—they test their emotional limits as it were. (The elderly, with their experience, have in contrast already done that.) On this reading, then, there would be no intrinsic connection between the power-testing and morality. But perhaps, as one scholar (Deimling) suggests, the youth are testing their abilities to resist (via imagination and sympathy) the dangers or struggles presented in the play, revealing how their own moral nature could be considered powerful enough to prevail even amid such challenging circumstances.[228] This line, while reminiscent of the views of Friedrich Schiller, also seems attributable to Kant, especially once he had developed his mature views of ethics and practical reason.

The second reason for the youth's preference is that after watching a tragic play the young can get rid of the bad aftertaste more quickly than the older viewers can. "Given the frivolity of youth, no melancholy is left over from the distressing and terrifying impressions the moment the play has ended. Rather, there is only a pleasant tiredness after vigorous internal exercise, which puts the youth once again in a cheerful mood."[229] For similar reasons, Kant maintains that it is hard to engage in profound or deep contemplation after we've just seen a comedy.[230]

Kant thinks the English were generally better at comedy than the French, and the French better than the English at tragedy.[231] At first glance this claim seems puzzling, since Kant characterizes the French as frivolous and capricious, and the English as stoic and serious. But in fact it is due to such generalizations (or stereotypes) about national character that leads Kant to think that English actors will excel at comedy. The background to this claim is that, just as the Merchant's Wig joke (No. 1) is to be told with an "assumed seriousness,"[232] actors are supposed to govern their affects.[233] Since the English actors are not very predisposed to laugh (think: dry English humor), they will not break out in laughter on stage but will be in a good position to evoke it in the audience. "We laugh most strongly when someone adopts a serious look."[234] Similar reasoning applies, with the necessary modifications, to the French actors and tragedy. The French are generally so "removed from sadness" that French actors can represent terrible events well on stage, evoking sadness in the audience.

Kant didn't write much on *physical* comedy, but it is interesting to speculate about how his line of reasoning would be applied to art forms such as mime, pantomime, and clowning. At first glance, it would appear that the intellectualist side of Kant's account would assign little value to them—if, that is, these forms lack substance and intellectual content. Wit that exhibits the latter is most admirable, since it gives the mind ideas to play with and toss about. However, even given Kant's premises, perhaps something can be said in favor of physical comedy. Some of the most important physical comedians brilliantly combine the physical and the intellectual.[235] For a twentieth-century example, consider the scene in *Modern Times* (Chaplin, 1936) in which the Tramp becomes a cog in the machine. Insofar as such a physical display is a critique of socio-economic injustice, it would be (to use a Kantian phrase) of interest to reason.

In fact, in his anthropology lecture Kant makes conceptual room for pantomime. To understand his claim, we need to understand his notion of a facial expression or mien (*Mien*). Facial expressions or miens are external signs that reflect inner processes or events in the mind. Kant thinks they are natural and universally understood. "Facial expressions are universally valid and natural signs of mental agitations. There is nothing as universal as facial expressions; words are not as universal." Since facial expressions make up a kind of universal language, "a pantomime comedy which could be valid for all peoples could be staged."[236] It is thus possible to have a universal communication of thoughts through facial expressions or miens, gestures (*Gebärde*), and other bodily signs. This universality as such, the fact that such communication is possible in the first place, would also be of interest to reason.

Whereas it is this capacity for universal communication that stands out when it comes to pantomime, Kant's analysis of harlequins and court jesters gets a different emphasis, for he focuses on the mechanistic and physiological effects on the audience.

> By his antics [*Einfälle*] a harlequin who has a nimble wit produces a beneficial shaking of the diaphragm and intestines, by which the appetite for the ensuing social supper is whetted, and thrives as a result of the lively conversation.[237]

> The position of a court jester [*Hofnarren*], whose function is to tease the king's distinguished servants and thus season the meal through laughter for the sake of the beneficial shaking of his diaphragm, is, depending on how one takes it, above or below all criticism.[238]

Perhaps the intellectual and physical sides of Kant's account of physical comedy are not incompatible. Given the interpretation offered in this chapter, we can make sense of both aspects. I have suggested that his account of humor contains intellectualist components: in entertaining the humorous we *play* with mental content, an *incongruity*. Yet Kant also gives physiological and mechanistic descriptions of the *release* in humor. And sometimes we even feel *superior* to the court jester and targets of harmless ridicule, or to our friends when we play a joke on them or tease them. To put it another way, Kant's account incorporates various elements of the principal theories of humor, thereby unifying "stimulus-side" aspects (incongruity) with "response-side" aspects (release, mental play, superiority).[239]

Chapter 2
Three Questions about Laughter at Humor

Although theoretical and empirical researchers of humor often acknowledge Kant as a major figure in the history of the study of humor, in the vast sea of Kant scholarship there are strikingly few investigations of humor and laughter. Yet Kant's remarks on laughter are not just tucked away in his minor writings. They sit right in the middle of the third *Critique*. Thus, one commentator is right that, while at first glance it might seem odd that Kant discusses jokes and laughter over the course of seven pages in the third *Critique*, it would be a mistake to conclude that Kant's account is irrelevant to his aesthetics or to his broader philosophical aims.[1] In addition, laughing at humor is an important, meaningful human experience, and it seems worthy of philosophical analysis and attention.

Today it is still possible to read all or nearly all of the Kant scholarship on humor and laughter, though one day this may no longer be true. Of those few studies directly offering sustained discussions of the topic, there are at least three kinds, broadly speaking. (There can be overlap among these three, and this is only a general, non-exhaustive typology.) The first kind asks whether laughing at a joke amounts to making an aesthetic judgment, and, additionally, makes comparisons to other feelings like the experiences of beauty, the sublime, or the grotesque.[2] The second type tries to understand laughter and humor in terms of Kant's systematic aims, identifying their role in the philosophical system.[3] In this chapter, I take up both sets of issues. The third kind of study examines Kant's theory in relation to the ethics of humor and related practical matters; I address these in the next chapter.[4]

Here I raise three questions, devoting a section to each. Does Kant consider laughter at humor to involve a pure aesthetic judgment—like the judgments of beauty and sublimity (section 1)? Technically, he does not, I show.

Yet Kant seems inconsistent here, since he calls laughter in response to a joke "a play" with aesthetic ideas and with representations of the understanding, a play with thoughts (*Gedankenspiel*). If, expanding Kant's account, we allow that laughter can be or lead to a pure aesthetic judgment, what kind would it be? It would not be a judgment of the sublime, nor the beautiful, nor the anti-sublime and grotesque, but would be *analogous* to judgments of the sublime and the beautiful (section 2).

Finally, how does Kant's theory of humor and laughter contribute to his broader philosophical aims (section 3)? Some scholars claim it helps Kant solve Descartes's mind/body problem, or even that Kant's Critical philosophy is ultimately a philosophy of laughter.[5] Such assertions strike me as exaggerations. Still, we can wish that Kant had drawn out the implications of his claim that in laughter at humor, the mind and body interact with and affect each other. As a play with aesthetic ideas, such laughter is of interest to reason as it gives a hint of reason's efficacy in the sensible world. Below, I explain these points in more detail.

1. Can Laughter at Humor be a Pure Aesthetic Judgment?

It seems incontestable that, for Kant, humor-induced amusement counts as an aesthetic experience in a broad sense.[6] As one scholar (Menninghaus) puts it, laughter at humor "shares the fundamental features of aesthetic experience."[7]

The notion of aesthetic experience is notoriously hard to define. Here I simply mean to refer to the perceptual-sensory, cognitive, and/or emotional responses to objects engaged with or attended to with absorbed attention, and carried out for the sake of the absorbed engagement or attention itself, a pleasant state which is self-reinforcing, that is, one in which one wants to remain. The object of the aesthetic experience may be natural or artistic-literary-conceptual, as it is in a joke.

We are comically amused when we listen to clever jokes or watch a funny comedic performance. To claim it is an aesthetic *judgment* of any kind, however, is to make a stronger and more controversial claim, since aesthetic judgments (as I here conceive of them) have a propositional structure and are voluntary acts of reflection. As I read Kant, not all aesthetic experiences consist in making aesthetic judgments in this sense. Further, to assert that it is an aesthetic judgment that is *pure* rather than agreeable is to make a still stronger claim. A "pure" aesthetic judgment is one that is (in Kant's senses) disinterested, subjectively universal, purposive without a purpose (or subjectively formally purposive), and necessary.

Are there sufficient grounds for maintaining that laughter is (or implicitly contains) an aesthetic judgment? Strictly speaking, Kant does not write of a "judgment" of humor.[8] Laughter at humor is at most an aesthetic experience or phenomenon in the aforementioned sense concerning a felt response to the humorous object or joke enjoyed in itself, not a judgment with propositional content that is the result of a voluntary, reflective activity (even if that propositional content need not be voiced or uttered).[9]

Laughter's status as an affect, for Kant, prevents it from becoming a judgment. (This kind of hearty, immediate laughter or smile is called a Duchenne laugh/smile in the empirical literature, following the work of the nineteenth-century neurologist Guillaume Duchenne. A non-Duchenne smile is forced.) An "affect" is a strong emotion that momentarily overcomes someone, say, an incontrollable flash of anger. In *Anthropology*, Kant defines "affect" as "the feeling of a pleasure or displeasure in the subject's present state that does not let the person rise to reflection (the representation by means of reason as to whether one should give oneself up to it or refuse it)."[10] Affect is "surprise through sensation, by means of which the mind's composure is suspended. Affect is therefore rash, that is, it quickly grows to a degree of feeling that makes reflection impossible (it is thoughtless)." In the third *Critique*, Kant likewise claims that affects are related merely to feeling, not to the faculty of desire. He calls them "tumultuous and unpremeditated."[11] In short, affects are 1) related to the faculty of pleasure or displeasure; 2) surprising, rash, fast, unpremeditated; 3) purely sensation or feeling; 4) overwhelming to the point where thought is suspended and reflection is impossible. As an affect, laughter is incompatible with reflection.[12] If it is an affect, and purely sensation, it is hard to see how laughter could *be* an aesthetic judgment. (It might give rise to a second-order aesthetic judgment about an affect, but that is another matter.)

But, for the sake of argument, let us grant that there are aesthetic judgments of laughter at humor, even if, strictly speaking, there are no aesthetic judgments of laughter insofar as laughter is an affect. Would it be a *pure* aesthetic judgment, or an aesthetic judgment of the *agreeable*? One part of Kant's account implies that laughter cannot be a pure aesthetic judgment and that it must be merely agreeable. At the beginning of his discussion of §54, he distinguishes between the pleasure in beauty ("merely in the judging") and *gratification* in feelings associated with joy and laughter (gratification being associated with the merely agreeable).

> Between that which pleases merely in the judging and that which gratifies (pleases in the sensation) there is, as we have often shown, an essential difference. The latter is something that one cannot, like the former, require of everyone.[13]

Kant elaborates: "All changing free play of sensations (which is not grounded in any intention) gratifies, because it promotes the feeling of health." One of these kinds of play is the "play of thoughts" (*Gedankenspiel*), i.e., the animating mental play in laughter. Since laughter is only gratifying and agreeable, Kant says—apparently ignoring that, as in beauty, what is at hand is a play with thoughts or representations or ideas—it cannot be required of everyone. If it were to lead to a judgment, this side of his account implies, laughter could result only in a gratifying judgment of the *agreeable*. Consistent with this, Kant claims that the art of eliciting humor-induced laughter is an aesthetic art of the agreeable. That's Kant's official story, or at least the one Kant usually emphasizes. The other side picks up on laughter's play with thoughts and aesthetic ideas, the *judging* in laughter, as I will do in a moment.

Several interpreters acknowledge that Kant stopped short of calling laughter a pure aesthetic judgment while wishing that he had gone further. Godfrey attributes to Kant the view that "the pleasure in laughter is merely an affect due to certain bodily conditions."[14] Godfrey rejects this position, opting to defend a more intellectualist reading (though some of the intellectualism, I think, is already in Kant's account).[15]

Godfrey recognizes that much of his interpretation goes beyond what Kant actually writes. He thinks Kant "regards laughter as agreeable, but not [pure] aesthetic" and that it "cannot claim universality or necessity."[16] This is of course true, even if there is a side to Kant's account that makes room for normativity in our responses to humor.

Likewise, Critchley stops short of calling (Kantian) laughter at humor an instance of pure aesthetic judgment. He wishes Kant had recognized its universality and necessity, that is, its normative claim on others. "Sadly, despite Kant's fascinating discussion of laughter, he confines humour to the domain of the agreeable rather than the beautiful, whose analysis is the proper business of [pure] aesthetic judgment."[17]

Meredith notices that Kant does not analyze laughter as a pure aesthetic judgment and that Kant considers laughing to be merely agreeable. Yet he wishes Kant had offered a transcendental analysis of the laughable, which would give rise to a disinterested contemplative pleasure. "It seems obvious that if the laughable is not placed on the same basis as the beautiful it turns Kant's whole *Analytic of the Beautiful* into ridicule."[18]

Here, then, is my modest proposal. Let us call the denial that laughter is a pure aesthetic judgment, and affirmation that it is only satisfying and agreeable (in Kant's senses), the "strict" interpretation. This is the side that Kant states as his considered view. But perhaps there is a way to reconcile the strict view with the more "reconstructive" readings that understandably wish Kant had gone further and had recognized the normative character of our responses to humor, a normativity that bursting out in affect cannot provide. This kind of reading picks up on that other element that is also in Kant's text: the play with thoughts and aesthetic ideas.

To pursue such a text-based reconstruction, we can refer to a distinction that Kant appears to make (in his discussion of beauty) between judging (*Beurteilung*) and judgment (*Urteil*). This is the difference between the *activity* of judging an object and the *product* of such activity: a judgment.[19] According to this interpretation, the act of judging in response to a beautiful object 1a) creates a harmonious free play between the imagination and understanding, and 1b) this harmonious free play produces, or is experienced as, pleasure. 2) Finally, a judgment is made on the basis of, and is about, this pleasure. Such a judgment asserts that the object is beautiful (as in the uttered statement, "Look at that—it's beautiful"). Note that this "judging-pleasure-judgment" complex need not be understood as occurring in temporal stages, but may be considered to be merely logically or conceptually distinct.

At least implicitly, the judgment makes a claim that the pleasure is intersubjectively valid and communicable. When you issue such a judgment, you take yourself to be speaking with a "universal voice."[20] This means that the claim applies as much to you, the person pronouncing it, as it does to others. It is not that you are lording it over other people or exhibiting a kind of aesthetic bossiness.[21] Rather, you (qua judge) are *also* constrained, like everyone else, to respond to and judge the object a certain way (to find it beautiful, sublime, elegant, graceful, amusing, and so on).

Not everyone agrees that Kant makes a judging/judgment distinction in his account of beauty, and space does not allow me to defend a position on this issue here. But for the sake of argument, let us assume that Kant makes the distinction and apply it to laughter, since it provides a way to resolve the disagreement between the strict and the reconstructive views.

On the proposed application to laughter, the judgment is *about* the judging activity in which one apprehends and makes sense of the contents of the joke or humor, as one "gets" the joke and plays with its contents. The judgment, made on the basis of the *judging* in laughter rather than the merely agreeable physiological response, is reflective and second-order. The judgment is a comment *on* this judging activity and response ("That's funny!"). The judgment posits (at least implicitly) that others should agree that the humorous object is worthy of laughter. It communicates with others: when you make such a judgment, you are implying that I too should find the object or event funny, even if you cannot prove it.

Imagine you find a joke funny. Let us further assume that you laugh, which is a common (but not necessary) expression of comic amusement. The *judging* (of the joke) gives rise to (and is logically prior to) the bodily response of laughter and its associated pleasure. But the judgment (*Urteil*) is *about* such pleasure and laughter, and logically posterior. It would be the judgment that the joke is funny and would involve the thought or claim that others should agree with you about it, that is, should respond with comic amusement. You don't want them to just "get" the joke. You also want them to find it funny. ("That's funny! Don't you see?")

This proposal offers a kind of middle way. We can recognize the element of truth in the strict interpretation. As an affect, laughter is not a judgment, and as agreeable, it is not pure. Laughing, insofar as one is in the throes of affect, is incompatible with making a pure aesthetic judgment. At the same time, we can agree with the reconstructive interpretation that the judging activity (as we contemplate and get a joke) can lead to a normative ("pure") aesthetic judgment, in which we want others to agree with us and likewise find the joke or object funny.

An advantage of this proposal is that it is compatible with Kant's claims about laughter. If laughter can lead to a pure aesthetic judgment, we would expect the imagination to be involved, namely, to be at play with the understanding or reason. This aspect enjoys textual support, as we saw in the previous chapter, and as we see in Kant's references to aesthetic ideas and the play of thoughts (*Gedankenspiel*).

It would be nice if there were further textual support for this distinction with regard to laughter. In fact, there is something like the judging/judgment distinction in Kant's discussion of laughter (not just beauty). It is found right at the beginning of §54, and Kant later repeats these claims in the *Anthropology*.[22] As I note in the commentary on Happy Funeral Mourners (No. 2), Kant holds that we can use reason to reflect on our feelings of gratification. Rationally reflecting on and assessing gratification, I suggest, is similar to making a judgment on the basis of a judging activity and its accompanying pleasure. They are both second-order reflections about some pleasure.[23] Sometimes we are displeased *that* we are happy about a misfortune. Kant gives the example of a beneficiary of an inheritance who is delighted that he is receiving money, but feels bad about his delight. Or, sometimes we feel sweet sorrow. Kant describes a widow who is pleased about her grief: she is pleased that she is having the appropriate negative response to her loss. Kant thus wants to distinguish between approval by reason and bodily gratification, and faults Epicurus for missing this distinction.

> One can explain how a gratification can even displease the one who feels it (like the joy of a needy but right-thinking person over the inheritance from his loving but tightfisted father), or how a deep pain can still please the one who suffers it (the sadness of a widow at the death of her praiseworthy husband), or how a gratification can in addition please (like that in the sciences that we pursue) or a pain

(e.g., hatred, envy, or vengefulness) can in addition displease us. The satisfaction or dissatisfaction here rests on reason, and is the same as approval or disapproval; gratification and pain, however, can rest only on the feeling or the prospect (whatever its basis might be) of a possible state of well-being or ill-being.[24]

To be sure, the second-order intellectual assessment discussed in this quote is a practical or moral evaluation about a given mental state (joy, sorrow), not a judgment attributing intersubjective validity to a certain pleasure. Still, the rational moral assessment and assessment of normativity about a pleasure share this second-order structure, as they both comment on the pleasure. If we combine this with what Kant says about a play of thoughts and aesthetic ideas in humor and joking, a play that stems from a reflecting activity, we begin to see how we might reconstruct a Kantian account of judgments of laughter at humor.

Applying this, we can ask about a joke's or event's moral aptness. Likewise, we can ask questions about its normative scope. Do others also find the joke or event funny? Are they, too, comically amused? On this proposal, assigning intersubjective validity is not part of the act of judging itself. Rather, in a second-order reflection, a person assesses the judging in laughter, just as in the quote above, reason evaluates a felt pleasure.

Insofar as laughter is an affect, there is little room for reflection in the act of laughing itself. Even so, Kant's remarks on feelings of gratification (joy, sadness, laughter) imply that we can reflect on and assess the judging's appropriateness and, by extension, its scope.

2. An Experience of Beauty, Sublimity, or Something Else?

Judgments of the beautiful and the sublime are the two principal kinds of pure aesthetic judgments analyzed in the third *Critique*.[25] They meet the necessary conditions of pure aesthetic judgment (disinterestedness, subjective universality, subjectively formal purposiveness, necessity), and both please in themselves.[26]

The object that is experienced as beautiful tends to exhibit harmony and symmetry. Our response to the beautiful object is a pleasant one:

we want the experience to continue, to linger in it.[27] The experience has a simple structure in that the pleasure is not mixed with pain or discomfort. There is no "negative" moment in the experience of beauty. We respond to the object with a "harmony of the faculties," a free harmonious play between imagination and understanding.[28] The experience of beauty involves a play with aesthetic ideas.[29]

In the sublime, however, the object that functions as the stimulus of the experience is vast and/or powerful. In trying to perceive the vast or powerful object all at once, we respond with a mixture of pain and pleasure. Although the overall experience of the sublime is pleasant, it has a complex, negative-positive structure. The negative moment arises because, on account of its size or power, the object initially appears overwhelming or menacing. In the case of the vast object (e.g., the starry sky, Egyptian pyramids), our imagination tries to bring into one representation the idea of infinity which the vast object brings to mind, yet the imagination fails in its efforts. But in so failing it gives a sensible impression of the power of reason. In the case of the powerful object (e.g., a mighty waterfall) our bodies feel threatened by the power of nature. We imagine what it would be like to match up to it, but we realize that in any such contest we would fail. Nevertheless, this stretching of the imagination awakens a feeling of an even greater ability: freedom as a capacity to choose among diverse courses of action. In these ways, the initially conflicting relation is overcome in an ultimately harmonious relation between imagination and reason. Kant describes this movement between the negative and the positive moments, or between feeling overwhelmed and overcoming that feeling, as an oscillation or vibration. In the sublime, "the mind is not just attracted by the object, but is also always reciprocally repelled by it." "This agitation (above all at its inception) can be compared with a vibration, i.e., with a rapid alternation of repulsion from, and attraction to, one and the same object."[30] Whereas in the experience of the beautiful, the imagination and understanding are in a harmonious free play, in the sublime the play is between imagination and *reason*.

If laughter is, or can give rise to, a pure aesthetic judgment, then what kind would it be? Some commentators maintain that laughter, for Kant, counts as an experience of beauty and/or sublimity. Some scholars consider laughter to be a kind of anti-sublime, and, finally, some claim that laughter is required for making judgments of beauty and sublimity at all. I will argue that, insofar as it is a play with aesthetic ideas, the judging in laughter is analogous to the experiences of sublimity and beauty.

The judging in laughter at humor is not an experience of beauty. Marmysz claims that, since laughter begins in the free play of thoughts, Kant treats laughter "as a subspecies of the beautiful rather than of the sublime." Marmysz writes that the "innocent jokes . . . seem to fit neatly into Kant's category of the beautiful."[31] This seems misleading. Meredith's blunt statement seems more accurate: "No one could maintain that the laughable falls simply under the head of either the beautiful or the sublime."[32]

While Kant's discussion of laughter comes in section §54, hence at the very end of the "Deduction" of the *a priori* validity of judgments of beauty, this does not justify classifying the judging in laughter as an experience of beauty. In fact, section §54 (that is, the oddly unnumbered "Remark") really functions as a *border* with the preceding sections and a transition to the upcoming discussion of teleology.[33] The section is not an extension of Kant's discussion of judgments of beauty, and its claims do not actually contribute to Kant's Deduction.

It is not a species of both beauty and the sublime. Hounsokou holds that laughter is a species of beauty and the sublime. Her article is "an inquiry . . . into laughter . . . as a species of beauty and the sublime, and consequently as point of reconciliation between nature and freedom, sensible and supersensible."[34] But if laughter is not a species of beauty, it cannot be a species of both beauty *and* of the sublime. There is a lack of textual support for this reading: Kant never claims that laughter is a species of the beautiful and the sublime. We can reject this position for conceptual reasons too. Giamario (persuasively) rejects Hounsokou's view on the grounds that the beautiful and the sublime are highly specific judgments that differ in fundamental ways. As can already be seen from my brief summary at the beginning of this section, the beautiful and the sublime involve different cognitive faculties that enter into different forms of play with each other.[35] So the suggestion that laughter is a species of both kinds of experiences or judgments seems to be conceptually incoherent.

The judging in laughter at humor is not anti-sublime or grotesque. Stephen Nichols argues that laughter at humor can be classified as anti-sublime, by which he means something like the grotesque or (to use a psychoanalytic term) abject. He holds that it is anti-sublime because in laughter the mind is actively questioning what an incongruity means, yet remains unable to come away with any meaning. In contrast, in the sublime the mind imposes order and unity on the initially chaotic experience of trying to take in all at once an impressively vast structure, such as St. Peter's Basilica in Rome. Nichols thinks Kant "first noticed" the notion of laughter-as-gesture.[36] Nichols endorses the allegedly Kantian idea that laughter produces a sense of the body as grotesque or abject.

However compelling a view of laughter this may be, or however appealing as an interpretation of the later writers Nichols discusses (Jean Paul, Nietzsche), it seems far from an accurate depiction of Kant's views of laughter. For Kant the bodily movement in laughter is invigorating and stimulating, not grotesque or abject. Moreover, Nichols does not acknowledge the positive moment or *uplift* in laughter (an element also noticed by Freud). If laughter just consisted in the frustration of the understanding, laughter would be unpleasant or confusing. But the judging in laughter requires a pleasant *play* with aesthetic ideas (thoughts, representations).

It is not a condition of the possibility of beauty and sublimity. Giamario argues that laughter at humor not only "constitutes an aesthetic judgment," it constitutes the *most basic* aesthetic judgment.[37] Laughter is the transcendental condition of possibility for both the beautiful and the sublime. In other words, the sublime and the beautiful presuppose laughter. Giamario thereby inverts Hounsokou's claim that laughter is a species of the beautiful and sublime. He claims that laughter is the genus, while the sublime and the beautiful are the species.[38]

While Giamario justly criticizes Hounsokou's position that laughter is a species of the sublime and the beautiful, Giamario's claim that laughter is the "cloth" from which both the beautiful and the sublime are cut, commits the error in the other direction. Kant does not claim that laughter is the condition of possibility of pure aesthetic judgments, nor does he give us good reason to extend his account in this way.[39] To his credit, Giamario recognizes that his reading is at odds with both Kant's own conclusions and conventional interpretations of Kant's project.[40]

Rather, the judging in laughter at humor is analogous to the experiences of sublimity and beauty.[41] Let us begin with the sublime, leaving open whether the elicitor is a natural object or a work of art such as Albrecht von Haller's "Imperfect Poem on Eternity" (1736), which Kant admired. Since the experience of the sublime paradigmatically involves a pleasure following an initial failure to comprehend,[42] and, going back at least to Plato, laughter has been conceived of as a mixed combination of pain and pleasure,[43] it is not surprising that the experience of the sublime and laughter have been compared. In his 1927 essay, Freud uses language of the sublime to characterize humor, though of course he would not accept a fully Kantian account of sublimity. For Freud, humor can be not only liberating, but also fine and elevating (*erhebend*). The latter has the same root as the sublime (*Erhabene*).[44] Humor, Freud claims, involves the ego's victorious assertion of its own invulnerability. Humor signals the triumph of the ego even in the midst of adverse circumstances.

This view that the experience of laughter is analogous to the experience of the sublime has been noted by many Kant scholars.[45] Meredith writes, "May not an intellectual pleasure supervene upon the momentary displeasure at the disappointed expectation analogous to that in the case of the sublime?" While admitting the similarities between laughter and the sublime, Meredith correctly chooses not to subsume one under the other. He asks, "Why, then, do we not laugh at the sublime? Apparently because there is not a reduction to *nothing*. . . . But in respect of its physical concomitants [e.g., bodily oscillation] Kant certainly brings the sublime very near" to the humorous.[46]

Citing Meredith, Godfrey calls laughter a species of taste that involves a breakdown between the cognitive faculties analogous to that which occurs in the sublime.[47] Schopenhauer, too, concludes: "The word *humour* is borrowed from the English, in order to single out and denote a quite peculiar species of the laughable, which . . . is even *akin to the sublime*."[48]

Finally, Marmysz's view is particularly worthy of comment since his conclusion that laughter is analogous to the sublime is correct, but for the wrong reasons. Marmysz holds that laughter at humor is similar to the sublime experience in that it involves the transformation of a potentially unpleasant perception into a pleasurable experience, a transformation that we can cultivate with practice and effort. Yet there is a crucial difference between the sublime and laughter, Marmysz claims. Given our sensible limitations, we cannot fully overcome a powerful thunderstorm even in the experience of the sublime; but in the case of humor, we overcome the incongruity. That is why, "sublimity is associated with feelings of awe and respect," whereas "humorous laughter is associated with feelings of superiority and contempt." This difference, he argues, arises from the fact that sublimity is an affective response involving an individual's perception of vulnerability, while laughter at humor involves perceived invulnerability.[49] So there is at most an analogy, not a subsumption of the one under the other.

This is the right conclusion, but the reasoning seems flawed. As noted in my summary above, for Kant the sublime ultimately involves a sensible awareness of one's powers of reason, in which the initial feeling of vulnerability is therefore *overcome*. According to Marmysz's characterization, the sublime is ultimately negative without a redeeming uplift. Another commentator, Borch-Jacobsen, also reads the Kantian sublime this way.[50] A defeated and overpowered mind may be a component of some theories of the sublime, but not Kant's. Thus, whereas Nichols (interpreting laughter as anti-sublime) does not sufficiently acknowledge the recovery in laughter at humor, Marmysz does not sufficiently recognize the uplift and overcoming in the *sublime*. And when it comes to laughter and humor, Marmysz makes Kant sound like a pure superiority theorist ("feeling of superiority and contempt"), when superiority is only one feature of Kant's account.

In short, laughter and sublime experiences can be said to be analogous on several fronts. 1) Laughter involves an initially *discordant* relation between two cognitive faculties, the imagination and understanding. The discord is produced by the initial misapprehension or illusion created by the joke or object of humor. Such a discord is also characteristic of the sublime, where the imagination and reason come into conflict. 2) In both laughter at humor and sublimity, the initial discord is *resolved*, even if momentarily. In the judging in laughter at humor, we feel pleasure once we have insight into the misapprehension or once the "illusion" disappears into nothing. In the sublime, we have an intense feeling of freedom or a sensible awareness of the powers of reason. 3) Both sublimity and laughter involve a vibration or oscillation: the body corresponds to the mind as it moves back and forth. In laughter, there is a comparable shaking of the diaphragm and viscera.[51] The oscillation seems in both cases to be produced by a (momentary) resolution of an initial discord, as the mind moves from the negative moment to the positive moment, and back again to the negative moment. The move from negative to positive is summarized nicely in a marginal note on laughter from Kant's handwritten manuscript of the *Anthropology*. "The striking, the remarkable, what puzzles, what excites the attention as unexpected and in which one cannot immediately find oneself, is an inhibition with an outpouring following thereafter."[52]

We can now turn to beauty. Scholars have noted that laughter and the experience of beauty are analogous.[53] Specifically, the experiences of beauty and laughter share several features. 1) Like that of beauty, the judging in laughter is overall pleasing and people want the experience to last or continue. 2) As with beauty, in laughter the faculties that are in an initial discord, but ultimate harmony, are the imagination and *understanding*.

3) As with beauty, in judging in laughter there is a mental play with "thoughts" and "aesthetic ideas." Here the play with aesthetic ideas in *poetry* that is "beautiful" (which Kant uses to designate artistic merit) makes for the best analogy to the play with thoughts in a joke that is funny. In particular, jokes and poetry both play with aesthetic ideas through a kind of illusion. Poetry "plays with the illusion which it produces at will, yet without thereby being deceitful; for it itself declares its occupation to be mere play."[54] While jokes likewise contain an illusion of a kind, they are not (in any bad sense) deceitful since (or when) one knows that the other person is joking. Such illusion is just part of the game. Moreover, a good ("beautiful") poem requires us to understand both the literal meanings of words and their figurative meanings, just as word plays and puns require us both to keep in mind (using imagination) distinct meanings of words and play them off against each other. Similarly, jokes require us to hold together various elements: a setup (creating expectations), the illusion or incongruity or misunderstanding, and the resolution of the latter (at least momentarily). Finally, just as poetry is in part produced by a play of imagination, for Kant, bon mots or witticisms "are the fruits of wit and are brought forth through the play of imagination."[55] One commentator (Silva) arrives at a similar conclusion, stating that there is an intrinsic connection between wit and poetry (understood broadly as *poiesis*). Wit, as a creative faculty and vehicle of imagination, as sheer inventiveness and freedom, is by its nature *poetical*: poetry may be seen in itself as a continuous wit (*Witz*).[56]

But, if this reading is plausible, where in a joke can we locate its aesthetic *form*?[57] If we could provide a compelling answer to this question, it would strengthen the case that a pure aesthetic judgment of humor is analogous to a pure aesthetic judgment of beauty. Whereas a beautiful poem (especially in Kant's day) has a form (e.g., meter and rhythm, alliteration, rhyme scheme, versification), it might not be immediately clear where, in a joke, such form is to be located. But consider the following. First, some jokes do use rhyme. For instance, my version of Abelard's Flying Ox (No. 16) is (I hope) improved by the rhyme introduced in my English translation of it but missing in the German. According to one study of poetry, rhyme seems to increase the humor of a poetic line, even if the *extent* to which it increases remains an empirical matter.[58] Likewise, I would submit that the introduced alliteration ("form of a fart") and rhyming ("depart/fart") improve joke No. 17.

If a wind rages in a hypochondriac's gut, what matters is where it does *depart*.
If it travels upwards, it is an inspiration from heaven.
If it travels downwards, it takes the *form of a fart*.[59]

The alliteration and rhyming bring it closer to the kind of verse found in Kant's source, Butler's *Hudibras*. Moreover, some jokes, namely narrative or fiction jokes ("Plato walks into a bar . . ."), clearly possess a kind of form, working within the constraints of a given setup/punch line structure. Indeed, the various kinds of joke forms have been widely studied and documented in both the psycho-linguistic and theoretical literature on jokes. Finally, as noted, some jokes and poems play with language in similar ways. Even if word play, punning, and ambiguity have to do more with meaning and semantics than with form and structure, they do strengthen the proposed analogy between a joke and poetry.

4) Like the experiences of beauty and sublimity, the judging in laughter at humor requires a person to be in a disinterested mindset or (if one prefers) to give it one's full, absorbed attention. 5) Finally, like judgments of sublimity and beauty, judgments of humor have a normative dimension. We want others to agree with us, to share our judgments. When they do not, it is disappointing, even unsettling.[60]

In the end, Kant is of two minds about laughter. While he admires laughter's beneficial effects for the body, mind, and even society, he hesitates to claim that it is (or leads to) a pure aesthetic judgment or that it is universally (or intersubjectively) valid and necessary. Why does he hold back?

There appear to be systematic reasons. Kant hesitates to pursue the implications of his account because he maintains (justifiably or not) that humor does not link up directly enough with morality. Without a connection to morality, the "play of the power of judgment" in humor seems to lack "seriousness."[61]

Specifically, as some scholars have noted, Kant does not regard humor as a symbol of the morally good.[62] Yet perhaps Kant missed an opportunity here. He might have drawn on the similarities between the free play in judging beauty and the free play in judging the humorous: both kinds of judging involve a freedom of imagination and a play with "aesthetic ideas." Like the judging in beauty, the enlivening of the mental powers in response to humor has a kind of immediacy and is thought to be valid for others, or intersubjective. Finally, the experiences of laughing at humor and enjoying beauty, for Kant, presuppose being in a disinterested mindset. Since these are the formal features of judging beauty that allow the latter to function as a symbol of the morally good, then perhaps the judging in humor, which shares these features, could act as such a symbol too. Whether or not these reasons are philosophically persuasive, at least they seem to have been available to Kant.

Banki points out an additional compelling reason for Kant's holding back. He maintains that Kant steps back from the implications of his account because he views the gratification in laughter as a mainly physical, corporeal response. Kant to some extent acknowledges the intellectual side of laughter, but in the end he sees it as an agreeable bodily response, worthy of (merely) mechanistic explanations.[63] The consequences of Kant's insight that in laughter we overcome the mind/body split and can get at the body through the soul and vice versa, Banki regrets, "are not explored because of the necessity (inherent to the system) to insist that the gratification here is purely corporeal, as distinct from intellectual or practical (moral)."[64] In the end, the physical and physiological side won out.

I agree that it would have been interesting if in the third *Critique* Kant had not only written more than seven pages on laughter, but had also been bolder and followed through on the implications of his claims. Laughter does seem to have a kind of normativity, even if it is not the kind that we can prove using concepts or symbols, as in logic or mathematics. This is what led several interpreters to go beyond the letter of Kant's text.

If we were to expand Kant's account, we would do well to follow Godfrey. Recognizing the reconstructive nature of his proposal, he aims to show that laughter leads to "an aesthetic judgment, akin to, though distinct from, the judgments of the beautiful and the sublime." Such a judgment (*Urteil*) appears to be a pure aesthetic judgment, an immediate enjoyment directed by reason. Thus, it rests on foundations common to (finite) rational beings. If laughter gives rise to a pure aesthetic judgment, the conditions of pure aesthetic judgment must apply to it. "Laughter in its pure or aesthetic use is universal, claiming validity, and it is necessary, for it fulfills a distinctive function in the rational."[65] Thus, we think that others ought to join in.[66]

If we must extend Kant's account, we should say that if there is a pure aesthetic judgment of laughter, it would be based on a mental play that makes up (part of) the subject's response to and judging of the humor (the joke, gag). The judgment (*Urteil*) would be merely analogous to judgments of the sublime and the beautiful, and would implicitly make or entail an analogous claim to intersubjective validity.[67] The judgment need not become a judgment of the beautiful to make such a claim.

Given the nature of the aesthetic for Kant, if jokes are objects of pure aesthetic judgment, it would be impossible to *prove* that a joke is funny.[68] True, you can give reasons for why you find the joke or event funny, perhaps even based on the kind of joke it is—its joke "genre," as it were.[69] For instance, you might like puns and consider a particular joke to be a good instance of punning. Nevertheless, finding something funny is not a merely conceptual matter and membership in a class is not sufficient for aesthetic success: a *play* with thoughts lies at the core of the proposed reconstructive reading.

3. How Does Laughter at Humor Fit in with Kant's Broader Philosophical Aims?

One of Kant's systematic philosophical aims is to show how it is possible to make what he calls a transition from nature to freedom, that is, to a world where the laws are governed by practical reason, the source of the moral law (see No. 29). As he clarifies in the third *Critique*'s Introduction, this so-called bridge building is one of his reasons why he thought it was necessary to write a third *Critique*. In that work, Kant wishes to prove that it is possible to make such a transition from the manner of thinking in accordance with the principles of *nature* to a manner of thinking in accordance with the principles of *freedom*.[70] In terms of concrete practice, our goal should be to create the conditions that lead to a harmonious realm of rational agents who together form a moral community. This process requires moral education (see No. 30). The human being, insofar as it is a moral being or an autonomous subject of morality, is the "final purpose" of nature to which all other purposes or ends are subordinated.[71]

It would appear that humor-induced laughter, insofar as it promotes socialization and even (indirectly) morality, has a place in Kant's philosophical system. Consider for a moment the following comments by Terry Eagleton.

> It is a republic of free and equal citizens that the bonhomie of the club or dinner table prefigures. In the fourth volume of *Tristram Shandy*, Sterne speaks of his ambition to construct 'a kingdom of hearty laughing subjects.' To laugh together is to share a bodily as well as spiritual communion, one whose closest analogy is a festive meal. In this unity of the physical and mental, laughter is a refutation of Cartesian dualism.[72]

Eagleton offers this passage as a commentary on Hutcheson, but it could also be applied to Kant. Indeed, in her article on Kantian dinner parties, Alix Cohen aptly notices a similar connection between festive dining and the larger aims of Kant's philosophy: "Dinner parties are not merely political communities, they are 'republics of diners' where the freedom of thought is guaranteed in order to produce an open exchange of ideas."[73] Kant would have supported the idea that the communion and solidarity found in festive and merry dining, replete with open intellectual exchange and jest as we simultaneously exercise our rational powers and satisfy bodily and social needs, can indirectly promote morality.

I do not wish to exaggerate the import of laughter to Kant's philosophical project. I would not say that for Kant laughter plays a "crucial, even decisive role" in the third *Critique* or that laughter is a "consequential piece of his critical aesthetic philosophy."[74] But laughter and humor do play *some* role, with section §54's claims about these topics sitting somewhere between, or straddling, anthropology and transcendental philosophy (that is, explaining the conditions of the possibility of a given experience or phenomenon, by identifying its *a priori* source in shared mental capacities).

Is Kant's account best seen as part of transcendental philosophy or as anthropology? Cardelli views section §54 (the "Remark") as belonging to Kant's transcendental philosophy, and thereby rejects Meo's statement that the section remains "merely a chapter from Kant's anthropology."[75] There is some truth to both positions. It seems hard to deny the anthropological elements in section §54, with its references to dining and the diaphragm. Many of its claims are repeated or elaborated in Kant's lectures and writings in anthropology. Kant never attempts to show how the judging in laughter could be or lead to a pure aesthetic judgment that is synthetic and grounded *a priori*. He does not offer anything like an "Analytic of the Comic."

On the other hand, the section is after all located in one of the *Critiques*; this alone should raise a few eyebrows. Moreover, with its remarks on how laughter at humor is beneficial for bodily health, §54 makes for a smooth transition to the subsequent discussion of organisms and teleology in the "Critique of Teleological Judgment." More importantly, the section identifies within humor-induced laughter intellectual and rational elements, not just its merely physiological aspects. Kant characterizes the judging in laughter as a play with infinitely rich aesthetic ideas, and thus of potential interest to reason. To put this another way, Kant's account describes the psychologically real (though not necessarily self-conscious or self-aware) activities of the mind that he thinks make possible the normative experience of laughter at humor. A necessary condition of such laughter is the disinterested, free play of aesthetic ideas and play of thoughts (*Gedankenspiel*), that is, a play between imagination (a source of the aesthetic ideas) and the understanding (the faculty of concepts and thoughts), faculties presumed to be standardly shared by human beings. Kant's explanation of laughter, insofar as it is transcendental, appeals to the interaction between these two faculties (as it does in the case of beauty), rather than to the merely empirical and agreeable physiological elements in the affect, laughter.

Finally, before concluding this chapter, I would like to assess some of the ways laughter's role in Kant's philosophy might be understood.

This role is not best understood as being metaphysical. Meredith speculates that the laughable could be regarded as furnishing us with a playful reminder that the world is a mere appearance of a thing-in-itself.[76] (For Kant, the thing-in-itself is an unknowable "thing" considered independently of observation, or to put it another way, considered in abstraction from the human sensible faculties of space and time. It somehow underlies the sensible world and makes appearances possible.) Although Meredith's suggestion makes a connection to a cornerstone of Kant's philosophical system, it strikes me as adopting too many unnecessary metaphysical assumptions, at least too many for a theory of humor to take in. Meredith himself offers it as a merely tentative remark.

Godfrey expands Kant's account in a more plausible direction. Although there is lighthearted playfulness in laughter at humor, he says, it is the rational being who is at play. All taste is the play of the rational being, who has everything under control, with the imagination properly subordinated to the understanding even as it plays with illusions or with the understanding's mistakes.[77] We have a sense of humor because, finite beings that we are, we have limited understandings. Unlike an omniscient being, we can be wrong. Many of our judgments are merely contingently true; they can be false. And sometimes our errors make us or others laugh. Laughter is one way of responding to and coping with such misunderstandings. In laughing at the incongruous or absurd, we tame it, we make sense of it. We see the mind's power of asserting its own unity, of keeping itself whole and sane, and of expressing this unity and sanity in appropriate and specific ways.[78] Laughter at humor, then, would ultimately serve as an indicator of the power and efficacy of reason broadly construed. Indeed, at one point Kant endorses provoking laughter in "rational people."[79]

John Zammito offers a similar line, employing Kant's idiom more directly. In his interpretation of section §54, Zammito claims that laughter might help Kant show how it is possible to make a transition from nature to freedom. Specifically, the feeling of life (*Lebensgefühl*) that is promoted by laughter somehow "leads to" a distinct intellectual feeling (*Geistesgefühl*), a feeling of autonomous spirituality, where we sense the rational authority of the moral law which rational beings legislate to themselves.[80] To develop this suggestion further, however, it would be useful to clarify if this process is to be understood in only psychological, or in some other, terms, and if possible, to describe in further detail the process by which the feeling of life leads to or brings about the spiritual-intellectual feeling.

Although he does not focus on laughter, Rudolf Makkreel emphasizes the import of section §54 for Kant's broader systematic aims. Makkreel writes that the idea of life can be used to point to the fundamental coherence of the two parts of the book, on aesthetics and teleology, respectively.[81] Structurally, Kant's discussion of life (not just laughter) functions as a bridge to the second half of the third *Critique*. On Makkreel's plausible reading, the subjective feeling of an objective state of bodily health is the logical hinge connecting the subjective purposiveness (aesthetics) and objective purposiveness (teleology) discussed in the book's two halves.[82] This is a compelling point about the structure of the book, but one wishes that Makkreel had devoted more than a page to laughter.

In her article on laughter, Hounsokou considers naiveté to be the most important of the three "arts" of laughter.[83] The naive person exposes the joker (*Schalk*) in us—human artificiality or even hypocrisy. In other words, the joke is on us. Since such exposure can be put to moral ends, it can help realize morality in the world and so contribute to what Kant calls the final purpose of nature. This seems Kantian enough.

More significantly, Hounsokou sees laughter, as a bodily phenomenon in response to aesthetic ideas, as contributing to Kant's systematic aims of unifying nature's lawful necessity and freedom. A Janus-faced phenomenon, laughter at humor reconciles the sensible and the supersensible.[84] In laughter, she maintains, the body and the soul engage in a free yet lawful play that is purposive for the whole human being, so that the body is in harmony with the mind.[85] Thus, she concludes, "the role that laughter could have played in the third *Critique* is that of a stepping stone towards the supersensible; a stepping stone situated a little lower, a little closer to the senses, and therefore more accessible to more people."[86] She wishes Kant had elaborated how laughter could play such a role.

Hounsokou is right that humor-elicited laughter, insofar as it is a pure aesthetic judging or experience, would play a crucial role in Kant's system, and a similar interpretation is also put forward by Birgit Recki.[87]

The ability to play such a role derives from such laughter's status as a kind of pure aesthetic judging, thereby containing intellectual-rational components and not just the corresponding bodily expressions. In fact, however, it would seem that *every* (Kantian) pure aesthetic judging would be intellectually interesting to reason, as it gives sensory intimations of freedom and reason. All pure aesthetic experiences or judgings, for Kant, are Janus-faced in this way. For instance, the experience of beauty, which is surely "close" to the senses (to paraphrase Hounsokou), becomes intellectually interesting (in Kant's sense) because it can act as a symbol of morality and gives a sensible hint or indication that nature will harmonize with our attempts to be moral. Sublime experiences, which involve a vivid bodily oscillation and are intense sensory experiences too, become intellectually interesting because they provide us with a feeling of freedom and of our power to act morally. Reason takes an interest in any such experience and act of judging.[88] Hounsokou identifies a way in which the judging in humor-induced laughter could support Kant's broader philosophical aims, but it is not unique to laughter.

Kant maintains that laughing together can sometimes build community and forge social bonds that can support morality. In addition, ridicule and literary satire can be used to criticize and improve the status quo. In other words, laughter, and some of the forms of humor that evoke it (satire), can be of indirect service to morality. We now turn to the ethics of humor and to the possible connections between humor and morality.

Chapter 3
Kant and the Ethics of Humor

According to Kant, not all laughter is good and proper. Inappropriate laughter can be a sign of mental illness.[1] In the form of scoffing and malicious ridicule, it can be a means of hurting others (*wehe thun*).[2] Kant states that we judge a person from the way they laugh.[3] This naturally raises the question: When is responding with laughter or amusement appropriate?

To address this, I would like to characterize Kant's position as "soft ethicism."[4] The term *ethicism* seems to be fitting for Kant's theory since he holds that there are ethical constraints on joking and that shared, wholesome laughter can promote socialization, one of the aids or supports of morality. Kant's ethicism is *soft* because, within limits set by his ethical principles and given an appropriate context, it allows for some joking about sensitive matters, including (as we might say today) race, ethnicity, sexuality, gender, age, class, and disability.[5] If, as Kant writes, humor is only a "momentary entertainment," there is some leeway or area for play (*Spielraum*) in joking.

Accordingly, I begin with some general remarks on Kantian ethics (section 1). I explain why the labels "ethicism" and "soft" are appropriate for Kant's account (sections 2 and 3). I discuss Kant's view of the permissibility of telling potentially offensive jokes (section 4). To make this concrete, I contrast one of Kant's racist claims with one of his sexist quips (section 5). Finally, I conclude this Part of the book with some practical Kantian questions on the ethics of joking (section 6).

This chapter is more a presentation of broader Kant*ian* arguments than an interpretation of Kant's actual claims in the strict sense. I am directly applying Kant's moral philosophy to humor, whereas he does not do this very explicitly.

1. A Review of Kantian Ethical Theory

Since Kant is one of the most important writers on ethics of all time, I take it that most readers either will be somewhat familiar with the fundamentals of Kant's ethical theory or, if not, can easily bring themselves up to date, allowing me to spend less space on it here.

An ethical orientation runs through Kant's entire philosophical thinking. Not surprisingly, some critics have charged his theories of even aesthetic matters with being overly moralistic. For instance, Malcolm Budd attributes to Kant "a tendency that led him to moralize, in one way or another, any experience he valued."[6] Is this also true of his theory of humor?

An ethical orientation can be found in his account of humor, but I don't think Kant's account is guilty of over-moralizing here. The ethical side to the account is balanced by the notion that there is a time and place for joking that allows the joke teller (or humor producer) and the audience (or humor receiver) to say or laugh at certain things that in another context they would find inappropriate.

This does not mean, however, that joking is exempt from the requirement to meet the basic principles of ethics. After all, Kant thinks that no human action is exempt from that. Moreover, we should bear in mind that what counts for Kant as a morally worthy act has to meet a very high bar. A morally worthy act is done for the right reason, namely, *because* it is the right thing to do (in Kant's terminology, "for the sake of the moral law"). Kant allots morality utmost importance in human affairs. Of all kinds of actions, the ones that are morally obligated have priority over and override all other kinds.

While we can't here study the finer points of Kant's ethics, we have to get clear about the core principles underlying Kantian ethical theory. Morality, for Kant, is determined by what he calls the moral law, as expressed in the categorical imperative. The categorical imperative,

Kant thinks, governs and acts as a moral constraint on all rational agency and human action. Here is one formulation of it.

> **Principle 1**. "There is, therefore, only a single categorical imperative and it is this: act only in accordance with that maxim [i.e., a subjective principle of action] through which you can at the same time will that it become a universal law."[7]

This means that we should not make exceptions of ourselves when we deliberate and act, when doing so would require us to violate an objective moral law. When we wrong or harm an innocent person, we act on the principle that although we don't want that wrongful or harmful act to be done to us, it is okay for us to do it to someone else.

A violation of the moral law, Kant maintains, *harms* humanity in general. A lie, for instance, causes harm in this way. As Kant states in *On a Supposed Right to Lie from Philanthropy*, a lie "always harms [*schadet*] another, even if not another individual, nevertheless humanity generally, inasmuch as it makes the source of right unusable."[8]

Kant expresses the categorical imperative in other terms. A second version of the Ethical Principle states that we should treat other people with moral respect, recognizing their dignity. We should treat them as "ends" rather than as mere means.

> **Principle 2**. "So act that you use humanity, whether in your own person or in the person of any other, always at the same time as an end, never merely as a means."[9]

In short, Kant's ethics requires 1) not making exceptions of ourselves when it concerns the application of objective laws, and 2) treating other people with respect, recognizing their dignity.

As should be clear from this, Kant's ethics rules out discriminatory acts such as racist acts. According to one definition, a person does a *racist* act when i) a person A carries out the act in order to *harm* another person B (a member of a certain group) because B is a member of that group; or ii) the person A doing the act can reasonably be expected (regardless of A's intentions or purposes) to *mistreat or wrong* B as a consequence of B's being a member of that group.[10] For similar reasons, Kant's account would also rule out sexism, ableism, ageism, and other forms of discrimination. In other words, the "group" above can be adjusted to apply to other classes of people.

While it might border on the obvious to state this, Kant's ethical principles imply that we may not physically harm someone in order to create or evoke comic amusement. We may *simulate* such violence on stage or on screen, but we should not carry it out in real life. Carrying it out in real life would violate the ethical limits imposed by the moral law. And it would be no justification to insist that we are in a disinterested space or area of play, that we are carrying out such violence for "art's sake," and thus that such real violence is justified. Rather, the proper response would instead be to adopt an interested mindset and to oppose the morally wrong violence against others. Kant would place similar ethical constraints, I will argue, on joking and jest.

2. Why Ethicism

Before proceeding, I would first like to point out that there is a related but distinct debate in contemporary philosophy of humor concerning "ethicism" or "moralism." I mention this because we should not confuse my use of "ethicism" with the term as it is used in that debate. That discussion revolves around this question: Does a joke's immorality make it less funny, funnier, or have no effect at all? There are three principal positions.[11]

> **Moralism**: the immoral joke is made *less* funny by its immorality.
> **Immoralism**: the immoral joke is made *funnier* by its immorality.
> **Amoralism**: there is *no* correlation between the joke's immorality and funniness.

According to moralism, a joke with a morally flawed outlook is to some extent deficient as a joke—precisely on account of its immorality. Thus, even if the joke could still be funny to some extent, its immoral features render it less funny. Moralism has stronger and weaker forms, but the distinction between high-octane moralism *simpliciter* and moderate moralism need not concern us here.[12]

Immoralism holds the inverse of moralism: a moral flaw improves the joke.[13] The more a joke violates and disrupts ethical norms, the more its value as a joke increases (the funnier it is). Ethical flaws do not detract from the funniness of a joke occasion, but instead enhance its comic effect.[14]

Amoralism holds that there is no influence of morality on humor.[15] A joke's morality or immorality has no effect on how funny or amusing it is. This position could also be called "autonomism" since it maintains that morality and humor are independent of each other, that is, autonomous. Ted Cohen and Al Gini, for instance, hold that comic amusement is untouched by a joke's moral shortcomings. Cohen writes, "Wish that there were no mean jokes. Try remaking the world so that such jokes will have no place, will not arise. But do not deny that they are funny."[16] Gini claims that a joke that is "unethical" can still be funny, given the right audience.[17] In other words, the unethical aspect has no bearing on the funniness.

The morality/funniness relation contains a noteworthy asymmetry. Whereas there is considerable controversy about whether an *immoral* joke is thereby less funny, no one claims that a *moral* joke is thereby funnier.[18] A joke with a moral perspective or content (i.e., a moral joke) may be better for practical-moral reasons and may be morally edifying, but nobody holds that it is better as a joke.

So, which of the above three positions would Kant adopt? Unfortunately, he does not frame his account in these terms, so it is not easy to say, although it seems fair to rule out immoralism. Perhaps moralism? Maybe even amoralism? Kant's position does not precisely match up to this debate, so I won't spend more time on it here.

Even if I am using the term "ethicism" in a way that differs from "moralism" in this recent debate, I think my use of the term is appropriate for four reasons. In explaining these reasons, the sense of "ethicism" should become clear.

1. There are ethical constraints on humor

For Kant, ethical principles place constraints on what we are permitted to joke about. In jest and joking, we should never treat people as mere means, but always with moral respect. Humor should be carried out in a morally permissible way, where morality is understood in terms of what is allowed or prohibited by the categorical imperative (Principles 1 and 2). There is no strict duty to joke, but if and when we do joke, we must be sure we do so in an ethically permissible way.

Although this chapter presents broader Kan*tian* arguments, it is nonetheless grounded in and inspired by his writings, so let us examine them. Kant claims that there are (ethical) limits placed on what can be said at a dinner party. For instance, if (potentially harmful) gossip is exchanged in this private setting, it should not be repeated outside of that context. The party goers have what Kant calls a "duty of secrecy." As one commentator (Alix Cohen) puts it, there is a "covenant" shared by the dinner guests, a trust that they can reveal their thoughts to each other without fear of later disclosure.[19] Kant thereby implies that there are ethical principles that govern our speech in informal settings.

It is not merely a social *taste* that must guide the conversation; there are also principles that should serve as the limiting condition on the freedom with which human beings openly exchange their thoughts in social interactions.[20]

Kant does not explicitly state which principles he has in mind, but we can read them as applications of Principles 1 and 2—we should treat everyone, even people who are absent, with dignity and respect. We should not talk badly about others or hurt their reputations when they are absent.

How might this apply to joking? Talking negatively about others is not the same as joking. For when one gossips in a negative way, one is making claims about real people in the world, and these assertions can be either true or false, whereas in telling a joke the claims are often about a fictional joke world in which the claims (at least according to a prominent philosophical approach) are neither true nor false (in that same sense of truth and falsity). Still, I think it is fair to extend Kant's reasoning about gossiping at a dinner party to jest and joking. If so, the ethical limiting "principles" would act as a condition on what we should or should not say in jest and joking. Specifically, the principles would rule out our treating people as mere means and without moral respect. One commentator (Godfrey) arrives at a similar conclusion. "If we recognize judgment in laughter at all, it cannot conflict with moral judgment, but must rather ally itself with it."[21] Cohen similarly notes that freedom of speech in a social conversation should be restricted by respect for other guests.[22]

Principle 2 implies that it is unacceptable to treat people as mere means and to disrespect their humanity, even if one is "only" joking. This could be summarized by invoking Kant's means-end distinction as expressed in the categorical imperative: jokes that treat people or groups of people as mere means are morally wrong, while jokes that treat people as ends having dignity are permissible. Kant's account entails that we cannot joke in just any manner we please, but instead that there are ethical limits on what we can do or say in jest and joking.

But the fact that joking is constrained by ethical principles does not (*pace* Kivy) make appropriate joking simply a matter of following a "moral rule."[23] For what is also needed to treat people with moral respect when joking, is judgment and prudence. What is required is the proper use of judgment in a particular situation, in order to determine what would (or would not) cause harm and wrong to the another person, that is, what would violate their dignity. And there is no higher-order rule for that. It is useful here to bear in mind the *Anthropology*'s characterization of the faculty of judgment.

> But the . . . faculty . . . of discerning whether something is an instance of the rule or not—*the power of judgment (judicium)*—cannot be *instructed*, but only exercised. . . . It is also easy to see that this could not be otherwise; because instruction takes place by means of communication of rules. Therefore, if there were to be doctrines for the power of judgment, then there would have to be general rules according to which one could decide whether something was an instance of the rule or not; which would generate a further inquiry on into infinity.[24]

The power of judgment "is aimed only at that which is feasible, what is fitting, and what is proper (for theoretical, aesthetic, and practical power of judgment)."[25] Knowing how to joke and tease, in the right way and to the right extent, is a skill. Even if Kant does not exactly put it that way, I think his broader ethical theory implies this claim. For, analogously, Kant holds that we have some latitude regarding how candid and how reticent we wish to be. We certainly should not tell lies to each other, he holds, but we also don't have to say everything that is on our minds. In other words, we should be candid to the right extent and in the right way. He calls candor and reticence "duties of virtue." These two duties

> have a latitude in their application (*latitudinem*), and judgment can decide what is to be done only in accordance with rules of prudence

(pragmatic rules), not in accordance with rules of morality (moral rules). In other words, what is to be done cannot be decided after the manner of *narrow* duty (*officium strictum*), but after the manner of *wide* duty (*officium latum*).[26]

Analogously, there is a similar latitude when it comes to jest. When we attempt to treat people with moral respect while joking with them, our actions are (or should be) governed by prudence and judgment. An anthropology lecture from 1784/85 reads: "Wit enlivens the social gathering; but the lack of the power of judgment makes the social gathering tasteless."[27]

There is additional textual support for attributing the "ethical constraint" position to Kant. In chapter one's discussion of mockery, I maintained that Kant identifies ethical limits on joking and teasing. He thinks that there is a point at which jest becomes harmful or violates someone's dignity. For the sake of space, these passages need not be cited again, but I refer the curious reader back to them.

Other passages can be mentioned. Kant's view is nicely summarized in a passage from the *Anthropology*. He claims that malicious laughter is hostile and, by implication, ethically impermissible. "Good-natured (openhearted) laughter is sociable (insofar as it belongs to the affect of cheerfulness); malicious (sneering) laughter is hostile."[28] Moreover, although it is not evidence of bad taste or moral wrongdoing if we are amused by an absent-minded professor figure, it is wrong to feel *real* contempt for the person.

> The distracted person (like Terrasson entering solemnly with his night cap instead of his wig on his head and his hat under his arm, full of the quarrel concerning the superiority of the ancients and the moderns with respect to the sciences) often gives rise to the first, good-natured kind. He is laughed at [*belacht*], but still not mocked [*ausgelacht*]. We laugh at the intelligent eccentric, but it doesn't cost him anything; he laughs with us.[29]

The ethical constraints on humor go beyond the general principle that we should not deride and mock people. Kant's account also implies that, specifically, there are ethical constraints to joking about sex, gender, and sexuality.

He appears to have held this view long before the publication of the third *Critique* in 1790. In the mid-1760s, Kant repudiated what we might now call "locker room humor" insofar as it becomes offensive or uncivilized. "Jokes told in the company of just men have no real life, and become uncivilized too."[30] Kant deplores those who "get just as lively a joy from vulgarities and a crude joke," and he praises "persons of nobler sentiment."[31] Lewd jokes about others seem to be reproachable because they make people into mere means, for instance by treating them as mere objects or reducing them to their sexuality and sexual organs.[32] One could say that such jokes become *disgusting* from a moral point of view. They are at the very least blameworthy from the perspective of civility and etiquette. But on Kant's account they seem to be morally reproachable as well, for they do not treat people as ends in themselves, but reduce them to their sexual organs.

In addition, such jokes may even violate duties to *oneself* in that they can be self-degrading. By treating and interacting with other people merely in terms of their sexuality and sexual organs rather than in terms of their rational capacities to set and act on ends, one may be implicitly disrespecting the humanity in oneself, since one is likewise a rational yet embodied being.

According to *Observations* (1764), "vulgar jokes" or "obscenities" should not be told in the presence of women either.[33] As Kant puts it decades later in *Anthropology*, "At a festive table . . . the presence of ladies by itself restricts men's freedom within the bounds of good manners."[34] Although we may well justifiably criticize the broader context and the views of women that lead Kant to make this claim, in this section that is not my aim. My point is rather to note that there are social-civil and ethical restrictions on what we should joke about and say in conversation.

In short, the fact that Kant's account places ethical constraints on humor is a reason why it counts as a kind of ethicism.

2. Jest and joking are dispensable, overridden by ethical constraints

As much as he appreciates and identifies a positive role for humor and wit, Kant considers jest to be "dispensable," to be controlled by reason and governed by ethical principles. Of course, this view enjoys a long tradition in the history of western philosophy, going back at least to Plato. For Kant, jest's being overridden by ethical principles seems to follow from the first point: humor is constrained by the moral law. (Hence we can be much briefer here.)

Joking is like a luxury—it is superfluous. "For the joke is very delicate and is only fitting for the nobleman's supper, as Rabelais says."[35] Kant extends this "sauce" metaphor in another passage (No. 21). "Sound reason and understanding are like a dish of beef and mutton. They are fit only for the peasant's table. But a ragout of folly, accompanied by a sauce of wit, is fit for an emperor's table."[36] Humor is important, but it is only an accessory. Garnishes should be used wisely and not be mistaken for the main dish.

Because it sees jest as dispensable, something that can be overridden by ethical principles, Kant's account counts as a kind of ethicism.

3. Any moral content in a joke or jest increases its practical-moral worth

Jokes sometimes have a moral message. They can endorse a moral outlook or perspective. An example of this would be Abelard's Flying Ox (No. 16). Kant probably admired the Flying Ox joke because it makes the wise and upright Abelard look even wittier and smarter than the jocular priest, who told a kind of lie for the sake of a prank. Some humor, in other words, has moral content, and this adds practical-moral value to the joke. The moral content can have a moralizing effect on the readers or audience. When that happens, the moral content adds a kind of value to the joke. Given their potential to promote morality, jokes that have such a moral content or effect on readers or audience are better (in that they support morality) than those that lack such content or effects. If a joke has a moral effect, then that ethical quality gives it more ethical value, though it does not necessarily make it funnier. This implies the following corollary.

Corollary: any moral flaws exhibited by the joke worsens the joke, since it can have a morally harmful effect.

In the corollary, "worsening" the joke does not mean making it less funny, but only less valuable, morally speaking.

Ethical-social reform has long been recognized as one of the functions of ridicule and satire.[37] By making fun of vices and morally reprehensible characters who embody them, satirists (Fielding, Butler) help us identify moral shortcomings and potentially encourage us to have the desire to avoid them. Such humor contains an implicit ethical judgment.[38] It has the potential to support morality (indirectly), by containing "moral messages" or by ridiculing vices. It criticizes and potentially corrects the presumed claims and ways of the morally reprehensible characters. A joke can bring to attention cultural, social, and ethical-political issues and criticize the status quo, helping to bring about reform. On a more individual level, humor is able to deflate arrogance and pride by poking fun at our acquired cultural conceits and our unexamined social practices and habits.

For Kant, humor cannot effect moral change immediately or directly. Ethical reform does not happen without the effort of each individual, and it comes about only as a result of choices that we take to be free. But a morally-oriented joke, Kant implies, can still be of assistance to morality.

Note that Kant never implies that jokes need to have some intellectual-moral content in order to be funny. The three jokes presented in the third *Critique* — The Merchant's Wig (No. 1), Happy Funeral Mourners (No. 2), and Foam in a Bottle (No. 12) — lack a moral message. Despite the absence of moral content, Kant considers them to be comically amusing. He even claims that The Merchant's Wig will send us into "peals of laughter."[39]

Because Kant holds that a joke's moral content and its moralizing effects (if any) would add value to a joke, his account counts as a kind of ethicism.

4. Joking and jest promote sociability, one of the supports and allies of morality

The person who cannot laugh with us, to paraphrase Aristotle, is either a beast or a bore. As Kant puts it, "Whoever never laughs at a social gathering is either sullen or pedantic."[40] Even if joking may be dispensable and is overridden by moral constraints, the ability to joke and jest is important for human beings. Like Aristotle, Kant thinks that we are social animals, even if Kant gives this idea a modern and post-Hobbesian twist, calling it *unsociable* sociability.[41] Although qua social beings we need each other and rely on each other, we also have a tendency to annoy, frustrate, compete with, and even threaten and harm each other. In *Lectures on Pedagogy*, Kant illustrates this point with an anecdote taken from a Laurence Sterne novel.

In *Tristram Shandy*, Toby says this to a fly that had been bothering him for a while, as he was letting it out the window: "Go, you annoying creature, the world is big enough for both of us." And everyone can make this into their motto. We must not bother one another; the world is big enough for us all.[42]

Like Hutcheson, Kant thinks that laughter and jest can nevertheless help us get along better.[43] Of course, Kant never endorses buffoonery: "A mechanical (spiritless) burst of laughter is insipid and makes the social gathering tasteless."[44] Yet he values laughter and joke telling for promoting and developing our social sides.[45] In this section I would like to elaborate this point.

Let us first note that the framework for Kant's discussion of laughing at humor is generally more *socio-anthropological* (and ethical) than it is political. This is not to deny that the socio-anthropological dimension overlaps to some extent with a political one. Kant makes some connections between wit and politics. I can mention three. First, he tells a story (quoted in No. 4, Dying of Good Health) in which King Frederick displays some degree of wit in a conversation with the philosophical aesthetician Sulzer.[46] Kant thus suggests that a sense of wit (accompanied by judgment) can help politicians reach their aims. Second, as I note in my commentary on joke No. 3 (on Jonathan Swift's wit), Kant also makes a connection between a nation's sense of wit (a type of free thinking) and certain forms of government. The English political system encourages originality and wit, since the people do not have to follow the tone set by the monarch or court. Third and finally, Kant is reported to have stated (in an anthropology lecture) that "knowledge of the human being" is "indispensable" for politics "in order to be able to rule human beings." "Without knowledge of the human being the sovereign cannot lead" people from different ranks and classes.[47] While Kant doesn't exactly put it this way, I would suggest that possessing an awareness of what amuses people, a sense of humor, counts as part of what it means to have (practical) knowledge of human nature, to have prudence and an ability to influence others. Such know-how, no doubt useful for anyone, would be particularly beneficial for a sovereign or political leader. Notwithstanding these three connections, however, it is probably true that this association of politics and humor does not amount to the tight link that one finds in British accounts from the early modern period, when authors such as Hobbes and Shaftesbury, in addition to recognizing and commenting on the social aspects of humor, more directly addressed the uses of humor in the political realm.

It is worth recalling here that humor in general has many functions. It can censure, debunk, and transform, but it can also bring together and consolidate.[48] Humor is both a weapon and a bond, and the social aspects of humor have been widely recognized not just by Kant, but also by his predecessors and successors.[49]

Kant recognizes both sides of humor: censure and social communion. I here focus on the latter. For Kant, humor can help socialize us when it leads to shared pleasure in response to a story or narrative. A core function of humor, after all, is to have fun together. Kant holds that if humor and wit are used properly, they have the potential to cultivate and refine humanity. To put it another way, humor can reinforce social norms. (Even incongruity jokes that are based on the *violation* of social norms and values can strengthen those very norms and values. "Like art," Eagleton writes, "humor can estrange and relativize the norms by which we live, but it can also reinforce them."[50] In itself, reinforcing norms is not necessarily bad: it depends on the norm.) Even if humor and joking can become instruments of exclusion rather than of intimacy, humor can, in addition to relieving tension, boost social bonding. This is important to Kant, since it means humor can help create a context that can allow us to perfect ourselves and become better people. It is on account of humor's socializing and (indirect) moralizing potential that many of Kant's jokes and stories collected in this guide come from Kant's course on anthropology, for that course was intended to help students become not just prudent and well-mannered but also upright and informed citizens of the world.

Since humor has the ability to promote our social capacities, Kant reasons, it can ultimately be of service to morality. It can create a milieu that is conducive to morality, an environment whereby we can both perfect ourselves and create a moral community. In *Anthropology*, Kant lists some guidelines for giving a refined dinner party; significantly, he thinks that it should conclude with laughter and jest (*Scherz*). He then states:

> No matter how insignificant these laws of refined humanity may seem, especially if one compares them to pure moral laws, nevertheless, anything that promotes sociability, even if it consists only in pleasing maxims or manners, is a garment that dresses virtue profitably, a garment which is also to be recommended with serious consideration.[51]

Since laughter at humor is something that promotes sociability, humor and jest can "dress virtue profitably" (i.e., support it). Significantly, Kant thinks that the activities that promote sociability are to be taken and recommended quite seriously. And in one of his lectures on anthropology, Kant specifically mentions "artful jest" (*artige Scherz*) as something that can help promote self-mastery. "Well-mannered social intercourse and artful jest conquer the otherwise hard to overcome inclination."[52]

The "garment" or "dress" metaphor should be understood in the wider context of Kant's views, according to which our social interactions require some degree of affectation or acting (which is not the same as outright lying).[53]

> On the whole, the more civilized human beings are, the more they are actors. They adopt the illusion of affection, of respect for others, of modesty, and of unselfishness without deceiving anyone at all, because it is understood by everyone that nothing is meant sincerely by this. And it is also very good that this happens in the world. For when human beings play these roles, eventually the virtues, whose illusion they have merely affected for a considerable length of time, will gradually really be aroused and merge into the disposition.[54]

Such affectation and "innocent illusion" is acceptable, since everyone knows how to understand it. Moreover, it is even good preparation for actual virtue. "Even the illusion of good in others must have worth for us, for out of this play with pretenses, which acquires respect though perhaps without earning it, something quite serious can finally emerge."[55]

In his late work on ethics and practical philosophy, *The Metaphysics of Morals*, Kant states even more clearly that we have a duty to develop our social sides and to do so in a virtuous manner. In an appendix entitled, "On the Virtues of Social Intercourse," Kant claims that social interaction with fellow human beings involves duties to self and others. There is, in the first place, a duty not to isolate oneself but instead to engage in socializing activities of some kind (including, I would add, joking and light banter). One thereby perfects and improves oneself: by putting on good appearances, one is getting a kind of practice for, or doing a simulation of, genuine virtue.

> It is a duty to oneself as well as to others not to *isolate* oneself (*separatistam agere*) but to use one's moral perfections in social intercourse (*officium commercii, sociabilitas*).[56]

In socializing with fellow human beings, one participates in a community that is analogous to the moral community that is made up of "citizens of the world."

> While making oneself a fixed center of one's principles, one ought to regard this circle drawn around one as also forming part of an all-inclusive circle of those who, in their disposition, are citizens of the world—[. . .] [in order] to cultivate a disposition of reciprocity—agreeableness, tolerance, mutual love and respect (affability and propriety, *humanitas aesthetica et decorum*) and so to associate the graces with virtue. To bring this about is itself a duty of virtue.[57]

But, consonant with what he writes in *Anthropology*, *The Metaphysics of Morals* states that we should not be misled into thinking that such social graces have moral worth.

> These are, indeed, only *externals* or by-products (*parerga*), which give a beautiful illusion resembling virtue that is also not deceptive since everyone knows how it must be taken.[58]

There is a degree of illusion ("beautiful illusion") created in such social interactions and pleasantries, even though it is not deceptive in the bad sense, since everyone knows what is going on and is playing the same game. These social graces, Kant thinks, indirectly support morality. Although "affability, sociability, courtesy, hospitality, and gentleness" are only amoral accessories,

> they promote the feeling for virtue itself by a striving to bring this illusion as near as possible to the truth. By all of these, which are merely the manners one is obliged to show in social intercourse, one binds others too; and so they still promote a virtuous disposition by at least making virtue well-liked [*beliebt*].[59]

Thus, such sociability-promoting activities—including joking and jest—can indirectly promote a virtuous disposition and a feeling for virtue.

To be sure, socialization is not the same as moral cultivation. According to *Anthropology*, the "cultivation of social qualities" promotes virtue and constitutes a kind of progress and a "higher step," but it does not count as either virtue or morality.[60] For Kant, morally worthy action is always a matter of deliberate effort and activity; there is no replacement for respect for the authority of the moral law. But socialization is a step in the direction of morality since it helps create an amenable setting that is conducive to moral cultivation in oneself and in others.

It will be helpful to recall Kant's doctrine of prudence.[61] According to Kant, one uses prudence in order to aim at achieving one's own happiness. This seemingly self-serving capacity has a beneficial effect that extends beyond self-interest, however, for it forces us to be "well-mannered." While not the same as virtue, this activity is good preparation for it.

> Making the human being *well-mannered* for his social situation to be sure does not mean as much as forming him into a *morally good* person, but nevertheless it prepares him for the latter by the effort he makes in his social situation to please others (to become liked or admired)."[62]

Even if prudence aims at one's own happiness, it gets us to think from the position of other people, to adopt a broader perspective, and attempt to satisfy the inclinations of others, since after all we frequently need their help if we are to obtain what we think will lead to our happiness.[63] Prudence, because it involves the ability to use people (while hopefully still treating them with respect) in order to get what we think will make us happy, forces us to become well-mannered and to develop qualities such as affability, propriety, and friendliness. Significantly, it leads us to develop a sense of *taste*, a sense of beauty and the fine arts. As Wilson notes, Kant was especially "enamored of the role that taste can play in a prudent life."[64]

Now, I would add that a sense of humor, like taste and a sense of beauty, can play a role here. As we have seen, the quickening of the mental capacities in response to humor would appear to share several of the formal features of the judging of beauty that, for Kant, allow the latter to function as a symbol of morality (immediacy, intersubjectivity, disinterestedness, freedom of imagination). Engaging in jest and humor requires us to think from the perspectives of others, as we ask: Will this joke work? Was it fitting in that context? Was that an appropriate thing to say in front of that audience? Kant would consider such reflection to be good practice for the kind of perspective shifting that is required of morality, even if it is not to be identified with morality. In knowing when and how to deliver a joke, we are exercising our capacities of good judgment. Here we can recall the three maxims of the "common human understanding" or ways of thinking presented in the third *Critique*: 1) to think for oneself (be unprejudiced), 2) to think from the standpoint of everyone else (adopt a broadened perspective), and 3) always to think in accord with oneself (think consistently). Significantly, Kant associates the second one with the power of judgment. "One can say that the first of these maxims is that maxim of the understanding, the second that of the power of judgment, the third that of reason."[65]

Before concluding this section, I would like to draw attention to an analogy between our socially-grounded interests in art and in humor. In §41 of the third *Critique*, Kant identifies an "empirical" interest in beautiful art that is rooted in our need to be social and, in turn, promotes our sociability.[66] Kant implies that we can likewise take an (empirical) interest in *humor* that is both grounded in and supportive of our social sides. Note that in both cases, art and humor, it is possible to promote sociability in morally permissible and impermissible ways. There is always the risk that we will take a socializing tendency that in itself is neutral and misapply it, hurting or wronging others, or violating a duty to self. In the case of art, for instance, we might go listen to or see (or collect) artworks just to impress our peers with our taste and thus in order to satisfy a misguided sense of pride. In the case of humor, we might tell jokes just to make others think we are clever (again out of pride), or use humor in order to exclude people wrongfully.

We can now take stock of the reasons for characterizing Kant's account as "ethicism." Reason 1 stated that there are ethical constraints on what jokes we may tell. In a similar vein, reason 2 claimed that joking or jest can be overridden by ethical principles, placing a relative value on joking. Reason 3 concerned the moral content or effects of a joke (including satire) and its corresponding practical-moral value. Reason 4 addressed the fact that humor has the ability to promote one of the supports of morality (socialization).

3. Why Kant's Ethicism is Soft

Kant's "ethicism" with regard to humor is soft. The term "soft" is fitting because Kant thinks we should listen to the joke *as* a joke, that is, at a distance from the narrative recounted, and that we have some context-dependent leeway or latitude (*Spielraum*) in joking. There are several passages that suggest we should read Kant this way.[67]

An interesting early statement supporting this reading comes from an ethics lecture recorded by Johann Gottfried Herder. Perhaps Kant was thinking of something like the pranking priest in Abelard's Flying Ox (No. 16), when he reportedly said this in a lecture from the mid-1760s: "Joking [*Scherzhafte*] lies, if they are not taken to be true, are not immoral." Even when they are taken to be true, they do not always cause harm. "But if the other person is supposed to believe it, then, even if no harm is done [*schadete nicht*], it counts as a lie, since at least there is always deception."[68] Thus, although lying in general is immoral because it violates the principles of morality, not all lies cause harm. (The joking priest does not harm Abelard, even though the priest lies to him.) Since "joking lies" do not cause harm, Kant reasons, they are "not immoral." Now, I recognize that this passage comes from an early stage of Kant's thinking about ethics and that his views of lying developed further after the 1760s. Still, this account of playful joking and lying agrees with what the *Critique of the Power of Judgment* states about joking as occurring in a playful arena in which we have a degree of latitude. More generally, we can take the Herder passage to entail that when it comes to jest and joking, what is most important to Kant, ethically speaking, is that we avoid causing harm, or that we avoid wronging and wrongdoing and instead always treat people with "dignity" and "respect" (concepts Kant presented in a publication from this time, the *Observations*).[69] ("Harm" should therefore here be understood more broadly than just physical or bodily harm, making worse off, decreasing benefits, or diminishing welfare and well-being, or the like.)

This textual support derives only from student lecture notes, of course. But there is other textual evidence. Joking at the end of a dinner party, *Anthropology* states, should not be serious business, but "only play."[70] In playful jest, we put aside our ordinary concerns and do not feel either threatened or annoyed. As Carroll puts it, we listen to the joke in "an arena of playfulness" while not solving a real puzzle or genuine problem.[71] Kant formulates a version of this in the third *Critique*:

> by means of jokes and laughter a certain tone of merriment [is produced], in which . . . much can be chattered about and nobody will be held responsible for what he says, because it is only intended as momentary entertainment.[72]

When we listen to the joke as a joke, we put to the side our ordinary (e.g., social, ethical-political) concerns. In order to attend to a joke properly, we accept ahead of time that we are hearing a joke and listen to it as such. The joke does not *create* a distanced attitude in the audience. Instead, being in that state of mind is the prerequisite for hearing it as a joke rather than as a report of an unfortunate event or as something bizarre. Thus, one commentator (Wicks) has it backwards when he claims that the 'transformation into nothing' *puts us* into a disinterested position.[73] In the third *Critique*, Kant accordingly gives cues that he is starting to tell a joke ("If someone tells this story: An Indian . . ."). In real life, we signal this by saying something like, "Stop me if you've heard this one . . ." or "Did you hear the one about . . .?" Thus, whereas Kant holds that games of chance are engaged in in an interested way (from "vanity or selfishness"[74]), humorous content is entertained from a disinterested perspective.

To put it another way, in listening to the joke as a joke, we "bracket" our sympathy and moral concern.[75] If the object or idea is something serious or of import to us, or if it affects us personally and we cannot put aside our social, bio-psychological ("fight or flight"), or ethical-political concerns, we won't be in a position to find it humorous. Instead we will be confronted with what is called "imaginative resistance," which blocks our ability to entertain imaginatively the incongruity in the joke. We would then feel the usual emotions that are appropriate to the case at hand. We would feel empathy when learning about a stroke of bad luck, anger when hearing of some injustice, and so on. If we are having these typical, ordinary responses to the recounted narrative, we are no longer perceiving the joke as a joke and in a play space; this makes it difficult to find it funny.

Kant uses The Merchant's Wig (No. 1) to make precisely this point.[76] After telling the joke, Kant offers a more realistic version: the merchant's hair (not wig) turns gray. When we hear that version, he thinks, we shift into a mode of concern and empathy with the merchant. We take the anecdote as descriptive speech, not a joke. We hear it as a story that, unlike a joke, could be either true or false. When it is only a wig and the story is "otherwise indifferent to us," we are in a better position to find the anecdote amusing and engage in a playful reflection on the content. Kant describes the experience metaphorically as playing with a ball.

> It gives us gratification, because for a while we toss back and forth like a ball our own misconception about an *object that is otherwise indifferent to us*, or rather our own idea that we've been chasing, while we were merely trying to grasp and hold it firm.[77]

Being removed from the situation is required even to be in a position to find it humorous. As Godfrey puts it, laughter involves a "detached, disinterested point of view."[78] In judging a joke and responding with laughter, we enjoy the free play of our cognitive faculties from a standpoint that is "undisturbed by passion." If we hear about someone falling, it is not the actual story (*Geschichte*) *that someone fell* that makes us laugh.[79] Rather, it is the unexpected divergence from the ordinary course of events, an incongruity or absurdity that is relished or enjoyed in itself.

The notion that appreciating humor requires distance both was formulated before Kant and continues to be maintained today. Hutcheson and Mendelssohn defended the idea that in appreciating humor, our ordinary social and moral concerns do not affect us. Mendelssohn put it in terms of being neutral: "The foolishness of our friends commonly vexes us, pleases enemies, and amuses persons who are neutral."[80] After Kant, Bergson maintained a similar idea, as have contemporary philosophers. According to Carroll, the ordinary or typically appropriate emotion (e.g., fear) disappears when the "comic frame" brings about the evaporation of the burden of moral concern we would usually feel for the well-being of the characters in a story (i.e., joke narratives).[81] According to Morreall, in responding to humor we "suspend our ordinary" practical and theoretical concerns.[82] Gimbel, in a similar Kantian vein, makes use of the notion of a "play frame," a concept developed by Gregory Bateson and William Fry in the 1950s.[83] This frame is a layer that surrounds the joke telling. It separates the joke world from the real world. For instance, the play frame would be thicker at a comedy club than at a cafeteria at work. At the comedy club, we are not as justified in taking offence to an otherwise disturbing joke, because qua patrons of the club we are in a mindset that is more tolerant of offensive jokes, especially those told by comedians about themselves or groups they identify as their own. In contrast, we are more likely to be justifiably offended by a degrading racist, sexist, homophobic, or ableist[84] joke heard at the workplace or in a more public space.

Kant implies that a questionable or borderline joke could be morally acceptable in one context, while being ethically reproachable in another. This seems to follow from his claim that in jest "much can be chattered about and nobody will be held responsible for what he says, because it is only intended as momentary entertainment."[85] In such playful and informal settings and contexts, we implicitly agree to more joking and teasing, even kidding that is directed at us.

But how soft is Kant's ethicism? In other words, where do we draw the line?

Before answering this, let us first observe that Kant's "Incongruity" jokes—which make up the largest portion of the "Jokes" collected and numbered in Part Two (eleven out of twenty)—tend to be quite innocent and mild. Kant's "Incongruity" jokes could here be contrasted with what Freud calls a *tendentious* joke. For Freud, the tendentious joke must be intrinsically transgressive and shocking, since it leads to the release of repressed drives.

But let us return to the question and examine how thick or wide Kant considers the play frame to be, by looking closely at one of Kant's controversial jokes, Foam in a Bottle (No. 12).[86] Some readers consider this joke from the third *Critique* to be racist. Critchley, for instance, refers to this joke as (one of) "the tiresome and indeed racist examples of jokes that Kant recounts, involving Indians and bottles of beer."[87] Indeed, to acknowledge that interpretation, in Part Two of this book I classified it as an ethnic joke.

But it is worth asking if the joke is in fact racist, that is, immoral on account of either harming or mistreating a person or group (violating their dignity) based on their ethnicity or genetic background. The joke would be morally defective, for Kant, if it contravenes the categorical imperative, that is, if it follows a course of action or leads to acts that cannot be universalized (against Principle 1) or that treats human beings as mere means (against Principle 2). If the joke treated people from India as mere means, or induced us to accept or endorse the belief that Indians do not deserve moral respect, for instance, it would thereby become morally defective.

Yet, there may be a more innocuous way to interpret the joke. First, the Indian man appears to be at the Englishman's table, presumably to *share* a beer. This implies that at least some kind of friendship exists between the men. And in fact, the Indian man addresses the Englishman using the informal German pronoun *Ihr* rather than *Sie*. One commentator (Giamario) even uses the revealing phrase, "the Indian guest."[88] If the Indian man is a guest at the Englishman's table, or if they share a form of friendship, it is harder to characterize the content of the joke as racist.

But one might point out that the joke asks us to accept a colonial distribution of power, and thus to condone the oppression of the Indian man. Given the colonial context, it might be conjectured that the Indian is the Englishman's servant, and that the joke implicitly endorses the unjust colonial power structure. However, the joke simply does not call the Indian a "servant." Second, if he were a servant, it is questionable that he would have spoken up that way. (And wouldn't he have seen beer before?) In addition, to refer to or acknowledge a certain political structure is not the same as to endorse it. Even if the joke can be read as referring to a colonial power structure, insofar as this is the joke's setting, that is not equivalent to asking the audience to accept it or approve of it.

Even if one is not willing to accept the foregoing, perhaps there is another way to interpret the joke charitably. The punch line of the joke requires the person who is watching the beer bottle being opened for the first time to be unfamiliar with beer. Hence the joke teller is forced by the very structure of the joke to find a culture that did not have a tradition of drinking beer. That in itself need not be racist, since it is not necessarily an insult or harmful to accuse someone of being unfamiliar with beer or of belonging to a culture lacking that tradition. Indeed, any culture could be unfamiliar with some of the practices of another culture. On this reading, we might see the Indian as expressing humorous *naiveté* (in Kant's sense) and think that the Indian's innocent understanding of beer foam unintentionally leads to a comical situation.

Finally, we could read it as a display of *intentional* wit on the part of the Indian. Perhaps *he* is the one being witty. We do not have to see him as being stupid, and Kant's joke never states that he is. In fact, Kant explicitly adds that we do not laugh because we consider ourselves to be cleverer than the Indian. Rather, Kant clarifies, we laugh when our expectation suddenly disappears into nothing as we hear the punch line. Of course, the joke would become morally unacceptable if it were told with malicious intentions or if the joke made a slur, or if the joke referred to the man as "another stupid Indian." But it does not do that. The joke only refers to the Indian as unacquainted or unknowing (*Unwissenden*)—which can be read, more innocently and charitably, as a reference to being unfamiliar with the English cultural practice of bottling ale, that is, with India Pale Ales (IPAs). In fact, Kant's anthropology lectures repeatedly state that ignorance (*Unwissenheit*) should not be confused with stupidity (*Dummheit*).[89]

In any case, it seems a stretch to accuse Kant of having deliberate ill will or malicious intent toward Indians when he included this joke in the third *Critique*.

On the positive side, there are at least two reasons why Kant probably liked this joke. First, the exploding froth symbolizes the release in laughter. The beer foam illustrates the sudden reversal accompanying comic relief. The tension bottles up—until our expectation disappears into nothing. Second, the joke is set at dinner, a feature of the joke that Kant surely relished. Jesting, Kant thought, makes up the third and final stage of any good dinner party (following going over the news and some heated arguing). "And so the meal ends with laughter, which, if it is loud and good-natured, has actually been determined by nature to help the stomach in the digestive process through the movement of the diaphragm and intestines, thus promoting physical well-being."[90] In such a setting, the joke would have been especially fitting.

4. The Relative Permissibility of Joking

A sizable portion of recent philosophy of humor has been devoted to the question: Is it always ethically objectionable to tell questionable jokes about groups of people (women, ethnicities, etc.)? There are three principal positions here.[91]

> **Universal impermissibility**: it is *never* allowed to tell such jokes. There are always ethical limits on joking.
>
> **Universal permissibility**: it is *always* allowed to tell such jokes. There are no ethical limits on joking.
>
> **Relative permissibility**: it is *sometimes* allowed to tell such jokes. It depends on the context or situation.

I won't go over the arguments supporting each of these positions. Given the aims of this guide, I am instead trying to make an argument about which position Kant would hold.[92] I think Kant would subscribe to the third, which could also be called "contextualism": the ethical permissibility of the joke telling is relative to and depends on the context. Let me explain why.

Given what was written above about the ethical constraints of joking, clearly the second position cannot be attributed to Kant, even though Gimbel, rather surprisingly, attributes a version of universal permissibility to Kant.[93] It should be obvious from the foregoing discussion in this chapter that Kant would not hold that there are no ethical limits and that it is always permissible to tell off-color jokes about other groups. The real question, then, is why Kant's position is not the first one, universal impermissibility.

One critic of Kant, Merrie Bergmann, defends a version of universal impermissibility, and exploring her arguments for this position will help shed light on Kant's account and show why we should not attribute such a position to Kant. Bergmann focuses on the universal impermissibility of telling sexist jokes (in other words, the "group" she discusses is women). She defines sexist humor as "humor in which sexist beliefs, attitudes, and/or norms either must be held in order to *perceive* [not just see or "get"] an incongruity or are used to add to the fun effect of the incongruity."[94] In such cases, she maintains, there is real harm done. She holds that a sexist joke is not an isolated event in which a woman is harmlessly teased or ridiculed. It is rather one instance among many in which women are belittled or disparaged.[95] Whenever somebody tells or laughs at a sexist joke, it is an insult to the people who have been hurt (or wronged) or who will be hurt (or wronged) by sexist beliefs, *whether the insult is intended or not*. This move (in italics) is, I think, in part what separates Bergmann's from Kant's position. For Kant, the joke teller's intention, while not the only ethically salient feature when it comes to joking, is of utmost significance in determining moral worth or failure.

In addition, Bergmann holds, laughing at (and telling) sexist humor may suggest to peers and friends that it is *acceptable* to hold the beliefs that are presupposed by the humor.[96] Surprisingly, Peter Kivy thinks there is "no evidence" that hearers of a prejudiced joke are more likely to *believe* the denigrating stereotype and become more prejudiced.[97] In fact, Kivy puts the point even more strongly. "Far from encouraging belief in such stereotypes, jokes based on them, to the contrary, *discourage* belief," since the joke's punch line reduces the underlying stereotype to absurdity, evoking laughter.[98] While I think the issue of the harmful effects brought about by a particular off-color joke is an empirical matter (and could be fruitfully studied by social scientists), my own intuition goes in the other direction and sides with Bergmann here.

In any case, Bergmann maintains that in sexist humor, sexist attitudes or norms must be "held" or "used" for the fun. Though she does not use the term, she appears to be what more recent literature refers to as an *attitude endorsement theorist*. An attitude endorsement theorist maintains that in order for a person to feel comic amusement in response to a joke that is sexist (etc.), the adoption of the questionable attitudes, beliefs, or norms is required. "Adoption" here means that the attitude is held and endorsed.

This leads to a second departure from Kant. I don't think the attitude endorsement approach to humor can be attributed to Kant. (Whether or not Kant has the *best* philosophical position is another matter, of course, and I am not assessing that here.) Rather, Kant's view would be that the questionable attitude can be merely *entertained* in imagination.[99] According to Bergmann, because feminists[100] and like-minded people are aware of sexist beliefs, they may see or "get" why particular episodes or jokes are thought to be funny, but they don't have to find them funny. Sexist humor, Bergmann holds, does not just *incidentally* incorporate sexist beliefs for the sake of having fun. Rather, it depends on such beliefs essentially and crucially. Having sexist beliefs is required for finding sexist humor amusing, and it is likewise required for the telling of a sexist joke, insofar as one tells jokes that one finds amusing. Accordingly, the offense in sexist humor is a "real offense committed by the person who finds fun in sexist humor."[101] Moreover, Bergmann explicitly singles out the Bearded Woman joke (No. 14) and reproaches Kant for telling it.

But there is actually something quite Kantian about Bergmann's argument. It is a kind of deontological argument, which I reconstruct as follows.

Premise 1. People have an ethical duty not to wrong other people.

Premise 2. Some jokes wrong other people.

Therefore, people have an ethical duty not to tell or encourage those jokes that wrong people.

Premise 2 is bound to raise some eyebrows, even when viewed from a Kantian perspective. For to know whether a joke wrongs other people, good judgment is required, and I doubt that Kant would agree that all off-color jokes constitute actual wrongdoing. The question is *which* jokes do so.

Moreover, a Kantian would hold that a morally inappropriate attitude need not be endorsed in order to find an off-color joke funny; the attitude need only be entertained. A Kantian could make an analogy with joking about things that we know do not exist—wigs that suddenly turn gray, oxen that fly—and ways of acting that we do not endorse. For instance, although lying is immoral, Kant holds that "joking lies" and self-contradictory "bull" are morally acceptable, for we know (or ought to know) that people who say such things are joking and that we are in the arena of playfulness. In support of this view, Kant could thus offer the following claim. Just as adults can make jokes involving Santa Claus, Mrs. Claus, the elves, and flying reindeer without believing that these exist, and atheists can appreciate jokes involving God, heaven, and hell without endorsing the notion that they exist,[102] we can joke with and tease each other, and the other sexes (groups, etc.), without endorsing everything expressed in our exchanges or said in the joke.

Of course, it is conceivable that joking may well reach a point where it becomes morally reproachable within the constraints set by Kantian ethical principles. There is a point at which it is no longer either psychologically feasible or morally appropriate to be disinterested. That is after all the *ethicism* in Kant's account. Certain kinds of mockery and ridicule, Kant thinks, can be harmful, as we have seen. If an immoral attitude is endorsed or propagated in the joking, the jest itself becomes morally compromised. Even otherwise playful practical jokes can be taken too far. They can do harm. We read in an anthropology lecture from 1784/85 (thus, coeval with the *Groundwork of the Metaphysics of Morals*): "Practical jokes or April Fool's jokes do not make everybody laugh, for they are often harmful [*schädlich*] to the other person."[103] In this sense, Kant's "ethicism" runs against those who maintain that in the arena of playfulness "anything goes" and that there are no limits. It likewise contravenes those who, like Kivy, think there is little evidence that actual harm is done to the members of a group who hear an offensive (racist, etc.) joke.[104]

The moral status of a particular instance of joke telling depends on several interrelated factors about the situation. In applying Kant's Ethical Principles, we have to take into account numerous particulars to adjudicate the issue: the situation and context, the comic timing, the intention of the humor producer or joke teller, the attitude of the audience, and the actual content of the joke. Each of these components functions as a necessary (but not sufficient) condition of the permissibility of the joke telling.

For instance, the intention of the joke teller matters. It would clearly be a violation of Kantian ethical principles to tell a racist joke to an audience in order to stir up racist views in them, but it may be permissible (if other conditions also hold) to mention such a joke in a presentation or paper in order to make a didactic point, or to include it in a study of humor as an object of analysis. As Carroll puts it, "It matters who is telling the joke and for what reason."[105] The aforementioned components (context, timing, etc.) should be considered when evaluating the ethical permissibility of a particular instance of joke telling. The *occasion* of the joke—not just the joke itself (the content)—should be considered when assessing if telling a joke is acceptable or not. The occasion (or, as it is sometimes called, the joke "token") will depend on the specific context in which it is told and on whether or not the other necessary conditions obtain. A joke kind (or "type") may be permissible in one context but not in another, Kant's account implies.

If the endorsement of immoral content is prohibited by a Kantian account, but entertaining it in imagination is allowed, one (but not the only) key question that has to be answered in a particular situation is: Is a racist/sexist or prejudiced attitude being endorsed and accepted by the joker or audience, or is the incongruity merely being entertained? If the audience is expected to agree with or endorse the immoral content, telling the joke would be morally defective.

Since a joke's context matters, it will be useful to say something more about the circumstances that would make a particular instance of joking acceptable on the Kantian account. I here offer three Kantian guidelines. (We can call these "guidelines" in order to avoid confusion with the core Ethical "Principles.") I emphasize that while these guidelines are Kantian in spirit, they are nothing more than that. I am not claiming that Kant explicitly formulated these guidelines, but only that some of his jokes illustrate or employ the guidelines, and that some assertions found in Kant's writings and lectures seem to entail them.

Group Membership: it is morally acceptable to joke about oneself or one's own group.

Duty to Self: telling the joke is morally unacceptable if it makes you a worse person, such as if it habituates you to think in a prejudiced way (since prejudice violates the Ethical Principles).

Punching Up: it is morally acceptable to target members of groups (or groups) that possess a relatively large share of the wealth, power, or social capital in a society, but it is morally unacceptable to target people who are at a lower level in the hierarchy.[106]

The first guideline probably requires little commentary. One of Kant's jokes illustrates it. When Kant, a German, tells German Fools (No. 13), it seems unproblematic. This is due to Group Membership. The guideline gives permission to make fun of oneself (or one's group), but it does not create an obligation to do so. It is a may, not a must. There may be times when it is best *not* to make fun of oneself or one's group. For instance, African-American comedian Dave Chappelle was once working on a skit in which the character he played exhibited qualities considered to be stereotypical features of African-American men. Although in the skit Chappelle was aiming to question and ridicule such stereotypes, he realized that his skit could too easily be misinterpreted and could reinforce prejudice.[107] So he stopped production of the skit. In other words, in this case membership in the group was not sufficient to justify the humor.

The second guideline (Duty to Self), which is in fact stronger than a guideline insofar as a duty is an application of an Ethical Principle, should be clear to those familiar with Kantian ethics. Self-regarding duties, for Kant, include obligations not to harm ourselves, to take proper care of our bodies, and to cultivate our talents, to name a few. Here, the Duty to Self principle refers to a duty to refrain from causing ourselves a kind of moral harm or wrongdoing through jest, such as by worsening our characters by telling (or listening) to jokes that endorse prejudiced attitudes.

As we have seen, Kant thinks that not only is caustic, cruel mockery of others morally wrong, so is letting *oneself* be used as an object of mockery. "If it happens to a suck-up who, just to be center stage, abandons himself to the mischievous game or allows himself to be made a fool of, then it is a proof of bad taste."[108] It is not just bad taste, the passage implies, it is also morally inappropriate as it violates a duty to oneself. The free-loader or suck-up (*Schmarotzer*) reveals a lack of self-respect when he lets himself be used in this manner.

When an off-color joke violates the dignity of the joke teller, or even the idea of humanity in itself ("humanity generally"), telling the joke violates a self-regarding duty. Loosely speaking, this amounts to a kind of wronging oneself. It can wrong the teller by reinforcing an inaccurate view of the world, habituating them to think of the world a certain way — as different from how it actually is. Whereas in reality we all have equal moral value, the racist (sexist, etc.) joke can sometimes lead us to think that some people have more, and some less, dignity and worth. We have a responsibility, Kant once reportedly said in an ethics lecture, to see the (moral) world as it actually is, to "judge things at their true value."[109] The racist joke is wrong if, by endorsing racism, it encourages us to adopt an inaccurate view of the moral world.

According to the third guideline (Punching Up), it is okay to poke fun at those who have more socio-political or economic power than you or your group, but it is not okay to punch down at those below you.[110] One of Kant's jokes, King Louis' Gate (No. 7), is an example of punching up. Comedian Hannah Gadsby was once asked if comedians had a responsibility to figure out the most deserving target for a joke. She responded, "The most deserving people are the powerful, and they're all straight white men."[111] In other words, she applied a principle that it was acceptable, even desirable, to punch up, targeting those with power. (For ease of exposition let us assume that it is relatively easy to determine who is "up" and who is "down" in a particular society, though in reality people may fit into more than one group or section of society, and this hierarchy may not be well defined.)[112] The disadvantaged who are the butt of punching-down jokes by definition hold a less advantageous place in a society. Jokes may condone or aid their persecution either by reinforcing the pejorative stereotypes holding them back, or by making people indifferent to the circulation of those stereotypes. It thus turns the joke tellers and listeners into accessories to further oppression of the group.[113] Kantian ethical theory would oppose such wronging.

Due to Punching Up, it seems that the defender of a Kantian account has no grounds to object when Ted Cohen tells this joke about the Germans, a riff on the observation that some ethnic foods leave you hungry after an hour:

> The thing about German food is that no matter how much you eat, an hour later you are hungry for power.[114]

Given the Nazi Holocaust and the horrific events of the twentieth century, it seems okay to punch up at the Germans here. In contrast, the joke Two Moneylenders (cited in No. 13) seems thoroughly problematic in that it contravenes this guideline.

Before concluding this section, I would like to mention briefly a comparison between a joke's content and a derogatory term, say, a racial or sexist slur. If a person—even someone that is otherwise kind and gentle—uses a slur or derogatory term for a group, we would typically fault them for it. We would say that they simply should not be using the term. We reason that the meaning or reference of the word or slur matters, and that it seems nearly always inappropriate to use such a term. (To be sure, one could think of a case where something about the context makes it acceptable for someone to use it. For instance, members of a group could use a term to address each other or in order to subvert its use by an oppressive group. Or, perhaps, the term could be used for didactic-scientific purposes as noted.) But prima facie the offensive content, the hurtful denotation or connotation of the slur, makes it such that the term should never be invoked, on grounds laid out in Kant's Ethical Principles. When it is used to label others (rather than as a form of peer address), we think that the user has done something morally unacceptable. For we think that, prima facie, i) the derogatory term should not be used, and ii) that when it is invoked the user should have known better. When they keep using the offensive language, in other words, they display a kind of epistemic failure, a failure to know what is appropriate, which leads to our moral disapproval.

Now, it seems that a controversial joke's *content*, such as what happens in the joke (i.e., the narrative) and the words it employs, is in important respects like the slur or derogatory term. There can be analogous ethical concerns regarding both i) the content of the joke and ii) the joke teller (however apparently innocent or neutral their intentions). For the Kantian account, some jokes are so offensive they should prima facie never be told, and sometimes the tellers of such jokes should have known that it would have been better to have refrained from telling them. Still, even here I hesitate to attribute to the Kantian account universal prescriptions and unbending rules. For just as with slurs and labels, there can be contexts in which the telling of the controversial joke could be acceptable, namely, when the play frame allows it. As noted, it is always necessary to use one's judgment.

In short, Kant's position is able to accommodate the intuition that we should not tell jokes that promote racism and sexism (etc.) by endorsing racist/sexist beliefs or leading others to endorse them, or that do actual harm to people or wrong them (including the teller and audience). On the other hand, it also accounts for the common intuition that there is an arena of playfulness in which we can sometimes joke without actually harming or wronging people.

5. A Racist Claim, a Sexist Joke

Kant makes indisputably racist claims in various places throughout his writings, including his relatively early treatise, *Observations* (1764).

They deserve our scrutiny in general to be sure, but here I raise the issue in order to contrast one of his racist claims with one of his sexist quips. Kant relies on Hume to make a comparison between (African) "blacks" and (European) "whites."[115]

> The Negroes of Africa have by nature no feeling that rises above the ridiculous [*Läppische*]. Mr. Hume challenges anyone to adduce a single example where a Negro has demonstrated talents, and asserts that among the hundreds of thousands of blacks who have been transported elsewhere from their countries, although very many of them have been set free, nevertheless not a single one has ever been found who has accomplished something great in art or science or shown any other praiseworthy quality, while among the whites there are always those who rise up from the lowest rabble and through extraordinary gifts earn respect in the world.[116]

The reference to a feeling for the "ridiculous" is not a reference to an African sense of humor. As the context and rest of the passage make clear, Kant is referring to his view that black Africans engage in a "religion of fetishes" bordering on idolatry, involving the fetishization of animal objects (feathers, horns, shells). In short, Kant is disparaging them.

Kant concludes this passage with a disturbing practical suggestion, an endorsement of beating, in turn based on a stereotype that African blacks are talkative. "The blacks are very vain, but in the Negro's way, and so talkative that they must be driven apart from each other by blows."[117]

So far there is no joke, but something like one comes in the form of a racist quip. It is preceded by a report by Jean-Baptiste Labat (1663–1738), who lived for some time in the colonies of the West Indies.[118]

> Indeed, Father Labat reports that a Negro carpenter, whom he reproached for haughty treatment of his wives, replied: "You whites are real fools, for first you concede so much to your wives, and then you complain when they drive you crazy." *There might be something here worth considering, except for the fact that this guy* [Kerl] *was completely black from head to foot, a distinct proof that what he said was stupid.*[119]

Is Kant joking here? The reasoning ("black from head to foot ... [therefore] stupid") is such an absurd *non sequitur*, it is tempting to see Kant as trying to make a tongue-in-cheek one-liner. He is not. The racist passages preceding it offer resistance to such an attempt to save Kant. The passage as a whole seems to be carried out in the spirit of cultural anthropology, and to be executed with utter seriousness. Sure, perhaps if read on its own, the italicized statement could be interpreted as a joking quip, but in the wider textual context it comes across as racist plain and simple. Nor, moreover, does it help Kant's case to point out that he is quoting other authors (Hume, Labat), for Kant clearly seems to accept their racist views. Finally, perhaps there remains one last way to defend Kant: maybe Kant is being sarcastic and using sarcasm to *subvert* a stereotype about black Africans. Unfortunately, this too seems doubtful. For this stunning passage only seems only to endorse, and to reinforce, racist views. In the end, it seems that Kant is making the racist claim and generalization: everything black Africans say is stupid.[120]

True, in a footnote placed at the beginning of the section (Section Four, "On National Characters, Insofar as They Rest upon the Different Feeling of the Sublime and Beautiful"), Kant suggests that his "criticism [*Tadel*] that might occasionally be cast on a people can [i.e., should] offend [*beleidigen*] no one, as it is like a ball that one can always hit to his neighbor."[121] He apparently wishes to excuse himself for the potentially offensive generalizations that he makes about the various nations or peoples (*Völkerschaften*) in the section. It is true that this remark is reminiscent of his other claims about jest and joking. After all, it employs the same "ball" metaphor. Nevertheless, his caveat does not seem sufficient to justify the passage in question, since the latter seems to be put forward as a kind of cultural anthropology; the play frame does not appear to be wide enough. The passage ultimately makes a racist claim that, in the context of the section, seems to be offered as indicative of a people (*Volk*). Moreover, the claim appears to be inconsistent with Kant's own Ethical Principles (Principles 1 and 2) and with the notions of "dignity" and "respect" for humanity that Kant defends in Section Two of the *Observations*.

In contrast, The Bearded Woman (No. 14) comes across as a jesting quip. Bergmann refers to this as a sexist joke, and this characterization seems correct. She does not let Kant off the hook for this quip, however, and does not think the "it was just a joke" defense works.

Nevertheless, perhaps there is another plausible reading of the passage. As can be seen from my commentary on No. 14, in the *Observations* Kant proposes a moral ideal that goes beyond stereotypes associated with men and women, an ideal of acting on moral principles for which both men and women should strive. This suggests that Kant's position is not outright misogynistic or sexist. In fact, elsewhere in the *Observations* he comes to women's defense. He criticizes the inhabitants of the "Orient" and Africa for imprisoning or beating women, while he praises the North American Indians for giving women decision-making power in councils. He even sympathizes with the North American Indian women, saying they pay "dearly enough" for it because they "have all the domestic concerns on their shoulders" and in addition "share all of the hardships with the men."[122] Kant then defends women in their "relationship between the sexes"—though in so doing he adopts a Eurocentric perspective.

> The European has alone found the secret of decorating the sensuous charm of a powerful inclination [i.e., sexuality] with so many flowers and interweaving it with so much that is moral that he has not merely very much elevated its agreeableness overall but has also made it very proper.[123]

In the *Observations*, Kant criticizes any treatment of a woman that does not show her both respect and love.[124] "Presumably, as such a great defender of the fair sex, Rousseau felt indignant that a woman was not treated in France with more real respect."[125] Kant thinks that even when engaging in light banter with women or teasing them, they should be given proper respect. Jest is to be used in a manner that conforms to this ethical constraint.[126]

This is not to say that Kant's attempt to "defend" women could not be subjected to justified criticism. It could be faulted for being, in the end, sexist and for reflecting Kant's view that women are second-class citizens who are weak and in need of protection. Or, alternatively, it could be faulted for being inconsistent with sexist claims that he makes elsewhere and that underlie his thinking about women.

In any case, we see a call for respect of women in *Anthropology*'s advice on how to create appropriate jest at a dinner party. At the conclusion of the conversation, in order in part to please women guests, small and deliberate—but "not humiliating"—provocations (*Angriffe*) of the women should be made among the participants, presumably in a kind of playful battle of the sexes. It is very important, he says, that these affronts not be humiliating (*beschämenden*). In the end there is a *reversal* of the power held by the men, an inverting of the relation between the powerful and the subjugated. These teasing provocations will enable the women to respond, showing "their own wit" and doing so "to their own benefit."[127] Perhaps that is why he thinks that this lighthearted banter is introduced in part to *please* women. It is not serious and does not do actual harm, he thinks, but is agreeable to everyone.[128]

The fact that women and men are joking in each other's *presence* also seems to be an ethically salient feature of the situation Kant has in mind. When such potentially harming jest occurs face-to-face rather than behind the back, any alienation expressed by the jest could be counterbalanced by a sense of community created by the jest. As de Sousa puts it, any estrangement would be "offset by the reality of [the] community signaled" or created by sharing the joke.[129]

The view that some playful, mutual teasing is acceptable was held by Kant at various points in his career. In a 1784/85 lecture he is reported to have said this about teasing in general: "One applies wit when one is teasing somebody, and it is pleasant if it is refined and the other replies. If he doesn't reply, it is offensive. Wit is the most excellent kind of amusement in society." And later in the lecture: "When one person teases another person and he answers back with teasing, it is amusing. But one must be cautious and first see whether he is in the right mood [*Laune*]."[130]

About teasing between the sexes in particular, we have marginalia that go back even earlier. According to notes that Kant wrote in his personal copy of the *Observations* (around 1765), "Woman interprets a satire of her sex as just having fun (*Spaß*), because she knows well that the ridicule (*Spott*) of her sex's little shortcomings actually applies to the men themselves, who only love them all the more for it."[131] Light ridicule is allowed as long as it does not becomes "serious" and so long as there is no "truth" to it: jokes should not be taken as descriptive speech with a truth value. Such mocking banter should not become insulting or limit women's actual freedom, for in that case "her sex would be reduced to the will of men."[132] Whatever one thinks of it, this view of the relations between the sexes is far from simple.

This is not to say that Kant's views of women are impervious to serious criticism. It may well be that, as Pauline Kleingeld suggests, Kant's view that women, while physically weaker than men, are superior to men in that they use coquettish techniques to control and govern them, is ultimately guilty of "damning with faint praise."[133] Unfortunately, dismantling Kant's views of women and the sexes would constitute a much larger project than can be undertaken in this guide to Kant on humor. What seems clear is that Kant's treatment of sex and gender is not only far more complex than it might first appear, it also differs from his handling of race.

Kant saw himself as being playful in the Bearded Woman quip. Given the playful tone of the *Observations*, he thought that the frame was wide enough to allow for such jest. Regrettably, he seems to have been wrong about the thickness of the play frame in this case. If that assessment is correct, this instance of quip-making reveals an error in his judgment.

6. Closing Kantian Questions

Taking up the Kantian notion that anthropological considerations should be "pragmatic," I would like to conclude the last of my chapters with some questions that bring together a few of the themes covered in this guide—humor from a pragmatic point of view, as it were.

What does Kant's account imply about whether, and when, it is okay to tell a potentially inappropriate joke?

As indicated, a set of necessary conditions have to be met. An unethical attitude should not be endorsed or adopted by the joke teller (or humor producer). For instance, a racist shouldn't tell racist jokes (and shouldn't be a racist in the first place).

The timing and context have to be right. When the context is undefined and we don't know the status of the audience, we should probably not tell the joke. When the context is clearly defined and the audience holds the immoral views that the joke invites the audience to entertain (even if only imaginatively), the joke should not be told because it is too likely to reinforce the immoral views.

When jesting we would do well to bear in mind our intentions, how others might interpret these intentions, and the jest's context and play frame. What, beyond evoking amusement or laughter, are the joke teller's intentions? How might the joke be interpreted and later used? Then we have to use our judgment in the particular situation to apply the standards of right and wrong (as defined by the Ethical Principles), and determine if someone is actually harmed by the jest or their dignity violated. The ability to assess these elements and aspects of the situation, to know when humor is appropriate or misplaced, belongs to our practical, social know-how. It requires prudence and good judgment.[134] There is, alas, no simple or final formula for this, and, insofar as a joke is a phenomenon that cannot be reduced to concepts and rules and that requires the faculty of judgment, Kant's account never implies that there should be.[135]

But here are two Kant-inspired questions you might ask yourself if you are unsure about a joke at a particular time.[136]

1) Ask if the play frame is thick enough to make it acceptable to tell the joke. Keep in mind the joke's content, the audience, your intention, and the timing and setting. If the play frame is not thick enough, don't tell it. For instance, if you don't think the joke could comfortably be shared with strangers or acquaintances in an ordinary public space such as the workplace and they are your audience, refrain.

2) If the original play frame seems to be wide enough, next ask yourself whether a joke that you are comfortable telling in the right setting (etc.) *could potentially be removed from its original frame*. This is especially important if the joke telling is being recorded, published, or broadcast on media such as Instagram, Snapchat, Facebook, YouTube, and Twitter. One of the problems with joking via texts, chats, emails, recordings, videos, and tweets, is that the jesting or quip can easily be taken out of context, moving the frame from the one that was originally intended and into a wider public space. If an off-color joke could be so removed from the originally acceptable frame, it is probably better simply to refrain from telling the joke.[137]

If a questionable joke can be published or broadcast, perhaps it is better just to be innocently playful, such as when Kant added to the title page of the 1787 edition of *Critique of Pure Reason*: "Second edition, improved here and there."

PART TWO
Jokes

Incongruity Jokes

1. The Merchant's Wig

There was once a young merchant who was sailing on his ship from India to Europe. He had his entire fortune on board. Due to a terrible storm, he was forced to throw all of his merchandise overboard.

He was so upset that, that very night, his *wig* turned gray.[1]

This joke comes from the *Critique of the Power of Judgment* (1790), one of Kant's three *Critiques*. He contrasts this version with another version: the merchant's *hair* turns gray. But in that version, we listeners or readers become more concerned and involved. We empathize with the merchant and feel his pain more than in the first version. When it's just a wig, we are in a better position to find the story amusing. We hear the narrative as a joke rather than as descriptive speech, a real story about the world that can be either true or false.

Kant thinks that when we hear or read a joke *as* a joke, we need to be removed from the situation or story; we cannot have something at stake in it. He calls this *disinterestedness*, which turns out to be a key principle in his aesthetic theory and account of beauty. "Taste is the faculty for judging an object or a kind of representation through a satisfaction or dissatisfaction without any interest. The object of such a satisfaction is called beautiful."[2] While the humorous is not the same as the beautiful, Kant thinks that our response to both of them requires a kind of disinterestedness. A notion of disinterestedness can be found in the writings of Shaftesbury (Anthony Ashley Cooper) (1651–1713) and other eighteenth-century aesthetic theorists. Today the notion of disinterestedness remains controversial. Some theorists think that the idea can be better captured by the concept of absorbed attention or focus.

2. Happy Funeral Mourners

A man's rich relative dies. Suddenly he is rich. To honor his relative, the man wants to arrange a solemn funeral service. But he keeps complaining that he can't get it quite right.

"What's the problem?" someone asks.

"I hired these mourners, but the more money I give them to look grieved, the happier they look."[3]

This is a second joke from the *Critique of the Power of Judgment*. (The third one is No. 12.) Kant is using it to illustrate his incongruity theory of humor. When we learn that the mourners are happy because they are getting paid, he says, our expectation is suddenly "transformed into nothing."

The philosophical underpinning is that there are at least two levels of satisfaction at work: we feel sadness, joy, etc. (first-order satisfaction) and then can approve or disapprove of it using reason (second-order). A man can be glad that he is receiving an inheritance from a deceased relative, yet disapprove of his gladness. "The object can be pleasant, but the enjoyment of it displeasing."[4]

The joke turns on something similar happening with the mourners. They are so happy that they are getting paid (second-order) that they are no longer able to look sad (first-order).

There is a similar anecdote in Plato's *Ion*, a dialogue about a professional reciter (a "rhapsode") named Ion, who aimed at moving his audience. Ion says that when he looks out at the audience and sees them weeping, he knows he will laugh because it has made him richer, and that when they laugh, he will be weeping about losing the money.[5]

3. Swift Wit

Jonathan Swift was speaking before Parliament about the benefits of understanding, wealth, and the like. He finally arrived at the topic of *good sense*. He said:

> "Since in this esteemed assembly nobody will claim to have any, I'll just stop now and conclude."[6]

Jonathan Swift (1667–1745) was an Anglo-Irish writer and satirist, author of *Gulliver's Travels* and other satirical works. Swift didn't maliciously jibe at particular individuals, for he preferred to criticize vices we all have.[7] The intent of his satire was therapeutic; he aimed to reform.[8]

Kant told this joke in his anthropology course, one of his most popular university courses. (He taught anthropology a total of about 24 times between 1772 and 1796.) Kant is giving an example of English or British wit, since he thinks (overlooking Swift's upbringing in Ireland) that Swift exemplifies English humor. Kant makes a connection between a nation's sense of wit (a kind of free thinking) and politics. The English political system encourages "originality" and wit, since the people do not have to follow the tone set by the monarch or court. Humor and thinking for oneself go hand in hand. Kant comments on the joke: "The capricious wit rests upon an original disposition of mind. We find this among the English, for the court does not set the tone there. The trickster mood [*Laune*] is a quite peculiar part of some people."

This kind of joke survives today. Michelle Wolf opened her set at the 2018 White House Correspondents' Dinner with a Swift jab at the audience. (President Trump did not attend.) "I'm here to make jokes. I have no agenda. I'm not trying to get anything accomplished. So, everyone that's here from Congress: you should feel right at home."

4. Dying of Good Health

There was a physician who was always consoling his patients, giving them hopes of a speedy recovery. He told one patient that his pulse would grow steadier. He predicted to another that his bowel movements would improve. He told a third that his sweat would get better.
 One day the physician received a visit from one of them.
 "How is your illness?" the physician asked.
 "How should it be? I'm dying of *improvement!*"[9]

This anecdote is found at the end of Kant's late essay on politics and history, "An Old Question Raised again: Is the Human Race Constantly Progressing?". Kant considered armed conflicts, especially wars of offense and preemptive strikes, to be among the greatest impediments to progress toward peace and the establishment of international justice. The nations *seem* to be doing better, he suggests, but in the end they are "dying" from such improvements. No real progress is being made. Kant is hopeful that there will eventually be progress in politics, perhaps even in morality. At the same time, he recognizes that in light of wars and hostilities, not everyone will be able to share his hope in progress.
 Good leaders are needed for progress, Kant thinks, and wit can be beneficial to them. Kant relates a story about Frederick the Great in which the king displays a kind of wit, at least in a broader sense—his quip is not terribly funny. The Prussian king met with the celebrated philosophical aesthetician Sulzer. Sulzer suggested that humans were good by nature. The king replied, "My dear Sulzer, you don't really know this wretched race to which we belong."[10] While the politician should not be a clown or a buffoon, a sense of wit (accompanied by judgment) can be useful. Even if their main task is to enact just laws and protect rights, it helps if, like a good dinner party host, they can conduct a lively conversation and create a cheerful tone.
 In a letter to the renowned physician, Hufeland, a 73-year-old Kant included another wisecrack about aging. "It is a great sin to have grown old, but no one is spared the punishment for it: death."[11]

5. £200

What convinces someone of a thing's truth and goodness?

200 pounds sterling.

And what convinces that person of just the opposite?

Another 200 pounds.[12]

Kant cribs this from English poet Samuel Butler (1612–80).[13] Butler wrote *Hudibras* (1663–78), a satire on Puritanism inspired by the seventeenth-century Spanish novel *Don Quixote*. The knight Hudibras is the hero of the poem; Ralpho is his squire.

Kant considered Butler to be a model of wit. Kant thinks this joke illustrates how incongruities can sometimes be funny. It is an example of lighthearted wit that pokes fun at human fickleness. Kant comments on it: "The strength of this joke consists in the fact that one puts forward quite unexpected things." Still, the point is not so much that we are *surprised* by the unexpected; rather, the point is that an incongruity is enjoyed in itself. After all, we could be amused repeatedly by the same joke. Even when we know what's coming, a good gag continues to "work" on account of the incongruity.

6. Of Juice and Justice

A server once spilled some juice on the chancellor of France. He immediately apologized, saying:

> "*Summum ius, summa iniuria.*" (Too much juice, too much injustice.)[14]

This involves a play on words: *ius* can mean either law/justice or soup/broth (juice). The original phrase was *Extreme law is extreme injustice*, or *The strictest justice is the greatest injury*. In *On Duties*, Cicero calls it a proverb that was already "quite familiar" to people.[15]

Although Kant maintains that wit typically employs some kind of contrast, he thinks puns can become nauseating. "All acts of wit are called play. But wit and play are dull when wit produces a *false* similarity, and then it is quite disgusting. This kind of dull wit can be seen in word play. It was once very fashionable in France."[16] He faults abbot Nicolas Trublet (1697–1770) for content-light writings, but praises Henry Fielding for a pleasing use of contrast.[17] Yet Kant liked the following story; call it The Stuffed Aunt.

> A certain foreigner, Count Sagramoso, was visiting Countess Keyserling. By chance a schoolmaster appeared who was a native of Königsberg and had returned for a visit. He had been working in Hamburg as curator of a natural history collection of animals. Using broken German, Count Sagramoso tried to make small talk with the curator: "*Ick abe in Amburg eine Ant geabt, aber die ist mir gestorben*" [Translation: I had an aunt in Hamburg, but she died]. But instead of hearing the word *Ant* (*Tante*), which means aunt, the curator heard *Ente*, which means duck. Regretting the loss of a very rare specimen, he asked: "Why didn't you have her skinned and stuffed?"[18]

It might initially look like Kant is defending puns here, but in fact he uses this example to show that humor can arise from unintentional misunderstandings.

If Kant had been familiar with Abbott and Costello's "Who's on First?" routine, perhaps he would have thought more highly of puns and word play. Or maybe lines like this one from the Marx Brothers' *A Night at the Opera*:[19]

"It's all right, that's in every contract. That's what they call a sanity clause."
"You can't fool me! There ain't no Sanity Claus."

And it would be amiss if I didn't quote Oscar Wilde here:

"Immanuel doesn't pun, he Kant."[20]

7. King Louis' Gate

To honor King Louis XIV, they built a magnificent gate on the bridge he had to cross. On the gate, they placed an angel holding a crown in his hand.

But a jokester from the region of Gascony pointed out, "You can't tell whether he is giving him the crown, or taking it *away*."[21]

Louis XIV of France (1638–1715), the "Sun King," ruled for 72 years, the longest reign in the history of France. He is reported to have said "The state? I am the state." Gascony is in southwest France.

This is one of several jokes involving France. Even when the joke is told by a German, it's mainly a French-on-French joke. It's also a David/Goliath joke: it punches up at monarchical power and pokes fun at the king.

Kant uses this King Louis joke to explain his account of humor. When we find something humorous, we first have an expectation about something (the king to be *given* a crown). This then suddenly "disappears into nothing."

In the same lecture course, Kant reportedly said: "Laughter. This arises out of the sudden but harmless [*unschädlichen*] reversal of expectation." Kant then illustrates this with another joke that pokes fun at a king:

Charles II of England once visited a famous schoolteacher, Busby. Busby was very impolite toward the King—he did not allow him to sit. When the King was leaving, the teacher said outside, "Your Majesty, I'm sorry I was so rude. I just couldn't let the students see that I was not the most powerful person in the room."[22]

8. Thinking with One's Body

Aristotle says that when one thinks about the future, one looks up at the sky. When one thinks about the past, one looks down at the earth. My father is looking straight *ahead*, so he's not thinking at all.[23]

Kant is paraphrasing a passage[24] from *Tristram Shandy*, a novel by Laurence Sterne (1713–68) that Kant admired for its comic episodes.[25]

Kant comments: "We can infer what someone else is thinking based on body language." Kant told this in his anthropology course not only to illustrate his theory of humor, but also to comment on the view that the body mirrors the mind. People seem to be thinking through, or with, their bodies.

For the most part, Kant was skeptical of physiognomy, a pseudoscience that tried to infer personality and character traits on the basis of outer appearances and movements. Still, Kant couldn't resist some physiognomic speculations. He thought that ways of life and habits could change a person's looks and demeanor. Kant told a quip about a father who said to his son, who was about to depart for his academic studies: "My boy, come back to me with the same face."[26]

9. The Happy Cuckold

One of Voltaire's characters says this about marriage.

"Finally, I returned to my fatherland, Candia. I took a wife there. I quickly was cheated on—and found that this life was the most comfortable of all."[27]

The Kingdom of Candia was the name of Crete when ruled by the Republic of Venice. Kant is paraphrasing the final lines from the narrator in Voltaire's short story, *The History of the Travels of Scarmentado* (1756).[28]

This saying illustrates Kant's thoughts on incongruity in humor. (The husband learns that he was deceived and betrayed—yet he finds happiness.)

A biographical aside: Kant never married. We know next to nothing about his sex life. According to an early biographer, he appears twice to have been interested in a romantic relationship with a woman.[29] Yet it appears that he hesitated or never acted on it,[30] and his hopes were dashed.

10. Full of Bull

Here is an example of what the English call *bull*. One says, "I went on a walk with someone . . . completely alone."[31]

Bull derives from Middle English *bull*, meaning "falsehood, trivial statements, fraud." The verb *to bull* (from around the year 1530) means "to mock or cheat."

Mel Brooks has a one-liner that not only shares the self-contradictory structure, it even uses the word. "I've been accused of vulgarity. I say that's bullshit!"[32] Then there's the classic Groucho Marx lyric: "Hello, I must be going." Or the Irish bull where the policeman says: "Hey you! If you're going to smoke here, you'll have to either put out your pipe, or go somewhere else."[33] Or Oscar Wilde: "I can resist everything but temptation."[34] Comic Steve Martin reported that he was fond of the technique. "I loved implying that the one thing I believed in was a contradiction."[35]

Kant comments that "bull" helps the English "be witty." He adds that German wit makes use of it too. In Schopenhauer's version of the "walking alone" quip, it's an Austrian—in other words, a speaker of German—who says the bull:

> When someone had stated that he was fond of walking alone, an Austrian said to him: "You like to walk alone; so do I; then we can walk together." He starts from the concept, "A pleasure which two people like can be enjoyed by them in common," and he subsumes under this the very case that excludes community.[36]

(Schopenhauer's version may well also count as an "ethnic" joke, poking fun at Austrians.) A similar structure can be found in statements made by the Yankees baseball player Yogi Berra. "Half the lies they tell about me aren't true."[37] The self-contradictory structure is also reminiscent of "liar's paradoxes." (Someone says, "I am lying." Is that statement true or false? If the statement is true, it is false. And if the statement is false, then it is true.) But liar's paradoxes are not on their own funny. Contradictions like saying out loud, "I am being silent" need something more to be humorous. The Marx Brothers seem to find that something in *A Night at the Opera* (1935):

"What'll I say?"
"Tell them you're not here."
"Suppose they don't believe me?"
"They'll believe you when you start talking."

11. With Friends Like These

"My dear friends: there is no such thing as a friend."[38]

Following Diogenes Laertius, Kant attributes this view to Aristotle.[39] Laertius attributes to Aristotle this version: "My dear friends, there are no friends." Unfortunately, that version is based on a textual corruption. Aristotle's *Eudemian Ethics* in fact reads, "One who has *many* friends has no friend."[40] (It would surely be devastating to Facebook to learn this.)

In any case, this version was a favorite saying of Kant's and he repeated it in writings, lectures, and correspondence.[41] Students in his anthropology course recorded an even stronger version: "Hence Aristotle *correctly* said: My friends, there are no friends."[42]

Kant apparently had some close friends. He even believed we have a "duty of friendship." So why did he think that the statement was true and that there were no friends? While he thought friendship was a worthy *ideal*, he thought there were great difficulties in reaching it. Kant doubted that friends would be loyal in times of need or fully honest with each other. Even if your friend would help you out when needed, it is hard to find the right balance between love and respect, between exposing yourself to your friend, and maintaining the appearance of self-reliance. And, unlike marriage, friendship requires no formal, public statement of mutual commitment.

Kant was also ambivalent towards "courteous" signs of friendship such as bowing, gallant gestures, and declarations of friendship. (It is easy to think of updated versions of these today.) True, they provide "relief" from the "cloak of selfishness." They make us look like we are polite, caring, and courteous; they help us live together harmoniously. But they are merely external formalities. Even if they may be indirectly beneficial for morality, they don't have any value in themselves.

Ethnic and Sexist Jokes and Quips

12. Foam in a Bottle

A man from India watches an Englishman open a bottle of ale at the Englishman's table in the city of Surat. When he opens up the bottle, it explodes in a wave of froth. The Indian looks amazed.
"Well, what's so remarkable about that?" asks the Englishman.
"I'm not surprised at its getting out," replies the Indian, "but at how you ever managed to get it all in."[1]

This is one of three jokes in the *Critique of the Power of Judgment*. The incongruity in a joke, Kant writes, is between the "something" of the setup and the "nothing" associated with the punch line. Assuming that the joke works, whenever we hear the punch line there is a pleasant reversal. The froth symbolizes this sudden reversal.

There is a corresponding bodily response to this unexpected change or reversal. If we laugh, there is an "agreeable oscillation of the diaphragm," a rhythmical response to the joke. "One feels the effect of this relaxation in the body through the oscillation of the organs, which promotes the restoration of their balance and has a beneficial influence on health."[2] If you laugh vigorously, you experience a vibration of the organs, which is why it can hurt when you laugh if you engage in it a little too enthusiastically.[3]

Some people find this joke racist. For instance, one commentator refers to this joke as one of "the tiresome and indeed racist examples of jokes that Kant recounts, involving Indians and bottles of beer."[4] But perhaps there is a more innocent way to interpret the joke. (The Indian man is at the Englishman's table, implying a form of friendship; in fact, he addresses the Englishman using the informal German pronoun *Ihr* rather than *Sie*. It's not an intrinsic shortcoming to be unfamiliar with beer. And maybe, after all, the Indian is being funny and making a witty quip.)

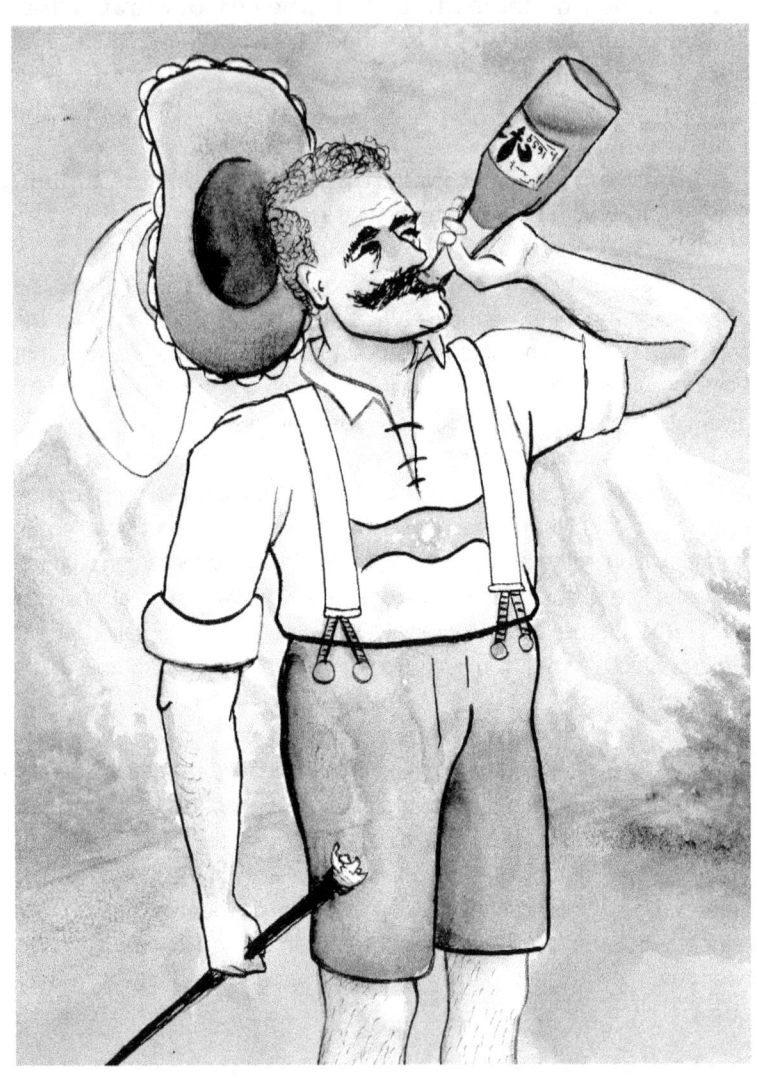

13. German Fools

Here's a truth about Germans:

> An *inexperienced* German fool went to Paris to learn how to become witty and refined. Instead, he just came home a fool *with experience*.[5]

This joke doesn't punch down, it punches laterally—at Kant's own group. It's mostly a German-on-German joke (with a touch of anti-French). To be sure, the self-mockery does not match that of the Southern humorist, Jeff Foxworthy. "If you remarry three times and still have the same in-laws, guess what? You might be a redneck!"[6]

Probably because it has a moral point, Kant liked the saying and often told it to his students (nearly all of whom never made it to Paris.) We find it in publications and personal notes from around 1765 as well as in various versions of his anthropology lectures.[7] "A *sot* [fool] is a German who travels to Paris to learn to be witty and how to live. A *fat* [dandy] is the experienced fool who returns from Paris with evidence of his folly."[8] When in his home country, the German is a foolish fop (*Laffe*) and lacks substance. When he goes to Paris he gathers material that allows him to look like a fool, but in a more refined way. He returns a vain and conceited dandy (*Geck*), full of ridiculous expressions and manners. The aphorism reveals eighteenth-century German ambivalence toward French culture, both esteemed for its refined customs and mocked for its alleged shallowness.

Kant tells a few jokes about avarice and greed. Here is one of them. Call it Two Moneylenders.

> A miser once heard a beautiful sermon about the shamefulness of usury. Afterwards, he went up to the priest, who knew him, and asked him to give the sermon again. The priest told him that he didn't see any need to do that, since he had just explained the matter quite clearly. "Yes," said the moneylender, "but there is still another lender out on the street. Perhaps he would like to convert—then I'd be the only one left."[9]

This is also an ethnic joke, specifically, an anti-Semitic joke. (Note that the person might *convert*.) It plays on the "greedy financier" stereotype. It's a joke about people outside of Kant's group, and counts as punching down.

14. The Bearded Woman

A woman who has a head full of Greek, like Madame Dacier, or who carries on deep disputations about mechanics, like the Marquise de Châtelet, is going for a look of profundity. So she might as well just wear a beard.[10]

Madame Dacier is Anne Dacier, born Lefèvre (1654–1720). She translated the *Iliad*, the *Odyssey*, and other Greek and Latin classics into French.

Marquise de Châtelet is Gabrielle Émilie la Tonnelier de Breteuil, marquise du Châtelet-Lomont (1706–49). She was a mathematician and physicist. She was Voltaire's host and companion at Cirey for the last fifteen years of her life. Her essay on the nature and propagation of fire won a prize in 1738 from the French Academy of Science.

This is more a wisecrack than a joke. One commentator suggests that Kant finds these scholar-scientists laughable because they are shattering the then-dominant norms.[11] While that may be true, Kant is *trying* to be lighthearted and funny. Regrettably, it flops.

The remark comes from the *Observations on the Feeling of the Beautiful and Sublime* (1764), a playful text. Does this change the context enough to legitimize his attempt to be witty? Probably not. Kant is making a sexist quip, drawing on traditional eighteenth-century stereotypes. It is one of Kant's many objectionable remarks about women, and the passage has been justly criticized.[12] It is sexist not just for implying that women should not be engaged in the arts and sciences, but also that they cannot be profound. It is about more than science and academics: it attacks women's character.

In the *Observations,* Kant uses an eighteenth-century (Burkean) distinction between the beautiful and the sublime to suggest that men are sublime (profound) while women are beautiful. Instead of exhibiting conventional femininity, Dacier and Châtelet incline toward the sublime. Such Burkean distinctions were quickly (and rightly) criticized by feminists such as Mary Wollstonecraft for being binary, limiting, and based on stereotypes about both sexes.[13]

Nevertheless, perhaps it is worth complicating matters somewhat. Kant argues that the moral character of women is beautiful because they tend to be governed by feelings of love and sympathy, while the character of men is sublime because they are capable of governing themselves by principle. So far Kant's view seems to be highly questionable. But Kant goes on to claim that men rarely act on principle either, and would do well to imitate women. In the end, Kant proposes a gender-neutral conception of moral character that makes room both for acting on principle and for sensitivity to feelings.[14]

15. Samuel Johnson's Wife

Johnson is said to have praised many women he would have hesitated to marry, and to have married one he was ashamed to praise.[15]

Samuel Johnson (1709–84) is best known as the author of the *Dictionary of the English Language* (1755), the first comprehensive lexicographical work on English. The above saying appears in *The Life of Samuel Johnson* (1791), written by James Boswell (1740–95).

Kant comments that the Johnson quip achieves its effect by way of "antithesis" or conversion. This technique involves the switching of terms, as in "Ask not what your country can do for you, but what you can do for your country." Kant uses the technique in this somewhat crude line: "When I needed a woman, I couldn't feed one; when I could feed one, I didn't need one any more."[16] Sometimes it can be amusing. "Why do we drive on parkways and park on driveways?"[17] Cicero wrote, "Words antithetically used are a great ornament to language; and the same mode of using them is often also humorous."[18] In 1711, Joseph Addison likewise noted, "For . . . the opposition of ideas, does very often produce wit: as I could show in several little points, turns, and antitheses."[19]

Like puns, humor arising from conversion sometimes comes across as cheap, lacking in substance. The following jokes are perhaps guilty of this.

> Why did the monkey go bananas?
> *He couldn't figure out whether he was his brother's keeper or his keeper's brother.*[20]

> What did one frog say to the other frog?
> *Time's fun when you're having flies.*[21]

Of course, Kant's quote of Johnson is also a version of another timeless genre, the spouse joke.

> Spouse A: Look at this beautiful dog I got for my husband.
> Spouse B: I wish I could make a trade like that.[22]

Kant is not a devoted follower of Johnson. Kant considers the Johnson quip to be "one of the *so-called* admirable sayings of Johnson about women." Kant clarifies: "Here the play of antitheses makes for the *only* admirable thing in the saying. But reason gains nothing from it." Kant thinks that profundity and wit ought to be combined, making the humor more stable and lasting. Despite his vast knowledge of language, Johnson is unable to unite wit and reason. Kant thinks it is best when a joke is able to make a point and is not just a play with an incongruity. But it shouldn't be overly didactic. The key is to find the balance between wit and reason. This is explored in the next section, "Jokes with a Point."

Jokes with a Point

16. Abelard's Flying Ox

One day Peter Abelard and a priest were riding together in a carriage. The priest suddenly exclaimed, "Look! There goes a flying ox!"

"Where? Where?" Abelard asked, looking up at the sky.

The priest scoffed and smirked. "It's hard to believe that such an intelligent and scholarly man, the great Abelard, could fall for that."

Abelard took a pause, and then responded: "It's easier for me to believe that an ox could fly, than that a priest could lie."[1]

Peter Abelard (1079–1142) was a renowned and influential medieval philosopher and theologian. He is also well known for his love affair with Héloïse, the subject of *The Letters of Abelard and Héloïse*.

In this joke, the priest pranks Abelard. "Even the cleverest minds can often be deceived," Kant commented on this joke in his lecture on anthropology. An honest man "is not necessarily stupid." Abelard is wiser and smarter than the priest, but he is also trusting and unsuspecting, because he himself acts from a "love of humanity." "The person who is tricked often puts up with the trickster. When he acts from love of humanity, he doesn't suspect anything bad." This may make him seem gullible—at least the first time around. "But when he uncovers the trickster the first time, he certainly won't be tricked by him ever again." Is Kant giving version of the old saw, "Fool me once, shame on you. Fool me twice, shame on me?"

Kant likes this story in part because the wit spices up a moral message. It's a joke with a point: goodheartedness doesn't imply stupidity or dullness. With his comeback or put down, Abelard turns out to be wittier than the jocular priest.

17. Which Way the Wind Blows

If a wind rages in a hypochondriac's gut, what matters is where it does depart.
If it travels upwards, it is an inspiration from heaven.
If it travels downwards, it takes the form of a fart.[2]

Kant attributes the above opinion to the "acute" knight Hudibras, the protagonist of the satirical poem by Samuel Butler. *Hudibras* is the inspiration of several of Kant's jokes (e.g., Nos. 5 and 20).

Like Steve Martin, Benjamin Franklin, and five-year-old boys, Kant was not above flatulence humor.[3] Around 1781, when he was living in France, Franklin wrote the piece, "Fart Proudly," also called, "To the Royal Academy of Farting." He suggested to the Royal Academy of Brussels that they adopt the following research agenda: "To discover some Drug wholesome and not disagreeable, to be mixed with our common Food, or Sauces, that shall render the natural Discharges of Wind from our Bodies, not only inoffensive, but agreeable as Perfumes." Franklin complains: "What Comfort can the Vortices of Descartes give to a Man who has Whirlwinds in his Bowels?"[4]

Such humor is not new, and goes back in the western tradition at least to Rabelais, if not Aristophanes. Kant's joke appears in a published work, *Dreams of a Spirit-Seer* (1766), written well before Kant's three *Critiques*. In this satirical piece from the middle of his career, Kant jokingly views fanaticism as a kind of brain fart. A windy gust in the gut results either in a moment of flatulence—or ungrounded ideas.

Kant thus engages in what Critchley playfully baptizes "post-colonial theory." It is fitting to quote Critchley here. Commenting on a scene involving scatological humor in Samuel Beckett's *Molloy*, he writes, "The whole scene seems to evaporate into nothing as Kant would put it, to go up in a cloud of rather odious smoke."[5]

18. Philosophy Detox

A bad poem is like a cleansing for the brain: the sick poet is relieved by the removal of all the harmful moistures. Isn't miserable and brooding *philosophical* writing just like that? If so, it would be a good idea to let nature use another path to cleansing. That way the author could be thoroughly and quietly purged of the ill—without creating a public disturbance.[6]

This comes in from an essay on mental illness, *Essay on the Maladies of the Head* (1764), a treatise more medical than most of Kant's writings. Purging the soul of "miserable and brooding" philosophy is like the detoxification of unhealthy elements in the body. The philosopher can prescribe a "diet of the mind" in order to cure "foolishness."

Philosophy and laughter sometimes have similar purgative effects. The idea that laughter is good for the mind is found in the third *Critique*: Through humor and "sallies of wit," which through pleasure promote "the business of life in the body," one "can get at the body even through the soul and use the soul as the doctor of the body."[7]

Above, Kant uses lighthearted wit to ridicule (and reform) brooding philosophy. In the 1760s, Kant was working on a remedy for melancholic philosophy; it involved showing the limits of reason, a view he expressed as early as 1766 in *Dreams of a Spirit-Seer*.

Yet Kant's thoughts would not appear in their mature form until about 15 years later. In criticizing fanaticism in the (1781) *Critique of Pure Reason*, he was much more solemn. "Of our own person we will say nothing," begins the motto to the second edition (1787) of the *Critique*, quoting Bacon of Verulam.

Kant's mockery of brooding philosophy in this text of 1764 is reminiscent of the affirmations of joy expressed by Friedrich Nietzsche. Solemn scholars, Nietzsche says, could use more laughter. "Not by wrath does one kill but by laughter. Come, let us kill the spirit of gravity!"[8] If Nietzsche had in mind the author of 1764, perhaps he could have imagined a laughing, jovial Kant.[9]

19. The Voltaire Bros

Somebody once congratulated Voltaire's father for his two famous sons.

He replied, "I have two buffoons for sons: One is a buffoon in prose, the other in verse."[10]

Kant comments: "One son, Armand, fell into Jansenism, and was persecuted. The other son, François-Marie, wrote satirical verses and was locked up in the Bastille."[11] It is the latter we know today as Voltaire. Jansenism was a Catholic theological movement inspired by the Dutch theologian Cornelius Jansen (1585–1638), with great religious and political repercussions in France. François-Marie Arouet, ten years younger than Armand, was imprisoned for 11 months (1717–18) in the Bastille for his verse. In his writings, Voltaire rarely mentioned his brother Armand.

Kant cites this witticism when explaining what a buffoon is. "A *buffoon* acts contrary to his own legitimate interests, even if in the end he only harms himself." "The *fool* places a greater value on things than he should; the buffoon places a greater value on himself."[12] The buffoon (*Narr*) is always going for laughs, bringing attention to himself. Even if Kant reserves a key place for humor in life, he repudiates joking in the wrong way or at the wrong moment.

20. The Life You Save May Be Your Own

There was once a knight named Hudibras. He was in danger, so his squire Ralpho advised him to flee. The Romans had promised to crown the man who saved a citizen. So, Ralpho reasoned, Hudibras would be praised and crowned if he fled. He would save a citizen's life—his own.[13]

Kant's source is again Butler's *Hudibras*. The *corona civica* was given to honor any soldier that, in battle, saved the life of a Roman citizen by killing an enemy.[14]

In his university lectures on anthropology, Kant aimed to help students become not just civilized and well-mannered, but also upright, informed citizens of the world. This quip makes fun of human hypocrisy and self-interest. Perhaps Kant liked it because he thought it made an ethical point, combining moral content with an incongruity. This brings us to Part Three, Sayings with a Message.

PART THREE

Sayings With A Message

21. Ragout, with Wit on the Side

Sound reason and understanding are like a dish of beef and mutton. They are fit only for the peasant's table. But a ragout of folly, accompanied by a sauce of wit, is fit for an emperor's table.[1]

Kant is quoting the French author François Rabelais (c. 1494–1553).[2] While Kant agrees with Rabelais about wit's utility, he thinks that wit should be used cautiously. It is best as an accessory.[3] Like a sauce, wit can enhance and improve the main dish (the "substance" of the conversation or text). But wit should not be overpowering. Ideally, jest should be combined with reason, making the result more enduring. This seems to be one reason why Kant was fond of the Abelard joke (No. 16).

For Kant, wit and jest are crucial to a successful dinner party. Dining should proceed in three main phases. "At a full table, where the number of courses is intended only to keep the guests together for a long time, . . . the conversation usually goes through three stages: (1) narration, (2) arguing, and (3) joking [*Scherzen*]."[4] Everyone contributes to the conversation together, without the party breaking up into smaller groups. First, the conversation should begin with a review of recent events and the local and national news (narration). After that, disagreements are bound to follow (arguing). But since this would get tiresome after a while, joking and playing games should follow (jest). "The conversation should not be business but merely play, one should avert such seriousness by means of a skillful and suitable jest."[5]

As Kant puts it in another text in 1786, "It is healthful for the body when, at dinner, the mind is not only free from cares but disposed to merriment and turned away from concentrating on any one subject. What best serves the body is conversation, amiable discussion, especially mirth breaking into hearty laughter. Here the mind exerts most strongly its force in moving the body."[6] The shaking of the diaphragm, the bodily movements accompanying jest and hearty laughter, help the digestive process. Just as tasteless joking leads to disgust, authentic jest aids digestion.

22. Hooped Skirts and Pruned Trees

The English magazine *The Spectator* claims it can predict women's fashions. They say it's just like with trees: when the branches are pruned below, the branches sprout up into the crown. When the hooped skirts and dresses become smaller, the head finery gets bigger and bigger.[7]

Kant is summarizing an entry from *The Spectator*, a popular English literary publication edited by Joseph Addison and Richard Steele between 1711 and 1712.[8] It aimed "to enliven Morality with Wit, and to temper Wit with Morality." This was an ideal Kant greatly admired, even if his understanding of ethics differed from that of British utilitarian moralists.

Kant contrasted fashion with "true" taste, which he thought was more enduring than fashion. Still, the correlation between above/below described by *The Spectator* might not be as eighteenth-century as it may seem (think of the 1980s).

23. Heidegger as a Woman

Heidegger was a celebrated singer and music performer from Switzerland. While at a party, it occurred to him to declare to a lord that he, Heidegger, had the ugliest face in all of London.

The lord reflected for a moment and then made a bet that he could find someone even uglier. Heidegger agreed. The lord sent out for an old drunk woman. When she appeared, the whole party burst into laughter. They cried out, "Heidegger, you just lost the bet."

"Not so fast," he replied, "Let the woman wear my wig. I'll put on her headdress. Then we'll see."

So they switched clothes. Everyone fell into laughter again, for the woman looked like a handsome and well-bred man, while Heidegger ended up looking like a witch.[9]

Having arrived in London in 1708, Heidegger became famous for organizing controversial masquerade balls and spectacles. The Heidegger in question is the Swiss musician and impresario Johann Jacob Heidegger (1666–1749), not the compromised German philosopher and Nazi-sympathizer Martin Heidegger (1889–1976).

Even if this story should be characterized as misogynistic and ageist, Kant's aim was not to be offensive, but to show that we can judge a thing's beauty or ugliness by comparing it with other members of its class and taking into account what kind of thing it is. Ugliness is not to be judged absolutely, he thought, only relatively.

Here, Kant thinks we judge the beauty of men and women from different points of view. We make an appraisal through the lens of gender. Heidegger, as a woman, was still ugly (in the version of the joke found in the Collins lecture transcription, *infinitely* so), whereas the lady came across as a decent-looking man. Ugliness lies in how we approach the object, under what class we see it. (See also No. 24.)

In the crowd's comparisons of the woman and Heidegger, there is an oscillation between disgust and ridicule.[10] When viewed as a woman, the lady was simply disgusting. When she was viewed as a man, she was acceptable and her ugly features were palatable. When Heidegger was viewed as a woman, the crowd laughed, making him the butt of a joke. But, unlike the woman, Heidegger was always ugly, never disgusting. They had fun with Heidegger and he laughed back — with them. But they simply laughed *at* her. This also reflects the sexism and ageism in Kant's anecdote: it employs the "fat old woman" archetype of the disgusting.[11]

24. There Are No Ugly Noses

There was once a soldier with a big nose, but it was blown off in combat. Since he thought his nose was too big for his face, he wanted to replace it with a smaller, more attractive one. So he had the best wax nose sent from Paris.

But when he had the new nose put on, he looked worse—ten times worse. So he ordered a version of his old nose, and he had that one put on.[12]

Kant was fond of telling this story to his anthropology classes over the years. He used the anecdote to explain that nothing in the world is actually ugly. What we think is ugly (an oversized nose) only appears to be so because we don't have the right perspective. Something seems ugly only in relation to individual specimens of its kind. But if one considers all of the specimens together, each one has a role to play.

A judgment of human beauty or ugliness is partly based on concepts of the human body, concepts in turn derived from observation. The beautiful bodily structure is the average for all specimens of its kind. Student lecture notes from 1784/85 read, "The perfect, proportioned, beautiful structure is the mean of the structure belonging to several things of one kind. The perfect, beautiful structure is thus the principle for the judging of the beautiful. Beauty lies in the concepts that we get from experience."[13]

Kant implies that what seems "ugly" has its place in the larger scheme of nature. An extremely short nose, and a very long one, would not be ugly, but would ultimately balance each other out. They both count in making up the beautiful average and thus help create a principle for judging.

25. A Whale Barrel

Nothing is accomplished by trying to use force over your inclinations and desires. Instead, you have to outsmart them. As Swift says, in order to save the ship, you have to surrender a barrel to the whale, so it can play with it.[14]

Kant's source is Jonathan Swift's *Tale of the Tub*.[15] He quotes this to give advice on how to pass time, to avoid idleness, even "nausea" with existence. You can't use force against boredom, but you can't just sit around either. You have to trick yourself by creating a diversion: Give the whale a barrel.

Kant recommended engaging with the "agreeable" arts, such as the joking, music, and games one might have encountered at eighteenth-century dinner parties. He praised laughing in response to joking ("play of thoughts"), feeling the affects created by music ("play of tones"), and experiencing the vivifying ups and downs created by playing games ("play of chance").[16] In the third *Critique*, Kant calls gaming one of the agreeable arts, that is, an art aiming to create pleasant bodily sensations.[17] (See also No. 26.) Kant himself preferred to play a card game called *ombre* (deriving from the Spanish for man), which involved bidding, similar to today's bridge.

26. To Each His Own

Let anyone ride his hobby horse up and down the streets, so long as he does not force you to sit behind him.[18]

Kant is endorsing a line from Laurence Sterne's *The Life and Opinions of Tristram Shandy, Gentleman*.[19] It's a version of "to each his own" or "live and let live." Tristram says there is no disputing about hobby horses; his own examples were fiddling and painting. Prigs and prudes who denounce harmless diversions deserve the Sterne "reprimand," Kant claims.

A hobby horse (*Steckenpferd*), Kant writes, represents[20] a "harmless little folly," a "fondness for occupying oneself industriously, as if it were a business, with objects of the imagination that the understanding merely plays with for amusement—a busy idleness, as it were."[21] Think of puzzle video games, crossword puzzles, Sudoku, Solitaire, making trinkets, knitting, stamp collecting, and other harmless diversions. Engaging in such activities can be good for one's overall health, Kant says, even charming. But when people take it a little too seriously, Kant thinks it crosses the line of sound understanding. Maybe that's why Kant thinks they sometimes evoke our gentle laughter and become laughable (*belachenswerth*).

As in the previous anecdote (No. 25), Kant gives advice on passing time. Following Sterne, he thinks that people should be allowed to play and amuse themselves as they please.

27. Pyrrho's Pig: That's What I'm Talking about

The philosopher Pyrrho was once on a ship in the middle of a terrible storm. Everyone else was anxious and scared. Pyrrho saw a pig eating calmly from his trough on the ship. Pointing to it, he declared: "The calm of the wise sage ought to be like this."[22]

Pyrrho of Elis (about 365 to 270 BCE) was a founder of Greek Skepticism. The anecdote can be found in Diogenes Laertius, *Lives of Eminent Philosophers*.[23]

According to this anecdote from *Essay on the Maladies of the Head*, the wise person is not ignorant of emotions and feelings—it's just that they know how to master them and reach a state of tranquility. The sage can sometimes come across as harsh or apathetic, but in fact they just have a high degree of self-control. Decades later, in the *Anthropology*, Kant endorsed the Stoic ideal according to which reason directs desires and passions. "The principle of apathy, namely, that the wise man must never be in a state of affect . . . is an entirely correct and sublime moral principle of the Stoic school."[24]

After this Pyrrho anecdote in *Maladies of the Head*, Kant refers to the story of an ambitious King Pyrrhus (319–272 BCE) and his wise and eloquent advisor, an Epicurean named Cineas. Kant doesn't tell the anecdote about them there, however, but in his early lectures on anthropology:

> Pyrrhus, a king of Macedonia some time after Alexander the Great, got it into his head to undertake many expeditions. He wanted to go to Italy: he told his advisor Cineas that he wanted to defeat Rome. Cineas asked him what he wished to do after that. Pyrrhus replied that he wanted to march on Sicily. After that, he said, he wanted to go to Asia Minor to subdue the people there. And then he wanted to conquer Syria. And so on. When Pyrrhus was done saying this, Cineas asked him what he wanted to do when all these conquests were over.

"We will want to drink a glass of wine, in peace," Pyrrhus answered.

"Well," Cineas replied, "why don't we just go ahead and relax and enjoy a drink now."[25]

Pyrrhus ignored Cineas's advice and went on to wage the Pyrrhic war. Kant views King Pyrrhus as a man enslaved by the passions (ambition) rather than governed by reason. Kant comments on the story, "Here it is clear that human beings who are in the throes of passion fail to see the whole, the larger context."

Kant doesn't just jump back to Greek Skepticism, Stoicism, or Epicureanism, however. For one, Jean-Jacques Rousseau (1712–78) stands in the middle. Kant closely followed the ideas of the Genevan author. He agreed with Rousseau that the natural inclinations should be in harmony with society.

Yet there are differences between their ideas. For Rousseau, humans in a state of nature have not yet been ruined by inept leaders and corrupt institutions, but in society they become tainted or even cruel. Kant is more optimistic than Rousseau concerning progress through social institutions. Humans can and should be cultivated by the arts and sciences, civilized by social decorum and propriety, and moralized by a proper education and way of thinking.[26] He thinks we are in the middle of the third phase, the moralizing process. Therefore, there is ground for hope. Not that Kant thinks the path will be easy (see No. 4, Dying of Good Health). Kant recognizes that civilization poses the risk of creating inequalities, oppressing others, and creating new opportunities for vice. Thus, Kant admits, out of the crooked wood of humanity, nothing entirely straight can be fabricated.[27]

28. Hobson's Choice

Hobson was a famous horse trader in London. He would keep a number of horses in his stables. When someone wanted to rent out one of them, he would say that one horse was tired, that a second one was sick, and a third had an injured leg.

Basically, he said that every horse had something wrong with it—except for *that* horse standing on the left-hand side of the stall. So, the customers had to pick that one.[28]

Kant comments, "Thus, it looked like Hobson allowed them free choice, but in fact the customer had only the appearance of it." Thomas Hobson was an English horse trader (1544–1631). Kant is paraphrasing a passage by Steele in *The Spectator*.[29]

In a Hobson's choice, only one option is available. American automaker Henry Ford offered people a Hobson's choice. Ford remarked on his vision for the Model T, "Any customer can have a car painted any color that he wants so long as it is black."[30]

Kant uses the example to illustrate the difference between true and apparent freedom. A Hobson's choice is not really a free choice. According to the *Critique of Practical Reason* (1788), the kind of freedom where a person is "driven around" by a series of "thoughts and representations" is likewise a "false" kind of freedom. It does not exceed the freedom of a dog running on a treadmill (a "turnspit"). The dog looks free, and it accomplishes its movements on its own, but is not in fact free since it's running in place.[31]

Kant defends a different conception of freedom. He thinks that although we cannot prove that we are free, the ideas of responsibility and agency require us to think of ourselves as if we are free, that is, free from determination by natural causes. Responsibility and agency require the thought that it is at least *possible* for a person to perform one action rather than another, and thus that it is possible for us to act morally.

29. Sex and Death

Suppose a man says that he cannot overcome his desire to have sex. If given the chance and the right moment, he just can't resist. But, ask him if he were to be hanged right after the act. Don't you think he would control his inclination? He would obviously say it was possible.

Now, consider the following. If his prince said to the man, "Either you offer false testimony against a good and honorable man I'd like to destroy (and I assure you that we would get away with it), or I will execute you."

What do you think he would do? The man would think it was at least possible to overcome his love of life, however great it was. He might not want to guess whether or not he *would* in fact resist, but he must admit that it would at least be *possible* for him to do so.[32]

Kant uses these two "what if" scenarios to argue for the possibility of human freedom to choose and act on adopted principles. He calls this *practical* freedom, a realm governed by practical reason, the source of the moral law. Kant is trying to get us to recognize that if we were in the threatened man's shoes, we could still say No to the prince and overcome even the love of life. Whether or not that would happen, of course, is another matter.

With thought experiments like these, we are supposed to be able to prove to ourselves that we are capable of recognizing the authority of morality over sensory gratification, even over life itself. If we ought to do something, Kant reasons, it must be possible for us to do it. As a well-known formula puts it, "ought implies can."

Freedom, Kant says, is not just following your intrinsic nature, as when a watch unwinds when left unhindered. That would be like the dog in the treadmill discussed in the previous anecdote (No. 28). Rather, it is the capacity to do "otherwise" (doing one action rather than another) and to set ends for oneself, including moral ends. The very idea of morality, Kant thinks, requires and presupposes the idea of freedom.

30. An Honest Man Is Hard to Find

There's an honest man. He is asked to join the adversaries of an innocent, but otherwise powerless, person (for instance, Anne Boleyn, who was accused by Henry the Eighth of England). The man, who is of modest means, is offered rewards such as great gifts and high rank. Yet he refuses them.

So the threats of loss begin. Among these enemies are his best friends; they stop being friends with him. Some are close relatives; they threaten to disown him. Some of them are powerful people who can hurt him at any moment. Another enemy of the innocent person is a prince who threatens to take away the man's freedom and, if necessary, to execute him. On top of this, the conspirators tell the man that his family is undergoing extreme distress and has run out of money. They inform him that his family is begging him to give in and join the conspirators.

He has a sensible heart, and feels genuine compassion for his family. He wishes that he had never lived to see the day that exposed him to so much pain.

—Nevertheless, he remains firm in his resolution to be truthful. He resists. He does not waver or doubt his decision not to join the adversaries.[33]

Anne Boleyn (1501–36): Queen of England between 1533 and 1536, mother of Queen Elizabeth I, Boleyn was beheaded after being found guilty of accusations made by Henry the Eighth.

This reads like a historical instantiation of No. 29. But Kant has a different aim here. Rather than employing it as a thought experiment to demonstrate human freedom, Kant uses the story to give an example of how moral education of the young might proceed. First, one evokes in a child a sense of awe for the aforementioned man's strength and purity of will. Second, the child realizes that they too possess such willpower or strength and that they can in principle act morally.

Kant's anecdote is an instance of gallows wit. Over a century later, Sigmund Freud too presented an account of joking, using gallows humor. "A rogue is being led out to his execution on a Monday. He observes, 'Well, this week's off to a great start'." (*Na, diese Woche fängt gut an.*)[34] The humor, Freud thinks, momentarily releases the energy normally spent to contain the fear of death and allows the person to jest about the very thing feared (death).

. . . And with that, we end on a happy note . . .

Appendix: Chapter Summaries

In the first chapter, I give an overview of Kant's theory of humor in its historical context. I survey the three major theories of humor (superiority, release, incongruity). Quoting from Kant's writings from various periods, I argue that his account has elements of all three of these theories, in addition to his own contribution, mental play theory. I explain his account of the "arts" of laughter (wit, naiveté, caprice), distinction between superficial and profound wit, and thoughts on the literary genre, comedy.

In chapter two, I give my answers to three main questions discussed in the scholarship on Kant and humor. Does laughter in response to humor count for Kant as a pure aesthetic judgment? Technically, it does not. But Kant seems to be inconsistent here, since the judging in such laughter is a play with aesthetic ideas. So, if we assume it can lead to a pure aesthetic judgment, what kind would it be? I argue that the judging in response to the humorous joke would be analogous, but not identical, to the experiences of the sublime and the beautiful. Finally, how does Kant's account of humor and laughter contribute to his broader philosophical aims? As a play with aesthetic ideas and thoughts (a *Gedankenspiel*), humor-elicited laughter is of interest to reason since it gives a hint of reason's activity and efficacy in the sensible world.

The final chapter is more a presentation of broader Kant*ian* arguments than an interpretation of Kant's actual texts in the strict sense; I apply Kant's moral philosophy to humor, although he does not do this very explicitly. I characterize Kant's position on the ethics of humor as *soft ethicism*. I give four reasons for calling his account a kind of ethicism, but add that this ethicism should be qualified as soft, since Kant holds that there is some leeway due to an aesthetic frame surrounding joking and humor. I argue that Kant is committed to the view that joking and jest over sensitive or controversial matters is sometimes, but not always, morally acceptable. To make this concrete, I discuss examples of questionable jokes from Kant as well as a racist passage. Finally, I conclude with some practical Kantian advice on joking.

Notes

Preface

1 Immanuel Kant, *Lectures on Anthropology* (Cambridge: Cambridge University Press, 2012), ed. Robert B. Louden and Allen Wood, trans. Robert R. Clewis, Robert B. Louden, G. Felicitas Munzel, and Allen W. Wood. The volume, *Lectures on Anthropology*, includes translations of several of the anthropology lectures that were published in *Vorlesungen über Anthropologie*, volume 25 (1997) of *Kant's gesammelte Schriften* (*Kant's Collected Writings*), a multivolume collection of Kant's works known as the Academy Edition (Akademie-Ausgabe, abbreviated throughout as "AA"). Each anthropology lecture is named after a (presumed) transcriber. For instance, the "Mrongovius anthropology lecture" was transcribed by a person known as Mrongovius, the "Friedländer anthropology lecture" by someone we call Friedländer, and so on.

Page references to Kant's works will be to *Kant's gesammelte Schriften* (1900–), cited by volume and, separated by a colon, followed by the page number. The translations not here carried out by me are taken from the volumes in the series *The Cambridge Edition of the Works of Immanuel Kant*, ed. Paul Guyer and Allen Wood (Cambridge: Cambridge University Press, 1992–), with occasional modifications. In my translations of jokes and anecdotes collected in Parts Two and Three, I have taken some liberties in order to improve Kant's set-up and delivery, modifying elements such as sentence transitions, punctuation, verb tense, and word order. Throughout this book, I refer to the collected jokes and anecdotes by their Numbers (e.g., "No. 3" refers to the joke I call "Swift Wit").

2 Friedrich Nietzsche, *Beyond Good and Evil*, in *Basic Writings of Nietzsche*, trans. Walter Kaufmann (New York: Random House, 1992), 422.

3 Friedrich Nietzsche, *The Genealogy of Morals*, in *Basic Writings*, 501.

4 Johann Gottfried Herder, *Letters on the Advancement of Humanity*, Letter 79, in Johann Gottfried Herder, *Sämtliche Werke*, 33 vols., ed. Bernhard Suphan (Berlin: Weidmann, 1877–1913), vol. 17, 404.

5 Herder, preface to *Kalligone* (1800). Johann Gottfried Herder, *Schriften zu Literatur und Philosophie, 1792–1800*, ed. Hans Dietrich Irmscher (Frankfurt am Main: Deutscher Klassiker Verlag, 1998), 651–2.
6 Kant, AA 13:96; my translation. A translation can also be found in Immanuel Kant, *Correspondence*, trans. Arnulf Zweig (Cambridge: Cambridge University Press), 565.
7 Manfred Kuehn, *Kant: A Biography* (Cambridge: Cambridge University Press, 2001), 114.
8 John Morreall, ed., *The Philosophy of Laughter and Humor* (Albany: State University of New York Press, 1987), 204.
9 Jim Holt, *Stop Me If You've Heard This: A History and Philosophy of Jokes* (New York: W. W. Norton, 2008), 94.
10 Jean-Baptiste Botul, *La vie sexuelle d'Emmanuel Kant*, ed. Frédéric Pagès (Paris: Éditions Mille et une nuits, 1999). "Botulism," alas, is not a real philosophical school. Pagès wrote this spoof using the made-up name of a fictional philosopher, Botul.
11 Norman Malcolm, *Ludwig Wittgenstein: A Memoir* (New York: Oxford University Press, 1984), 27–8.
12 This content-based classification of Kant's jokes is not meant to be an exhaustive taxonomy of all joke-kinds. Pursuing the latter, Lewis Black holds there are only five kinds of jokes: the long shaggy dog story (long-form joke), the shorter narrative joke, the formulaic joke, the quickie, and the one-liner. Black's typology seems to address more the *form* than the content of jokes. See Lewis Black, *History of the Joke, with Lewis Black*, DVD, History Channel, produced by Marc Etkind, May 9, 2008. Cited by Gini, *The Importance of Being Funny* (Lanham: Rowman & Littlefield, 2017), 123 n. 17. For a more comprehensive taxonomy of humor, wit, and jokes, see Debra L. Long and Arthur C. Graesser, "Wit and Humor in Discourse Processing," *Discourse Processes* 11, no.1 (1988): 35–60. They list ten categories (based on a joke's content): nonsense, social satire, philosophical, sexual, hostile, demeaning to men, demeaning to women, ethnic, sick, and scatological. Of these, Kant gives instances of all of these except the hostile and the demeaning to men.
13 Immanuel Kant, *Kritik der Urteilskraft*, with illustrations and photos by Andrea Büttner, ed. Museum Ludwig, Cologne (Hamburg: Felix Meiner, 2014).
14 Antje Herzog, *Lampe und Sein Meister Immanuel Kant* (Frankfurt am Main: Edition Buechergilde, 2017).
15 On Kant as a university lecturer, see Steve Naragon's informative website, "Kant in the Classroom." https://users.manchester.edu/Facstaff/SSNaragon/Kant/Lectures/lecturesIntro.htm [accessed March 25, 2019]. See also the 22-chapter volume covering each of the eleven disciplines in

which Kant taught: *Reading Kant's Lectures*, ed. Robert R. Clewis (Berlin: Walter de Gruyter, 2015), especially the editor's introduction. On Kant's lectures on anthropology in particular, see Holly Wilson, *Kant's Pragmatic Anthropology: Its Origin, Meaning, and Critical Significance* (State University of New York Press, 2006).

16 For historically oriented studies of Kant on wit, for instance, see the following contributions. Manuel Sánchez Rodríguez, "Witz und reflektierende Urteilskraft in Kants Philosophie," in *Kant und die Philosophie in weltbürgerlicher Absicht*, vol. 4, ed. Stefano Bacin, Alfredo Ferrarin, Claudio La Rocca, and Margit Ruffing (Berlin: Walter de Gruyter, 2013), 487–96. (This appears in Spanish in an expanded version: Manuel Sánchez Rodríguez, "Ingenio, Uso Hipotético de la Razón y Juicio Reflexionante en la Filosofía de Kant," *Anales del Seminario de Historia de la Filosofía* 29, no. 2 (2012): 577–92.) Fernando Silva, "'Zum Erfinden wird Witz erfordert'. On the Evolution of the Concept of 'Witz' in Kant's Anthropology Lectures," in *Kant's Lectures / Kants Vorlesungen*, ed. Bernd Dörfinger, Claudio La Rocca, Robert B. Louden, and Ubirajara Marques Rancan de Azevedo (Berlin: Walter de Gruyter, 2015), 121–32.

17 Diogenes Laertius, *Lives of Eminent Philosophers*, ed. Robert Drew Hicks, 2 vols. (London: William Heinemann, 1925). Around 2900 BCE, priests and scribes in ancient Egypt created a specific hieroglyph for laughter or laughing. Ancient Greeks were collecting jokes around the time of Philip II of Macedon (382–336 BCE), and the Romans continued the tradition. See Gini, *Being Funny*, 1, 3. On ancient Roman humor, see Mary Beard, *Laughter in Ancient Rome: On Joking, Tickling, and Cracking Up* (Berkeley: University of California Press, 2014). On the history of jesters, fools, and court wit in Renaissance Europe, Japan, China, and other parts of the globe, see Beatrice K. Otto, *Fools are Everywhere: The Court Jester Around the World* (Chicago: University of Chicago Press, 2001).

18 There have been several attempts to connect philosophy and humor, such as Thomas Cathcart and Daniel Klein, *Plato and a Platypus Walk into a Bar: Understanding Philosophy through Jokes* (New York: Abrams Image, 2006). But the present book is not an attempt to explain philosophy through jokes. It instead aims to understand Kant's account of humor, illustrated by his jokes.

19 Søren Kierkegaard, *The Humor of Kierkegaard: An Anthology*, ed. Thomas C. Oden (Princeton: Princeton University Press, 2004). Slavoj Žižek, *Žižek's Jokes (Did You Hear the One about Hegel and Negation?)*, ed. Audun Mortensen (Cambridge: MIT Press, 2014).

20 Consider, by contrast, *Kant zum Vergnügen*, ed. Volker Gerhardt (Stuttgart: Reclam, 2003). Without providing commentary or extensive analysis, this small book first reproduces nearly all of Kant's *Observations* (pages 9–75), and then collects excerpts from Kant's writings followed by descriptions of

Kant by his contemporaries (pages 77–173). Likewise, the short book, Immanuel Kant, *Il piacere di ridere*, ed. Mascia Cardelli (Firenze: Le Càriti, 2002), only contains an Italian translation of the third *Critique*'s remarks on laughter. It neither collects his jokes nor provides commentaries and illustrations.

21 Immanuel Kant, *Kant's Grosse Völkerschau: aus den Naturwissenschaftlichen Kollegs des Herrn Professor Immanuel Kant aus Königsberg*, ed. Eugen Skasa-Weiss and illustrated by Wolfgang Felten (München: Heimeran, 1960).

22 For ease of expression I sometimes also refer to Kant's "theory" of humor, but in reality Kant provides thoughts or considerations from which an account of humor can be constructed. In addition, we should resist the common characterization of Kant as the *first* major proponent of the incongruity theory of humor. The guest editors of a special issue on humor for instance write, "The earliest proponent of the incongruity theory is Immanuel Kant." Tom Brommage, Michael Cundall, and Elizabeth Victor, *Florida Philosophical Review* 15, no. 1 (2015): i–viii, iv. Hutcheson and Mendelssohn, among others, preceded Kant. The need for such corrections is also noted by Patrick Giamario, "'Making Reason Think More': Laughter in Kant's Aesthetic Philosophy" *Angelaki* 22, no. 4 (2017): 161–76, 174 n. 6.

23 Gini and Brown both attribute a version of this quip to E. B. White. See Gini, *Being Funny*, 19. Deborah Brown, "What Part of 'Know' Don't You Understand?" *The Monist* 88, no. 1 (2005): 11–35, 20. Strangely, Terry Eagleton begins a recent book on humor by *denying* that to analyze a joke is to kill it dead. Terry Eagleton, *Humour* (New Haven: Yale University Press, 2019), ix.

24 Francis Hutcheson noted that treating laughter *seriously* is rather odd. See *Eighteenth-Century British Aesthetics*, ed. Dabney Townsend (Amityville: Baywood Publishing, 1999), 145.

25 Gini, *Being Funny*, xx. "When you have to . . . explain how it [a joke] works, and why it's funny, then the joke ceases to be funny"; Gini, *Being Funny*, 37. The point is also made by Bob Mankoff, longtime cartoon editor at the *New Yorker*: "Although humor is a fascinating topic, academics being academics can take the fun out of it and make it boring." Quoted by Gini, *Being Funny*, 22. See Bob Mankoff, *How about Never—Is Never Good for You? My Life in Cartoons* (New York: Henry Holt, 2014), 4.

26 See Spinoza's remark on studying humanity using a mathematical method: "I have laboured carefully, not to mock, lament, or execrate human actions, but to understand them." See Benedict de Spinoza, *Tractatus Theologico-Politicus*, in *The Chief Works of Benedict de Spinoza*, vol. 1, trans. R. H. M. Elwes (London: George Bell & Sons, 1891), 288.

Foreword by Noël Carroll

1   Immanuel Kant, *Critique of Judgment,* translated by Werner S. Pluhar (Indianapolis: Hackett Publishing Company, 1987), 203; AA 5:332. Here Kant, like many traditional comic theorists, uses the notion of *laughter* where many comic theorists today would speak of *comic amusement* insofar as laughter arises in many situations in which humor plays no role.
2   See section 14 in *The Philosophy of Laughter and Humor*, ed. John Morreall (Albany, NY: Suny Press, 1987), 111–16.
3   Kant, *Critique of Judgment*, 203; AA 5:332.
4   It violates several of Grice's conversational maxims. See Paul Grice, "Logic and Conversation," in his *Studies in the Way of Words* (Cambridge, MA: Harvard University Press, 1989), 26–9.
5   Kant, *Critique of Judgment,* 204; AA 5:334. Here, in the name of historical charity, I am ignoring Kant's further biological speculations about the physiological concomitants of this experience.

Note on Text and Sources

1   In similar fashion, Jonathan Bennett provides more readable versions of some of Kant's writings, although not the third *Critique*. Bennett offers English translations even for works of modern philosophy that were originally written in English. Jonathan Bennett, "Early Modern Texts," http://www.earlymoderntexts.com/ [accessed October 4, 2019].

Part One Kant's Theory of Humor

Chapter 1: The Secret Soul of Kant's Joke

1   Nietzsche wrote in *The Gay Science* (sec. 193): "*Kant's Joke*—Kant wanted to prove in a way that would dumbfound the common man that the common man was right: that was the secret joke of this soul." Friedrich Nietzsche, *The Portable Nietzsche*, ed. Walter Kaufmann (New York: Penguin, 1982), 96.
2   Heinrich Heine, *On the History of Religion and Philosophy in Germany and Other Writings*, ed. Terry Pinkard (Cambridge: Cambridge University Press, 2007), 79.
3   Heine, *On the History of Religion and Philosophy*, 79.

4   Gini, *Being Funny*, 109. In contrast, Giamario concludes that "Attending to the account of laughter that Kant advances . . . demonstrates that Kantian critical philosophy is—despite its well-earned reputation as serious and uncompromising—a philosophy of laughter." Giamario, "Making Reason Think More," 173.

5   Kuehn, *Kant*, 115.

6   Kant held Voltaire in esteem for decades. Kant quotes the ending to Voltaire's anti-Leibnizian, anti-optimism work *Candide* (1759) at the end of his own satirical work (1766), *Dreams of A Spirit-Seer*. In a jab at the "school" philosophy of Leibniz and Wolff, Kant concludes *Dreams* by urging readers to cultivate their own gardens: "I will conclude with the advice which *Voltaire* gave to his honest *Candide* after so many futile scholastic disputes: *Let us attend to our happiness, and go into the garden and work*." See Kant, *Dreams of a Spirit-Seer*, AA 2:373; original emphasis. *Candide* concludes with the words: "'That is well put,' replied Candide, 'but we must cultivate our garden'." Voltaire, *Candide and Other Stories*, trans. Roger Pearson (Oxford: Oxford University Press, 2008), 88. In a treatise on the proofs of God, Kant recycles a Voltaire joke that pokes fun at Leibnizian optimism: "Why do we have noses?—So that we can wear glasses." Kant, *The Only Possible Argument in Support of a Demonstration of the Existence of God*, AA 2:131. (The glasses joke is reminiscent of a more serious, teleological line of argument about moss—which exists for reindeer—which exist for Laplanders, a line that Kant considers in the third *Critique* but ultimately does not accept outright. Kant, *CPJ*, AA 5:369.) Kant told a couple of Voltaire quips (No. 9, The Happy Cuckold; The Voltaire Bros, No. 19). Kant also mentions Voltaire at the end of his discussion of laughter in *CPJ*. The fact that at the end of his analysis Kant would mention only Voltaire, underscores the latter's importance for Kant.

7   On Hogarth, see Kant, *Observations*, AA 2:214; and Kant, Reflection 1498 (from 1775–77), AA 15:777.

8   Kuehn, *Kant*, 154.

9   Given the aims of this guide, I cannot wade into debates about the meanings of these core terms and concepts in the philosophy of humor. They are explained and/or debated in many of the sources and studies cited in my notes and listed in the bibliography. For general discussions of the philosophy of humor, see Noël Carroll, *Humour: A Very Short Introduction* (Oxford: Oxford University Press, 2014), and Simon Critchley, *On Humour* (New York: Routledge, 2002). See also the primary sources in Morreall's *Laughter and Humor* and in *A Source Book of Literary and Philosophical Writings about Humour and Laughter: the Seventy-five Essential Texts from Antiquity to Modern Times*, ed. Jorge Figueroa-Dorrego and Cristina Larkin-Galiñanes (Lewiston: Edwin Mellen, 2009).

10 Kant did not use the word "humor" in the contemporary sense. While "humor" has been used to refer to the funny or ludicrous in English since the late 1600s, in the German of Kant's day it was not used that way. Kant instead writes about jokes (*Scherze*), wit (*Witz*), laughter (*Lachen*), and caprice (*Laune*).

11 Going against the consensus of recent theories, however, Shaw argues that laughter and humor are intimately connected and should not be conceptually detached from each other. Joshua Shaw, "Philosophy of Humor," *Philosophy Compass* 5, no. 2 (2010): 112–26, 118–23. An important historical source for the laughter-humor connection is Schopenhauer's theory of humor. A version of the thesis ("Laughter is the most characteristic way of enjoying humor") was defended by Martin in a 1983 article, albeit with great qualification ("laughter is neither a necessary nor sufficient condition for amusement"). Mike W. Martin, "Humour and Aesthetic Enjoyment of Incongruities," *British Journal of Aesthetics* 23, no. 1 (1983): 74–85, 78.

12 Robert Sharpe, "Seven Reasons Why Amusement Is an Emotion," *Journal of Value Inquiry* 9, no. 3 (1975): 201–3.

13 Morreall, *Laughter and Humor*, 4.

14 This distinction between formula and fiction jokes is made (for instance) in Peter Kivy, "Joking Morality," in *Once Upon a Time: Essays in the Philosophy of Literature*, ed. Aaron Meskin (New York: Roman and Littlefield, 2019), 103–18, 103.

15 For Kant, a "bon mot" is a witty saying (*Witzwort*). It is to be distinguished from a proverb (*Sprichwort*), which is "a formula that has become common which expresses a thought that is transmitted by imitation, even though it could well have been a witty saying in the mouth of the first speaker." Kant, *Anthropology*, AA 7:222.

16 For an illuminating taxonomy of comedic styles, see Steven Gimbel, *Isn't That Clever: A Philosophical Account of Humor and Comedy* (New York: Routledge, 2018), 81–90.

17 Gini, *Being Funny*, 57.

18 See Rudolph Herzog, *Dead Funny: Telling Jokes in Hitler's Germany*, trans. Jefferson Chase (New York: Melville House, 2012). Steve Lipman, *Laughter In Hell: The Use of Humor During the Holocaust* (London: Jason Aronson Inc., 1991). A coping or defense mechanism thesis is also found in André Comte-Sponville, *A Small Treatise on the Great Virtues: The Uses of Philosophy in Everyday Life*, trans. Catherine Temerson (New York: Metropolitan Books, 2001), 217. Gini likewise argues that comedy, humor, and joke telling "are a means of dealing with the everyday problems of life as well as many of the more elusive and mysterious questions of existence," and that humor can "defend and

protect us against life." Gini, *Being Funny*, xiii; see also xx, 10, 49. This thesis concerns the *function* of humor in our lives, however, not what makes something funny.

19. One of the narrator's friends, Arthur, returns to the concentration camp with news from an old lady in the ghetto.

> "Does she know when we will get out of here? Or when they are going to slaughter us?"
> "Nobody knows the answers to those questions. But she said something else, something that we should perhaps think about in times like these. She thought that God was on vacation." . . .
> "Let me sleep," I replied. "Tell me more when he gets back."

The narrator then thought he heard his friends laughing, or perhaps just dreamed that they were. This uncertainty may be an admission that the joke does not so much amuse as help the prisoners cope. Quoted from Peter Banki, "Humor as the Inverted Sublime: Jean Paul's Laughter within Limitations," *Parrhesia* 21 (2014): 58–68, 64; translation modified. The quote is from Simon Wiesenthal, *The Sunflower: On the Possibilities and Limits of Forgiveness*, trans. H. A. Pichler (New York: Schocken Books, 1997), 7–8.

20. The bear joke is from Rob Elliott, *Laugh-out-loud Jokes for Kids* (Grand Rapids: Baker Publishing Group, 2010), 56. The Freud joke is from Ted Cohen, *Jokes: Philosophical Thoughts on Joking Matters* (Chicago: University of Chicago Press, 1999), 17. Cohen (12) describes the need for background knowledge in order to get a joke.

21. I made this one up, I admit.

22. F. la T. Godfrey, "The Aesthetics of Laughter," *Hermathena* 25, no. 50 (1937): 126–38, 126. Godfrey's essay, largely forgotten, is quite illuminating.

23. Jeremy Arnold, "Laughter, Judgment and Democratic Politics," *Culture, Theory, & Critique* 50, no. 1 (2009): 7–21, 17.

24. Gimbel, *Isn't That Clever*, 9.

25. A version of this joke is found at Gini, *Being Funny*, 20. Gini cites Scott Weems, *Ha! The Science of When We Laugh and Why* (New York: Basic Books, 2014), 23.

26. Plato, *Philebus*, 49d. Following convention, Plato is cited by the Stephanus page. For Plato's writings, see Plato, *Complete Works*, ed. J. M. Cooper and D. S. Hutchinson (Indianapolis: Hackett, 1997).

27. Aristotle, *Rhetoric*, bk. 2, ch. 12 (1389 b 1). All references to Aristotle will include Bekker pagination in parentheses. For Aristotle's writings, see Aristotle, *The Complete Works of Aristotle*, 2 vols., ed. Jonathan Barnes (Princeton: Princeton University Press, 1984). Hutcheson notes (plausibly)

that Aristotle is claiming only that this is one species of humor and that Aristotle's claim was "never intended as a general account of all sorts of laughter." Hutcheson, in Townsend, *British Aesthetics*, 138.

28 Aristotle, *Poetics*, ch. 5 (1449 a 31).

29 See ch. 9, sec. 13, in Thomas Hobbes, *The Treatise on Human Nature and That on Liberty and Necessity* (London: McCreery, 1812), 65; emphasis and spelling modified.

30 René Descartes, *The Passions of the Soul*, in *Philosophical Works of Descartes*, vol. 1, trans. Elizabeth Haldane and George T. Ross (Cambridge: Cambridge University Press, 1984), article 178. References to *Passions* will be to the article number. On laughter, see part 2, articles 124–7, and part 3, 178–81.

31 Paul Swift, "In-jestion: Intestinal Laughter in Kant and Nietzsche," *International Studies in Philosophy* 27, no. 1 (1995): 97–103, 98.

32 Nietzsche, *The Gay Science* (sec. 200), in Nietzsche, *Basic Writings*, 172.

33 Nietzsche, *Beyond Good and Evil*, in Nietzsche, *Basic Writings*, 422–3.

34 John Morreall, "Philosophy of Humor," *The Stanford Encyclopedia of Philosophy* (Winter 2016 Edition), ed. Edward N. Zalta. https://plato.stanford.edu/archives/win2016/entries/humor/

35 Roger Scruton, "Laughter," in *Laughter and Humor*, ed. Morreall, 156–71, 169.

36 For a recent version of superiority theory, see F. H. Buckley, *The Morality of Laughter* (Ann Arbor: University of Michigan Press, 2005).

37 Kant, Friedländer anthropology lecture, AA 25:601.

38 Quoted from Matthew Kotzen, "The Normativity of Humor," *Philosophical Issues* 25, no. 1 (2015): 396–414, 399.

39 Quoted from Eagleton, *Humour*, 79. ("Refuse" can also mean garbage.)

40 Merrie Bergmann, "How Many Feminists Does It Take to Make A Joke? Sexist Humor and What's Wrong with It," *Hypatia* 1, no. 1 (1986): 63–82, 69.

41 Henri Bergson, *Laughter: An Essay on the Meaning of the Comic*, trans. Cloudesley Brereton and Fred Rothwell (Oxford: Macmillan, 1911), 5. For Bergson, laughter can also be used as a social corrective, to bring others in line when they act in a mechanical way.

42 Carroll, *Humour*, 28.

43 Holt, *A History and Philosophy of Jokes*, 94.

44 For instance, Kant's personal library contained copies of German translations of *An Inquiry into the Original of Our Ideas of Beauty and Virtue* (1725) and *An Essay on the Nature and Conduct of the Passions and Affections* (1728). See Arthur Warda, *Immanuel Kants Bücher. Mit einer*

getreuen Nachbildung des bisher einzigen bekannten Abzuges des Versteigerungskataloges der Bibliothek Kants (Berlin: Martin Breslauer, 1922), 50.

45 James Beattie, "An Essay on Laughter and Ludicrous Composition," in his *Essays: On Poetry and Music, As They Affect the Mind* (Edinburgh: William Creech, 1778), 319–486, 344.

46 Alexander Gerard, *An Essay on Taste* (London: 1759, A. Millar, A. Kincaid, and J. Bell), 69, 66; emphasis modified. Like Kant after him, Gerard mentions both Samuel Butler (specifically, *Hudibras*) and Jonathan Swift; see *Essay*, 70, 73.

47 Moses Mendelssohn, "Rhapsody or Additions to the Letters on Sentiments," *Philosophical Writings*, ed. Daniel O. Dahlstrom (Cambridge: Cambridge University Press, 1997), 131–68. On laughter, see 149–50. The similarities between Kant's account and Mendelssohn's are notable.

48 Christian Wolff, *Psychologia empirica* (Frankfurt and Leipzig: officina libraria Rengeriana, 1732), §743. References will be to the section number.

49 Lessing: "Every absurdity [*Ungereimtheit*], every contrast of reality and deficiency is laughable." Gotthold Ephraim Lessing, *Selected Prose Works*, ed. Edward Bell (London: George Bell and Sons, 1889), 306. Goethe: "The ridiculous arises out of a moral contrast, in which two things are brought together before the mind in an innocent way." Johann Wolfgang von Goethe, *Elective Affinities* (New York: Henry Holt, 1872), 184.

50 Arthur Schopenhauer, *The World as Will and Representation*, 2 vols., trans. E. F. J. Payne (New York: Dover, 1969), vol. 1, §13, 59; and vol. 2, ch. 8, "On the Theory of the Ludicrous," 91. Schopenhauer endorses an incongruity theory, yet he also recognizes laughing at others and adds some elements of superiority theory (vol. 2, 98–9). Like Kant, he looks down on mere word play and "mere puns" (vol. 2., 95). Presumably criticizing Jean Paul (Johann Paul Friedrich Richter), Schopenhauer lampoons as an "empty phrase" the definition of humor as "the interpretation of the finite and the infinite" (vol. 2, 100).

51 Søren Kierkegaard, *Concluding Unscientific Postscript*, trans. David Swenson and Walter Lowrie (Princeton: Princeton University Press, 1941).

52 Annegret Braun and Siegfried Preiser, "The Impact of Disparaging Humor Content on the Funniness of Political Jokes," *Humor* 26, no. 2 (2013): 249–75, 250.

53 Winfried Menninghaus, Isabel Bohrn, Ulrike Altmann, Oliver Lubrich, and Arthur Jacobs, "Sounds Funny? Humor Effects of Phonological and Prosodic Figures of Speech," *Psychology of Aesthetics, Creativity, and the Arts* 8, no. 1 (2014): 71–6, 71. The difference between incongruity and incongruity-*resolution* theories need not concern us here.

54 Eagleton, *Humour*, 67.
55 Carroll, *Humour*, 53. Noël Carroll, "Two Comic Plot Structures," *The Monist* 88, no. 1 (2005): 154–83, 166. Many other philosophers defend versions of incongruity theory. One of the earliest attempts in analytic philosophy is Michael Clark, "Humour and Incongruity," *Philosophy* 45, no. 171 (1970): 20–32. Clark's proposal is partially endorsed and amended by Martin, "Humour and Aesthetic Enjoyment of Incongruities."
56 One might be tempted to cite puns as a counterexample to the theory. Puns actually presuppose incongruity, however, since they require us to see or use a single word in two distinct ways. It is the incongruity between the two senses that generates any comic amusement. See Carroll, "Two Comic Plot Structures," 173; Gimbel, *Isn't That Clever*, 18.
57 Cicero claims, "The most common kind of joke is when we expect one thing and another is said; here our own disappointed expectation makes us laugh." Cicero, bk. 2, ch. 58, in *On Oratory and Orators*, trans. J. S. Watson (New York: Harper and Brothers, 1860), 157; translation modified. Kant makes claims about laughter that are strikingly close to this.
58 Carroll, "Two Comic Plot Structures," 166. Eagleton, *Humour*, 73.
59 Shaftesbury, *Sensus Communis: An Essay on the Freedom of Wit and Humour* (London: Egbert Sanger, 1709), 18; format and style modernized. See also Carroll, *Humour*, 38. Eagleton, *Humour*, 10.
60 E.g., Kant, *The Metaphysis of Morals*, AA 6:209; Kant, "On the Use of Teleological Principles in Philosophy," AA 8:166; and Kant, *Announcement of the Organization of His Lectures for the Winter Semester 1765–1766*, AA 2:311.
61 Herbert Spencer, "On the Physiology of Laughter," in *Essays on Education and Kindred Subjects* (London: J. M. Dent & Sons, 1911), 305.
62 Meredith thinks that Kant's account "strikingly anticipates" Spencer's. James Creed Meredith, in Immanuel Kant, *Kant's Critique of Aesthetic Judgment*, trans. James Creed Meredith (Oxford: Clarendon, 1911), cxxxi. For Spencer on laughter and the "viscera" and "digestion," see Spencer, "Physiology of Laughter," 307. For Meredith's general comments on Kant and laughter, see Essay VI, "Art and the Artist," in *Kant's Critique*, cxviii–cxliv, esp. cxxx–cxxxii. Meredith also provides comments on laughter in his Notes, in *Kant's Critique*, 302–6.
63 Sigmund Freud, *Jokes and Their Relation to the Unconscious*, trans. James Strachey (New York: W. W. Norton & Company, 1960).
64 Critchley, *On Humour*, 3.
65 Sigmund Freud, *The Interpretation of Dreams*, trans. James Strachey (London: Penguin, 1976), 766. In 1927, Freud wrote a lesser-known paper, "Der Humor" ("Humor"), employing his theory of the super-ego and ego.

See Sigmund Freud, *Standard Edition of the Complete Psychological Works of Sigmund Freud*, vol. 21 (London: Hogarth Press, 1961), 161–6. For discussion of the short essay "Humor," see Critchley, *On Humour*, 94–6.

66 Quoted in Nietzsche, *Basic Writings*, 422.

67 John Dewey, "The Theory of Emotion," *Psychological Review* 1 (1894): 553–69.

68 Eagleton combines relief theory with an incongruity theory. An older defense of relief theory can also be found in J. C. Gregory, *The Nature of Laughter* (London: Kegan Paul, 1924). For a more recent version, see Robert Latta, *The Basic Humor Process: A Cognitive-Shift Theory and the Case against Incongruity* (Berlin: Mouton de Gruyter, 1999).

69 For instance, Clark approaches the question "What is humor?" by asking what *amusement* is. Clark, "Humour and Incongruity," 22. A close connection between humor and amusement is affirmed even by Clark's critics, Mike W. Martin, "Humour and Aesthetic Enjoyment of Incongruities," 74–5, and Roger Scruton, who tries to find the "pattern of thought" indicative of amusement. Scruton, "Laughter," in Morreall, *Laughter and Humor*, 169. Clark retains the humor–amusement connection in his response to Martin and Scruton. Michael Clark, "Humour, Laughter and the Structure of Thought," *British Journal of Aesthetics* 27 (3) (1987): 238–46, 243–5.

70 There are many variations of incongruity theory. Sometimes a variation goes by different names ("incongruence") or is made more complex by, for instance, discussing the *resolution* of the incongruity (incongruity-resolution theory). Moreover, there are "hidden sense" incongruity theorists (e.g., D. H. Monro, Arthur Koestler) who claim that in all humor we find either some apparent sense in the incongruity, or some element that makes the incongruity plausible. "Hidden moral" incongruity theorists (again, D. H. Monro) maintain that behind the incongruity in a funny episode, there is always a moral or point. See D. H. Munro, *The Argument of Laughter* (South Bend: University of Notre Dame Press, 1963). On hidden sense and hidden moral incongruity theorists, see Bergmann, "Sexist Humor," 67.

71 For a discussion of various theories from a psychological point of view, see Christopher P. Wilson, *Jokes: Form, Content, Use and Function* (London and New York: Academic Press, 1979).

72 Eagleton, *Humour*, 70–1.

73 The term "play" has been used in theories that see humor as a kind of relaxation or release from work and activity, but Kant's sense of play differs from this. For a brief discussion, and criticism, of play theory in Aristotle, Aquinas, and Max Eastman, see Carroll, *Humour*, 42–3. For the theory, see Max Eastman, *The Enjoyment of Laughter* (New York: Simon and Schuster,

1936). Johan Huizinga, *Homo Ludens* (London: Routledge and Kegan Paul, 1949).

74 Kant, *CPJ*, AA 5:532–3. In the first *Critique* (1781), Kant offered four ways of understanding the concept of "nothing." For his Table of the division of the concept of nothing, see Kant, *Critique of Pure Reason*, A292/B348. (References to Kant's *Critique of Pure Reason* follow the convention of citing the A edition followed by the B edition.)

75 Kant, *CPJ*, AA 5:332–3; original emphasis. On laughter, see also *Anthropology*, AA 7:262, 7:301, 7:323–4.

76 Building on Kant's distinction between free and adherent beauty, Canivet proposes a potentially useful distinction between free and adherent judging in laughter. Michel Canivet, "Le rire et le bon sens," *Revue Philosophique de Louvain* 86, no. 3 (1988): 354–77, 365. The proposal needs to be developed in another way, however, for Canivet misconstrues the free/adherent distinction. He seems to think that to apply the term "adherent" to beauty is to say that it either is grounded on or evokes an *interest*. To the contrary, there can be a disinterested play with the beautiful object even as one takes into account its usefulness or function and thereby estimates an object's adherent beauty. A judgment of adherent beauty can neither be based on, nor elicit, an interest. In fact, if it were, it would not be a judgment of beauty (in Kant's sense of the term) in the first place.

77 Kant elsewhere writes that it is an "illusion" that disappears into nothing. Kant, *CPJ*, AA 5:334. As I explain below, the disappointment of our expectations, and the disappearance of an illusion, can be seen as distinct (negative and positive) moments in the mental "play" with the content of the humor.

78 Carroll, *Humour*, 18.

79 Carroll, "Two Comic Plot Structures," 172.

80 Yet Arnold considers, then rejects, this reading. He instead emphasizes "a sense for the nothing" and non-sense. Arnold, "Laughter," 10.

81 Kant, Friedländer anthropology lecture, AA 25:601; translation modified.

82 Kant, *CPJ*, AA 5:334.

83 Kant, *CPJ*, AA 5:332. Note that the play "begins with thoughts," which then results in bodily oscillations.

84 Kant, *CPJ*, AA 5:335.

85 Kant, "Remarks," AA 20:187; my translation.

86 Kant, "Remarks," AA 20:188; my translation.

87 Kant, *Anthropology*, AA 7:262; translation modified.

88 Carroll, *Humour*, 39. Cristina Larkin-Galiñanes, "An Overview of Humor Theory," in *The Routledge Handbook of Language and Humor*, ed. Salvatore Attardo (New York: Routledge, 2017), 4–16, 10.

89 Critchley, *On Humour*, 6.
90 Eagleton, *Humour*, 10, 69.
91 John Marmysz, "Humor, Sublimity and Incongruity," *Consciousness, Literature and the Arts* 2, no. 3 (2001): no pagination. All quotations can be found at www.dmd27.org/marm.html [accessed August 26, 2019]. See also John Marmysz, *Laughing at Nothing: Humor as a Response to Nihilism* (Albany: SUNY Press, 2003).
92 Swift, "Intestinal Laughter in Kant and Nietzsche," 97.
93 Kant, Friedländer anthropology lecture, AA 25:601.
94 In parallel fashion, in Article 124 of *Passions* René Descartes offers a description of the physiological mechanism underlying "explosive" laughter.
95 Kant, *CPJ*, AA 5:332.
96 Kant, *CPJ*, AA 5:333.
97 Kant, Reflection 466 (from 1770–1 or 1773–5), AA 15:192.
98 Kant, Collins ethics lecture, AA 27:458.
99 Kant, *Anthropology*, AA 7:261.
100 Kant, *Anthropology*, AA 7:265; translation modified.
101 Kant, *Anthropology*, AA 7:265; translation modified. On *Schadenfreude*, see Kant, Vigilantius ethics lecture, AA 27:698. See also Kant, Mrongovius anthropology lecture, AA, 25:1350: "laughing about harm [*Schaden*] to another person is *Schaden Freude*."
102 Kant, *Anthropology*, AA 7:265; translation modified.
103 Kant, *Anthropology*, AA 7:211.
104 Kant, *The Metaphysics of Morals*, AA 6:467; translation modified.
105 Kant, *The Metaphysics of Morals*, AA 6:467.
106 Kant, *The Metaphysics of Morals*, AA 6:467.
107 In his own life, Kant apparently did not always live up to this ideal. In an affair involving negative, sarcastic treatment of his work by Friedrich Nicolai (1733–1811), Kant responded with biting, contemptuous wit. See the editor's introduction by Allen Wood in Immanuel Kant, *Practical Philosophy* (Cambridge: Cambridge University Press, 1996), 619.
108 Kant, *The Metaphysics of Morals*, AA 6:208–9; translation modified.
109 In surveying humanity, we are permitted a "good-natured laugh," but should avoid "contempt" for its character. Kant, *Anthropology*, AA 7:332.
110 Kant, *CPJ*, AA 5:331, 333.
111 Canivet, "Le rire et le bon sens," 373; my translation. His essay begins as a critical summary of, and commentary on, Bergson's theory of laughter, but he then attempts to improve Bergson's theory by appealing to Kant's:

Canivet emphasizes that laughter is a bodily pleasure, a disinterested play, and a response to an incongruity or absurdity.

112 Kant, *CPJ*, AA 5:333–4.
113 Kant, *CPJ*, AA 5:332.
114 Stephen G. Nichols, "Laughter as Gesture: Hilarity and the Anti-Sublime," *Neohelicon* 32, no. 2 (2005): 375–89, 377. This interpretation of Kant bears some resemblance to the thesis (in Martin and Shaw) that humor should not be conceptually detached from laughter. Martin, "Humour and Aesthetic Enjoyment of Incongruities," 78. Shaw, "Philosophy of Humor," 118–23.
115 On causality, see Kant, *Critique of Pure Reason*, A144/B183, and above all see the Second Analogy at A188ff./B232ff. where Kant claims that causes (typically) determine in time and precede their effects. Kant describes "the concept of the relation of cause and effect, the former of which determines the latter in time, as its consequence" (A188/B234). A195/B240: "If, therefore, we experience that something happens, then we always presuppose that something else precedes it, which it follows in accordance with a rule." At A211/B256, he describes "the series of causes and effects, the former of which inevitably draw the existence of the latter after them." But he recognizes that cause/effect can be simultaneous. A202–3/B248: "The majority of efficient causes in nature are simultaneous with their effects, and the temporal sequence of the latter is occasioned only by the fact that the cause cannot achieve its entire effect in one instant." However, this is not the same as claiming that the effect *precedes* the cause.
116 Godfrey, "The Aesthetics of Laughter," 132. On play, see also Giamario, "Making Reason Think More," 167. Schopenhauer attributes a similar view to Voltaire, and quotes him as saying, "I think I have observed in the theatre that hardly ever is there a general burst of laughter except on the occasion of a *misapprehension*." Schopenhauer, *The World as Will and Representation*, vol. 2, 96.
117 Kant, *CPJ*, AA 5:332.
118 Godfrey, "The Aesthetics of Laughter," 134.
119 Kant, *CPJ*, AA 5:332.
120 Kant, *CPJ*, AA 5:314; 5:342–3.
121 Swabey misconstrues Kant's point as being about our cognition of the world. Swabey thinks Kant is wrong to hold that in humor nothing is thought, since "at the very least there is negative learning, the discovery of what is finally excluded as contradictory from the structure of things, human character, and societies; while on the positive side our acquaintance is enriched with regard to the possibilities of actuality." Marie Swabey, "The Comic as Nonsense, Sadism, or Incongruity," *Journal of Philosophy* 55, no. 19 (1958): 819–33, 822.

122 Kant, *CPJ*, AA 5:332; translation modified and emphasis added.

123 Birgit Recki, "So lachen wir. Wie Immanuel Kant Leib und Seele zusammenhält," in *Kants Schlüssel zur Kritik des Geschmacks. Ästhetische Erfahrung heute – Studien zur Aktualität von Kants "Kritik der Urteilskraft*," ed. Ursula Francke (Hamburg: Meiner, 2000) 177–87, 182. Peter Fenves, *Late Kant: Towards Another Law of the Earth* (London: Routledge, 2003), 25. Fenves even refers to the material for laughter as "indeterminate."

124 Thanks to Winfried Menninghaus and Marcus Willaschek for independently raising this objection. Along similar lines, Menninghaus characterized the object of humor as "nonsense" rather than (like an aesthetic idea) "infinite sense." See the English translation of his *Lob des Unsinns: Über Kant, Tieck und Blaubart* (Frankfurt am Main: Suhrkamp, 1995), Winfried Menninghaus, *In Praise of Nonsense: Kant and Bluebeard* (Stanford: Stanford University Press, 1999), 24, 30. For similar presentations of his view, see also Winfried Menninghaus, "Le mouvement du rire chez Kant," *Dix-huitième siècle* 32 (2000): 265–77, 274; and Winfried Menninghaus, "Kant über ‚Unsinn', ‚Lachen' und ‚Laune,'" *Deutsche Vierteljahresschrift für Philosophie und Geistesgeschichte* 68 (1994): 263–86.

125 Kant, "Remarks," AA 20:187–8; my translation. Kant then follows this up with a reference to the Terrasson joke, on which see, e.g., Kant, *Anthropology*, AA 7:264.

126 Carroll, "Two Comic Plot Structures," 173.

127 Kant never clarifies *which* aesthetic idea is at play in a joke. If I had to pick one idea (in Kant's sense), I would propose that it is the idea of the *infinite*. But this only raises another question: Where in a joke can we locate the infinite? Maybe it is in this ongoing play itself, this unending back and forth, between illusion and resolution, a process similar to entertaining two sides of a paradox without ever being able to nail down one side. Interestingly, post-Kantian thinkers like Jean Paul and Kierkegaard explained humor in terms of the infinite. A possible historical connection between Kant's account of humor and later, especially Romantic, theories of irony merits further investigation.

128 Joseph Addison was one of Kant's favorite authors on humor, and he adopted a similarly intellectualist position. "Humour should always lie under the check of reason, and . . . it requires the direction of the nicest judgment, by so much the more as it indulges itself in the most boundless freedoms." Addison also distinguished true from false humor. "For as True Humour generally looks serious, while every body laughs about him; False Humour is always laughing, whilst every body about him looks serious." See Joseph Addison, no. 35, April 10, 1711, in Joseph Addison and Richard Steele, *The Spectator; With Notes, and a General Index. The*

Eight Volumes Comprised in One (Philadelphia: Hickman and Hazzard, 1822), 41.

129 In *Observations* (1764), Kant employs the eighteenth-century distinction between the sublime and the beautiful, in order to claim that the understanding furnishes jokes with substantive content. "Jokes and cheerfulness go with the feeling of the beautiful. Nevertheless *a good deal of understanding can show through*, and to this extent they can be more or less related to the sublime." Kant, *Observations*, AA 2:214; emphasis added.

130 Kant, Reflection 1515 (from the 1780s), AA 15:853.

131 Kivy, "Joking Morality," 107.

132 Annie Hounsokou, "Exposing the Rogue in Us," *Epoché: A Journal for the History of Philosophy* 16, no. 2 (2012): 317–36, 322. "The cause of wit is intellectual" (324). "With wit, we essentially express an intellectual pleasure in a bodily way" (327). Going against this tradition, however, Brown repudiates intellectualized understandings of "wit," and wants to preserve the traditional (pre-Victorian) connection between affect (emotion) and "humour." Brown, "What Part?" 20.

133 Music occupies an ambiguous position in Kant's view of the arts. Sometimes he calls it a beautiful/fine art, sometimes a merely agreeable one in that it moves the body and creates affects, even as it represents aesthetic ideas; Kant, *CPJ*, AA 5:332. He distinguishes between agreeable and beautiful music; Kant, *CPJ*, AA 5:329.

134 Kant, *CPJ*, AA 5:305.

135 Kant, *CPJ*, AA 5:305.

136 Kant, *CPJ*, AA 5:305–6. Kant gives advice for conducting a lively conversation at a dinner party; Kant, *Anthropology*, AA 7:281.

137 Wit is discussed first and continues to be presupposed throughout his analysis of joking; Kant, *CPJ*, AA 5:332. On naiveté and then caprice, see Kant, *CPJ*, AA 5:335–6.

138 See Wolff, *Psychologia empirica*, §332 (on acumen) and §476 (on ingenuity).

139 See Alexander Gottlieb Baumgarten, *Texte zur Grundlegung der Ästhetik*, ed. Hans Rudolf Schweizer (Hamburg: Meiner, 1983). See in particular §572, §648, and §649 in Alexander Baumgarten, *Metaphysica* (Halle: Hemmerde, 1739). English translation: Alexander Baumgarten, *Metaphysics*, trans. Courtney Fugate and John Hymers (London: Bloomsbury, 2013).

140 Georg Friedrich Meier, *Thoughts on Jesting*, ed. Joseph Jones (Austin: University of Texas Press, 1947), a translation of Meier's *Gedanken von Scherzen* (1744). Meier defines jest as: "a sensitive fine thought, concise, produced by a high degree of wit and acumen, and exhibiting something ridiculous or adapted to cause laughter." Meier, *Thoughts on Jesting*, 20.

141 On Wolff, see Alfred Baeumler, *Das Irrationalitätsproblem in der Ästhetik und Logik des 18. Jahrhunderts bis zur Kritik der Urteilskraft* (Darmstadt: Wissenschaftliche Buchgesellschaft, 1967), 146.

142 Baumgarten, *Metaphysica*, §572. Baumgarten, *Metaphysics*, trans. Fugate and Hymers, 215.

143 Baumgarten, *Metaphysics*, 216. According to Kant's anthropology lectures, wit likewise involves a "play" of representations. See Kant, Pillau, AA 25:754; Menschenkunde AA 25:969, 1063; Mrongovius AA 25:1266 (where wit has "free" play); and Busolt AA 25:1459 (where wit "pleases through free play").

144 See John Locke, "The Difference between Wit and Judgement," bk. 2, ch. 11, sec. 2, in John Locke, *An Essay concerning Human Understanding*, in 2 vols., vol. 1 (London: J. Buckingham, 1813), 145–6. For a list of writings by Locke, Shaftesbury, Home (Kames), Gottsched, and Aristotle that characterize wit and judgment, see Reinhard Brandt, *Kritischer Kommentar zu Kants* Anthropologie in pragmatischer Hinsicht *(1798)* (Hamburg: Meiner, 1999), 285.

145 Addison, no. 62, May 11, 1711, in Addison and Steele, *The Spectator*, 73–4. Addison there praises Locke's view that wit consists in seeing the resemblance between ideas, but adds that it is also necessary to elicit delight and surprise. Addison distinguishes "true wit" which consists in the resemblance of ideas from "false wit" which consists in the resemblance of words (word play). There is also a "mixed" wit, which consists partly in the resemblance of ideas and partly in the resemblance of words.

146 Kant, *Essay on the Maladies of the Head*, AA 2:260. See also Kant, Reflections 463–85, AA 15:190–205; and Kant, *Observations*, AA 2:211.

147 One translator of Kant's anthropology (G. Felicitas Munzel) thus opts for "ingenuity," on the grounds that Kant, following his predecessors, sometimes lists the Latin (*ingenium*) as a synonym for *Witz*. See Kant, *Anthropology*, AA 7:201, 220.

148 Kant, *Anthropology*, AA 7:220. On wit, see especially sections §54 and §55 in *Anthropology*, AA 7:220–3. For a quasi-biographical discussion of wit (including *Witz* as a source of jokes), see Wolfgang Ritzel, "Kant über den Witz und Kants Witz," *Kant-Studien* 82, no. 1 (1991): 102–9.

149 We find a similar view even in the first *Critique*. The principle of discrimination "severely limits the rashness of the first principle (of wit)." Kant, *Critique of Pure Reason*, A654/B682.

150 Kant, *Anthropology*, AA 7:220–1; translation modified.

151 Kant, *CPJ*, AA 5:179. On the reflecting power of judgment, see also (though these arguably do not count as bona fide "works" published by Kant), Kant, "First Introduction to the third *Critique*," AA 20:211 and Kant, *Jäsche Logic*, AA 9:131.

152 A similar conclusion is offered by Gottfried Gabriel, "Der 'Witz' der reflektierenden Urteilskraft," in *Urteilskraft und Heuristik in den Wissenschaften. Beiträge zur Entstehung des Neuen*, ed. Frithjof Rodi (Weilerswist: Velbrück Wissenschaft, 2003), 197–210, 199. Gabriel (201 n. 15) criticizes Wolfgang Ritzel's article "Kant über den Witz und Kants Witz" for too hastily equating "wit" (*Witz*) with "joke/jest" (*Scherz*). Gabriel's point is well taken, but itself limited. While it is true that the extension of *Witz* reaches beyond just *Scherz*, it is equally undeniable that a core dimension of the Kantian concept of *Witz* is its connection to jest.

153 Kant, Reflection 472, AA 15:195. "Witz: zu vorläufigen, Urtheilskraft: zu bestimmenden Urtheilen." A provisional (*vorläufiges*) judgment is like a working hypothesis or conjecture that precedes and guides an investigation or inquiry into a certain matter. On provisional judgment, see (e.g.) Kant, Reflection 473 (early 1770s), AA 15:195; *The Metaphysics of Morals*, AA 6:478; *Jäsche Logic*, AA 9:66; 9:74–5; Vienna logic lecture, AA 24:862; and Friedländer anthropology lecture, AA 25:516. On *vorläufiges* judgment, see Brandt, *Kritischer Kommentar*, 327. For a lengthier discussion, see Claudio la Rocca, "Vorläufige Urteile und Urteilskraft. Zur heuristischen Logik des Erkenntnisprozesses," in *Kant und die Berliner Aufklärung: Akten des IX. Internationalen Kant-Kongresses*, vol. 2, ed. Volker Gerhardt, Rolf-Peter Horstmann, and Ralph Schumacher (Berlin: Walter de Gruyter, 2001), 351–61. La Rocca usefully distinguishes between two levels of provisional judgment: the orienting, heuristic, regulative *maxims* or principles that guide a cognitive process or investigation, and the *products* of these maxims (the provisional conjectures or "anticipations" themselves) (354). See Kant, *Jäsche Logic*, AA 9:75, where Kant distinguishes between "maxims" and "anticipations."

154 La Rocca, "Vorläufige Urteile und Urteilskraft," 357; my translation. For additional textual support regarding the close link between provisional and reflecting judgments, see Reflection 3200 (from the 1780s), Kant, AA 16:709; and Dohna Wundlacken logic lecture, AA 24:737.

155 Kant, *Anthropology*, AA 7:201.

156 Brandt, *Kritischer Kommentar*, 284.

157 Gabriel, "Der 'Witz'," 200.

158 Gabriel, "Der 'Witz'," 199.

159 Rodríguez, "Witz und reflektierende Urteilskraft in Kants Philosophie," 494. (In the expanded, Spanish version: Rodríguez, "Ingenio, Uso Hipotético de la Razón y Juicio Reflexionante en la Filosofía de Kant," 586.) Rodríguez cautiously rejects a simple identification of wit and the reflecting power of judgment, however. He criticizes Gottfried Gabriel's main thesis that the "wit" [in the sense of the *quid*] of reflecting power of judgment is *wit* ("Witz und reflektierende Urteilskraft," 490 n. 14; in the Spanish version, 582 n. 17). Rodríguez concludes his paper by claiming, "Wit is not the reflecting power of judgment, which is considered an independent faculty in the system of reason only in the third *Critique*, insofar as Kant grounds its subjective validity through a critical analysis of taste." ("Witz und reflektierende Urteilskraft," 496; in the Spanish version, 589). Rodríguez admits that the Kantian concept of "wit" (*Witz*) at most addresses the same *issues* as reflecting power of judgment. "Kant's discussion of wit in the anthropology lecture transcriptions stands in connection with the problematic presented in the theory of the reflecting power of judgment" ("Witz und reflektierende Urteilskraft," 493; in the Spanish version, somewhat modified, at 586). (Translations of Rodríguez's article are mine.) Technically, there is little wrong with Rodríguez's cautious reading, but his conservative conclusion does seem to be in tension with the claim quoted in the main text to which the present footnote is appended.

160 Brandt, *Kommentar*, 327: "Der Begriff des reflektierenden Urteils bzw. der reflektierenden Urteilskraft wird nie außerhalb der dritten Kritik in Kants Druckschriften verwendet." A passage in *Jäsche Logic* (§81), AA 9:131–2, is an only *apparent* exception, for, according to Gabriel ("Der 'Witz'," 203 n. 26), it derives from Reflection 3287 (from the late 1770s or the 1780s) (Kant, AA 16:759) and was introduced by the editor of the volume, Jäsche. Since the wording in the *Jäsche Logic* passage is almost identical to that of Reflection 3287, Gabriel's claim certainly seems correct. According to La Rocca, moreover, Jäsche probably drew from Reflection 3200 (Kant, AA 16:709) in preparing the subsequent sections, §82–§84, in the *Jäsche Logic*. See La Rocca, "Vorläufige Urteile und Urteilskraft," 357 n. 9.

161 "In the transcendental philosophy's treatment of the power of judgment, the terminological replacement of 'wit' by 'reflecting power of judgment' underscores Kant's systematic aim of placing wit under the supervision of the power of judgment." Gabriel, "Der 'Witz'," 203; my translation.

162 Kant, *Anthropology*, AA 7:222; translation modified.

163 *The Universal Passion* is a collection of seven satires published by Edward Young between 1725 and 1727. See, e.g., Edward Young, *The Universal Passion, Satire 1* (London: J. Roberts, 1725). Kant also admires the profound (*tief*) wit in Young's *Night-Thoughts* (published between 1742 and 1745) and contrasts Young with Voltaire; Kant, Menschenkunde anthropology lecture, AA 25:967.

164 Kant, *Anthropology*, AA 7:222; translation modified.

165 In "To the Author of the Dublin Journal," Hutcheson discusses "grave" and "serious" wit. See Hutcheson, in Townsend, *British Aesthetics*, 143. Unlike Kant, however, Hutcheson does not ascribe to serious wit any *moral* content, but rather discusses "serious" wit in order to identify incongruity as a source of humor.

166 Likewise, eighteenth-century psychologist David Hartley rejects out of hand "low similitudes, allusions, contrasts, and coincidences, applied to grave and serious subjects, [that] occasion the most profuse laughter in persons of light minds," and that "weaken" reverence for sacred things. David Hartley, "Of Wit and Humour," in Morreall, *Laughter and Humor*, 41–4, 43.

167 Kant, *Observations*, AA 2:246 n.

168 Kant, *Critique of Practical Reason*, AA 5:153.

169 Kant, *Anthropology*, AA 7:157–8.

170 Kant, Parow anthropology lecture, AA 25:388.

171 Kant, *Anthropology*, AA 7:221; translation modified.

172 "Wit must serve the understanding, either for invention (analogies) or for elucidation. Examples. Similarities. But it must not substitute the understanding. Image-rich wit, empty wit." Kant, Reflection 472 (from 1769–71), AA 15:194; my translation.

173 Kant, *Anthropology*, AA 7:225; translation modified.

174 Kant, *Observations*, AA 2:246.

175 Kant, *Observations*, AA 2:247. Kant says that he is relying on Montesquieu and d'Alembert in making these claims.

176 Kant, *Anthropology*, AA 7:222.

177 In Giamario's opinion, Kant's analysis of naiveté and caprice is less philosophically rich than Kant's examination of the laughter generated by joking (wit); Giamario, "Making Reason Think More," 174 n. 5. Meredith, however, thinks that the (very brief) discussion of naiveté is "far the best in the whole section." Meredith, in *Kant's Critique*, 305.

178 Kant, *CPJ*, AA 5:335. On naiveté, see also Kant, Philippi logic lecture, AA 24:371; and Kant, Busolt anthropology lecture, AA 25:1439.

179 Kant, Reflection 886 (from 1776–78), AA 15:387–8.

180 Marmysz, "Humor, Sublimity and Incongruity."

181 Marmysz, "Humor, Sublimity and Incongruity."

182 Hounsokou, "Exposing the Rogue in Us," 326.

183 Kant, *CPJ*, AA 5:335.

184 Hounsokou, "Exposing the Rogue in Us," 327.

185 Kant, *CPJ*, AA 5:335; emphasis modified.

186 Meredith translates *Laune* as "humor," thereby picking up a sense associated with the Galenic four humors (black bile, yellow bile, phlegm, blood). This has some plausibility. We sometimes find things amusing, or describe them in a funny way, because we are in a certain temper or mood. Moreover, the English word "humour" originally referred to one whose temperament diverges from the norm. See Eagleton, *Humour*, 81. Finally, the three times Kant uses the term *Humor*, he does so in the Galenic sense. Kant, Reflection 1490 (from 1775–8), AA 15:735; Reflection 1540 (from 1799), AA 15:965; and "Remarks," AA 20:63. Nevertheless, if we translated *Laune* with "humor" we would lose the ability to distinguish *Laune* from *Humor* ("humor"), a word used by Schopenhauer, Freud, and others. Thus, I will follow Guyer/Matthews in rendering *Laune* as "caprice."

187 Kant, *CPJ*, AA 5:335.

188 Kant, Mrongovius anthropology lecture, AA 25:1264; translation modified.

189 The English poet Coleridge makes a similar claim. "People of humor are always in some degree people of genius." Samuel Taylor Coleridge, *The Complete Poetical Works of Samuel Taylor Coleridge, including Poems and Versions of Poems Now Published for the First Time*, ed. Ernest Hartley Coleridge (Oxford: Clarendon, 1912), 481.

190 See also the use of "caprice" in the phrase, "*caprice* of the genius" (*caprice* des genies). Refl 466 (around 1770–1) in Kant, AA 15:192.

191 Kant, Reflection 812 (from the 1770s), AA 15:361.

192 Kant, *CPJ*, AA 5:335.

193 Menninghaus, *In Praise of Nonsense*, 30, goes as far as to call this unique kind of sense a "nonsense." See also Menninghaus, "Kant über ‚Unsinn', ‚Lachen' und ‚Laune'"; and Menninghaus, "Le mouvement du rire chez Kant."

194 Hounsokou, "Exposing the Rogue in Us," 325.

195 Kant, Friedländer anthropology lecture, AA 25:506; translation modified.

196 In *Anthropology*, Kant reasserts his admiration for Henry Fielding. He refers to *The History of Tom Jones, a Foundling* (calling it *The Foundling*), in Kant, *Anthropology*, AA 7:164 and 7:232.

197 Kant, Friedländer anthropology lecture, AA 25:506; translation modified. On contradiction and contrast in humor, see also Kant, Collins anthropology lecture, AA 25:142 and Kant, Pillau anthropology lecture, AA 25:811.

198 Kant, *Anthropology*, AA 7:163; translation modified. Kant gives the further examples of Samuel Richardon's *Clarissa* and Aloys Blumauer's travesty of Virgil, *Abenteuer des frommen Helden Aeneas* (*Adventure of the Pious Hero, Aeneas*).

199 Kant, *Anthropology*, AA 7:249.
200 Ritzel, "Kant über den Witz und Kants Witz," 106.
201 Kant had followed the erroneous attribution of this work to Jonathan Swift.
202 *Anthropology*, AA 7:221–2; translation modified.
203 Although neither the first nor the second editions of the third *Critique* printed §54 for the "Remark," I will (following convention) refer to this section as §54, since it is found between sections labeled §53 and §55.
204 Kant, *Anthropology*, AA 7:262.
205 "Mutterwitz und Schulwitz. ienes Naiv." Kant, Reflection 480 (from perhaps between 1776–83), AA 15:203. On mother-wit, which is natural and unteachable, see also Kant, *Critique of Pure Reason*, A133/B172.
206 Kant, *Observations*, in AA 2:212.
207 Kant, *CPJ*, AA 5:274, 325. For such a reconstruction of Kant's theory of tragedy, see Wiebke Deimling, "Kant's Theory of Tragedy," *Southwest Philosophy Review* 35, no. 1 (2019): 17–30.
208 Deimling, "Kant's Theory of Tragedy," 26.
209 On *Nathan the Wise* (1779), see Kant, Menschenkunde anthropology lecture, AA 25:886. On Lessing's faults, see also Collins anthropology lecture, AA 25:388.
210 Kant, Mrongovius anthropology lecture, AA 25:1260.
211 Kant, Menschenkunde anthropology lecture, AA 25:858; Mrongovius anthropology lecture, AA 25:1213; and Friedländer anthropology lecture, AA 25:472.
212 Márcio Suzuki, "Des Herrn Professors Kants Paradoxon des Comoedianten," *Kant-Studien* 109, no. 3 (2018): 395–418, 408. Suzuki (418) claims that, although Kant was unfamiliar with Diderot's *Paradox of Acting*, it is surprising how much Kant's view of acting and the moral function of theater agrees with the account found in Diderot's work.
213 Kant, Collins anthropology lecture, AA 25:149.
214 Kuehn, *Kant*, 166. Kant mentions Molière at Kant, *Anthropology*, AA 7:121, and Goldoni at Kant, Collins anthropology lecture, AA 25:149.
215 Kant, *Observations*, AA 2:212.
216 Kant, Reflection 1384 (from 1772–75), AA 15:603.
217 Kant, Friedländer anthropology lecture, AA 25:593.
218 Kant, *Observations* in AA 2:212. In an obscure marginal note from about 1765, Kant writes, after "*Hudibras* parodies grimaces," "ludicrous sublime [*possirlich erhaben*]." It is tempting to think that Kant is referring to a kind of farcical or comical sublimity, but he never elaborated. Kant, "Remarks,"

AA 20:37. On the *poßierliche*, see also Blomberg logic lecture, AA 24:109.
219 Kant, Friedländer anthropology lecture, AA 25:560.
220 Kant, Menschendkunde anthropology lecture, AA 25:1135.
221 Kant, *Anthropology*, AA 7:232.
222 Kant, Reflection 476 (from 1776–79), AA 15:196–7; emphasis added.
223 Kant, *Anthropology*, AA 7:281; translation modified.
224 Kant, Friedländer anthropology lecture, AA 25:570; translation modified.
225 Cf. Martin, "Humour and Aesthetic Enjoyment of Incongruities," 81–2.
226 On Hume and an artwork's passing the test of time, the repeated viewing of works (films), and personal aging, see Robert R. Clewis, "What Can Hume Teach Us About Film Evaluation?" *Aisthema* 1 (2) (2014): 1–22; and Robert R. Clewis, "Film Evaluation and the Enjoyment of Dated Films," *Projections: The Journal for Movies and Mind* 6 (2) (2012): 42–63.
227 Kant, "Remarks," AA 20:185, 123. See also Kant, Reflection 1384 (from 1772–5), AA 15:603–4. Since this view predates the formulation of Kant's Critical ethics, it is not necessarily connected to the Critical understanding of pure practical reason and autonomy of the will.
228 Deimling, "Kant's Theory of Tragedy," 21.
229 Kant, *Anthropology*, AA 7:263. Kant made this claim repeatedly in his anthropology lectures. See: Kant, Collins, AA 25:186. Parow, AA 25:381. Friedländer, AA 25:571. Mrongovius, AA 25:1283.
230 Kant, Friedländer anthropology lecture, AA 25:554.
231 Kant, Parow anthropology lecture, AA 25:434–5; Collins anthropology lecture, AA 25:225. About six years later (1779), however, Kant may have changed his mind and reversed his assessment. See the footnote at Collins anthropology lecture, AA 25:225–6 n. 201.
232 Kant, *CPJ*, AA 5:334. Cf. the sly "wag" who does not join in the laughter. Kant, *Anthropology*, AA 7:262.
233 On Kant's view of the control of affect in acting, see Suzuki, "Kants Paradoxon."
234 Kant, "Remarks," AA 20:187; my translation. In fact, Kant's own delivery of jokes was reportedly dry and deadpan. Kuehn, *Kant*, 64, 106.
235 Brown's view comes remarkably close to this. "Slapstick, clowning and practical jokes, have to engage the mind as well as the senses in order to remain memorable." Brown, "What Part?" 29.
236 Kant, Friedländer anthropology lecture, AA 25:667; translation modified. Suzuki, "Kants Paradoxon," discusses facial expressions (*Mienen*). On

facial expressions, see Kant, Reflection 1519 (from the 1780s), AA 15:874–75; and Kant, Mrongovius anthropology lecture, AA 25:1293.
237 Kant, *Anthropology*, AA 7:263; translation modified.
238 Kant, *Anthropology*, AA 7:265; translation modified.
239 This phrasing in terms of stimulus and response sides comes from Latta, *The Basic Humor Process*.

Chapter 2: Three questions about laughter at humor

1 Robert Wicks, *Kant on Judgment* (London: Routledge, 2007), 141.
2 Representative commentators here include Banki, Canivet, Giamario, Godfrey, Hounsokou, Marmysz, and Nichols.
3 Representative authors include Canivet, Cardelli, Fenves, Giamario, Hounsokou, Makkreel, Meo, Meredith, Recki, Wicks, and Zammito. For instance, Wicks holds that the point of Kant's lengthy discussion of laughter is "the idea that beauty and sense-gratification are compatible with respect to the furtherance of moral interests." Wicks, *Judgment*, 142.
4 Representative authors include Bergmann, Carroll, Critchley, and Gimbel.
5 Giamario, "Making Reason Think More," 162.
6 Hounsokou, "Exposing the Rogue in Us," 317.
7 Menninghaus, "Le mouvement du rire chez Kant," 277; my translation.
8 Thus, it is technically incorrect to claim that, "The involvement of our powers of cognition in *judgments* of humor could also grant them the claim to universality," even if one might reconstruct Kant's account in such terms. Hounsokou, "Exposing the Rogue in Us," 330; emphasis added.
9 Morreall holds that humor is an aesthetic experience; Gordon denies this. Neither Morreall nor Gordon mention Kant in their articles. Mordechai Gordon, "Exploring the Relationship between Humor and Aesthetic Experience," *Journal of Aesthetic Education* 46, no. 1 (2012): 111–21. John Morreall, "Humor and Aesthetic Education," *Journal of Aesthetic Education* 15, no. 1 (1981): 55–70, 57.
10 Kant, *Anthropology,* AA 7:251. The next quote is from Kant, *Anthropology*, AA 7:252. Translations modified.
11 Kant, *CPJ*, AA 5:272 n.
12 Arnold, "Laughter," 9.
13 Kant, *CPJ*, AA 5:330.

14 Godfrey, "The Aesthetics of Laughter," 130. He writes "affection" rather than "affect."
15 Godfrey wants to revise Kant, but his amendments may already be in Kant's account. Kant is not committed to the claim that (as Godfrey puts it) "our pleasure in the ridiculous is due altogether to physiological conditions" (127). The *bodily satisfaction* may be due to physiological conditions, but that follows trivially. We laugh at a joke because we appreciate the point, Godfrey says (130–1); yet I think Kant would agree. Kant recognizes a component of mental play with a rich intellectual content (aesthetic ideas, thoughts, representations), as we have seen.
16 Godfrey, "The Aesthetics of Laughter," 127.
17 Critchley, *On Humour*, 85.
18 Meredith, *Kant's Critique*, 302.
19 For a defense of this distinction, see Paul Guyer, "One Act or Two? Hannah Ginsborg on Aesthetic Judgement," *British Journal of Aesthetics* 57, no. 4 (2017): 407–19. For its denial, see Hannah Ginsborg, "In Defence of the One-Act View: Reply to Guyer," *British Journal of Aesthetics* 57, no. 4 (2017): 421–35.
20 If one calls something beautiful, "one believes oneself to have a universal voice, and lays claim to the consent of everyone." Kant, *CPJ*, AA 5:216.
21 Thanks to Samantha Matherne for this point.
22 Kant, *Anthropology*, AA 7:237.
23 Hannah Arendt pays close attention to these (third *Critique* and *Anthropology*) passages in which Kant distinguishes between rational approval and gratification. Specifically, she defends a notion of second-order reflective judgment that assesses a pleasure. Hannah Arendt, *Lectures on Kant's Political Philosophy* (Chicago: University of Chicago Press, 1992), 69. Canivet likewise sees how these passages can be applied to judgments of beauty. Canivet, "Le rire et le bon sens," 362.
24 Kant, *CPJ*, AA 5:331.
25 There are many introductions to and studies of the sublime and the beautiful in the Kant literature, so I won't try to cover that terrain here beyond what is provided in the first three paragraphs of the present section. My views of the Kantian sublime as an aesthetic judgment were originally presented in Robert R. Clewis, *The Kantian Sublime and the Revelation of Freedom* (Cambridge: Cambridge University Press, 2009). I argue against the widespread view of the Kantian sublime as always involving attention explicitly directed at oneself in Robert R. Clewis, "Imagination, Vital Forces, and Self-Consciousness in the Kantian Sublime," in *Kant and the Feeling of Life*, ed. Jennifer Mensch (Albany: SUNY Press, forthcoming). For my own thoughts about

the sublime and an outline of a theory, see Robert R. Clewis, "Towards a Theory of the Sublime and Aesthetic Awe," in *The Sublime Reader*, ed. Robert R. Clewis (London: Bloomsbury, 2019), 340–54.

26 See Kant, *CPJ*, AA 5:244–5, where Kant compares and contrasts beauty and sublimity. Kant further divides the sublime into the mathematical and the dynamical sublime, but using this terminology is not crucial to the present discussion.

27 "We linger over the consideration of the beautiful because this consideration strengthens and reproduces itself." Kant, *CPJ*, AA 5:222.

28 Kant, *CPJ*, AA 5:218.

29 Kant, *CPJ*, AA 5:314.

30 Kant, *CPJ*, AA 5:245, 258. Actually, Kant offers *two* (not fully reconciled) accounts of the "movement" in the sublime: (what I call) the dam-and-release view, and the oscillation view. I emphasize oscillation here since it strikes me as phenomenologically more compelling. It will also make for a better comparison with the oscillations found in laughter. For the dam-and-release view, see Kant, *CPJ*, 5:226, 244–5.

31 Marmysz, "Humor, Sublimity and Incongruity."

32 Meredith, in *Kant's Critique*, 305.

33 Menninghaus, *In Praise of Nonsense*, 29. Rudolf Makkreel, *Imagination and Interpretation in Kant: The Hermeneutical Import of the* Critique of Judgment (Chicago: The University of Chicago Press, 1990), 88.

34 Hounsokou, "Exposing the Rogue in Us," 318.

35 Giamario, "Making Reason Think More," 169–70.

36 Nichols, "Laughter as Gesture." His abstract states, "Kant first noticed this dynamic." This seems questionable. But to be fair, Nichols's article is mostly a commentary on the German writer Jean Paul (Richter), Nietzsche, and on a study of Jean Paul by Max Kommerell.

37 Giamario, "Making Reason Think More," 168.

38 Giamario, "Making Reason Think More," 170.

39 *If* we had to offer an expanded reconstruction along such lines, it would be better to propose it like this: *wit*, which in the Critical system is substituted by the reflecting power of judgment, is the precondition of pure aesthetic judgments. Yet I don't think that Kant strictly speaking would accept this extension, insofar as for Kant wit remains an empirical-psychological, anthropological term rather than a transcendental faculty that makes claims (including aesthetic claims) possible. Unrestrained by such considerations, however, Friedrich Schlegel gave wit a much larger role, as Gabriel observes. Gabriel, "Der 'Witz'," 202.

40 Giamario, "Making Reason Think More," 172.

41 It is worth recalling that in a work of 1764 Kant associates cheerfulness and jokes (*Scherze*) with beauty, and, if the jest exhibits more understanding or intellect, with the sublime. Kant, *Observations*, AA 2:214.

42 For the sublime as a failure of comprehension (*comprehensio*), see Kant, *CPJ*, AA 5:251.

43 On laughter as a mixture of pain and pleasure, see Plato, *Philebus* 48a. At 50b, Socrates says this also applies to the comedy of life, not just to dramatic comedy.

44 Freud, "Humor," 163.

45 In addition to the scholars to be discussed, see also Makkreel, *Imagination and Interpretation in Kant*, 98. Makkreel claims that the convulsive movement in laughter is "similar in structure" to that of the sublime. A comparison between laughter and the sublime is also found in Mascia Cardelli, "Lachen e Piacere Estetico nella *Kritik der Urteilskraft*," in Kant, *Il piacere di ridere*, 9–26, 21. See also Fenves, *Late Kant*, 20; and Recki, "So lachen wir," 184 n. 17.

46 Meredith, in *Kant's Critique*, 304, 264. See also lxxxviii.

47 Godfrey, "The Aesthetics of Laughter," 130.

48 Schopenhauer, *The World as Will and Representation*, vol. 2, 101; translation modified.

49 Marmysz, "Humor, Sublimity and Incongruity."

50 Like Marmysz, Borch-Jacobsen does not properly acknowledge the uplift in the sublime, portraying the sublime as inferiority and laughter as superiority. "Laughter . . . is thus as sort of inverted sentiment of the sublime . . . [which] places me . . . *on-high*." Mikkel Borch-Jacobsen, "The Laughter of Being," *MLN* (1987) 102, no. 4, 737–60, 750. Borch-Jacobsen's essay, an interpretation of Georges Bataille on laughter, includes a passing remark on Kant that closely follows Kant's (somewhat misleading) "definition" of the sublime as "the absolute great," implying that relative to the sublime the subject feels merely inferior. The sublime is thereby understood as the idea of reason (infinite extent or might), not as an experience. Although Borch-Jacobsen's approach understandably follows one of Kant's official definitions of the sublime, it overlooks the wider context in which Kant is accounting for an aesthetic experience that contains a negative *pleasure*, where the initial frustration is followed by the positive elevation and where one does not feel simply inferior. After all, for Kant, reason is the source of the very idea of the infinite.

51 On this aspect of laughter, see Kant, *CPJ*, AA 5:332, 334. On this aspect of the sublime, see *CPJ*, AA 5:258.

52 Translated in Immanuel Kant, *Anthropology, History, Education* (Cambridge: Cambridge University Press, 2007), 365.

53 "Laughter becomes something analogous to what is at play in the experience of beauty." Menninghaus, "Le mouvement du rire chez Kant," 267; my translation.
54 Kant, *CPJ*, AA 5:326–7.
55 Kant, Mrongovius anthropology lecture, AA 25:1263; translation modified.
56 Silva, "'On the Evolution of the Concept of 'Witz'."
57 Thanks to Stefano Micali for raising this question.
58 Winfried Menninghaus et al., "Sounds Funny?"
59 Based on Kant, *Dreams of a Spirit-Seer*, AA 2:348.
60 The experience of laughter seems analogous to other affects, too, such as enthusiasm (that is, *Enthusiasmus/Enthusiasm*, not *Schwärmerei*). Enthusiasm is "the idea of the good with affect"; Kant, *CPJ*, AA 5:272. But since the judgments of beauty and the sublime are the only two official kinds of pure aesthetic judgments investigated in the third *Critique*, and because I am here considering the response to humor as a pure aesthetic judgment (not an affect), I won't pursue such potentially interesting comparisons here. For Kant's positive view about an *"Enthusiasm"* that is ultimately ambiguous, see Kant, *The Conflict of the Faculties*, AA 7:86 and Kant, *Anthropology*, AA 7:254. For my more recent interpretations of Kantian enthusiasm, see Robert R. Clewis, "The Feeling of Enthusiasm," in *Kant and the Faculty of Feeling*, ed. Kelly Sorensen and Diane Williamson (Cambridge: Cambridge University Press, 2018), 184–207. See also my argument, based on the writings of Shaftesbury, Hume, and Mendelssohn, that *even on historical* grounds *Schwärmerei* is better translated as "fanaticism" rather than "enthusiasm," in Robert R. Clewis, "*Schwärmerei* and *Enthusiasmus* in Recent English Translations of Kant's Lectures and Writings on Anthropology," in *Kants Schriften in Übersetzungen*, ed. Gisela Schlüter and Hansmichael Hohenegger (Hamburg: Felix Meiner, forthcoming).
61 "But that something that is infinitely better than every assumed custom, namely purity of the way of thinking (or at least the predisposition to it), has not been entirely extinguished in human nature, adds seriousness and high esteem to this play of the power of judgment." Kant, *CPJ*, AA 5:335; translation modified. In chapter three, I explore the possible links between morality and humor.
62 This reason for Kant's hesitation is proposed by both Meredith and Canivet. Meredith, in *Kant's Critique*, cxxxi. Canivet, "Le rire et le bon sens," 373. On beauty as a symbol of morality, see Kant, *CPJ*, AA 5:353–4.
63 Banki, "Humor as the Inverted Sublime," 61.
64 Banki, "Humor as the Inverted Sublime," 60.
65 Godfrey, "The Aesthetics of Laughter," 126.

66 Godfrey, "The Aesthetics of Laughter," 137.
67 Compare: "Humor too could legitimately claim the expectation of universal assent, just in the same way that judgments of taste claim universal validity." Hounsokou, "Exposing the Rogue in Us," 325.
68 Cf. Ted Cohen, *Jokes*, 82; see also 4, 26.
69 There are joke kinds: knock-knock jokes, shaggy dog stories, puns, and so on. There is a wide range of disagreement on which kinds of jokes people like to listen to and tell. Someone might not find a joke funny because they don't like its kind or genre, even if the joke is a fine exemplar of its kind and even if the joke is well told. For example, one can *acknowledge* that a certain pun is a good and clever instance of punning, and still think it flops because one doesn't like puns. I myself don't care much for knock-knock jokes, but I think I can tell the better from the worse ones.
70 "The concept of freedom should make the purpose that is imposed by its laws real in the sensible world; and nature must consequently also be able to be conceived in such a way that the lawfulness of its form is at least in agreement with the possibility of the purposes that are to be realized in it in accordance with the laws of freedom." Kant, *CPJ*, AA 5:176; translation modified.
71 Kant, *CPJ*, AA 5:435 and 436 n.
72 Eagleton, *Humour*, 114–15.
73 Alix Cohen, "The Ultimate Kantian Experience: Kant on Dinner Parties," *History of Philosophy Quarterly* 25, no. 4 (2008): 315–36, 329.
74 Giamario, "Making Reason Think More," 161.
75 Cardelli, "Lachen e Piacere Estetico," 19, 24; my translation. Oscar Meo, *Kantiana minora vel rariora* (Genova: Il Melangolo, 2000), 17.
76 Meredith, in *Kant's Critique*, 304.
77 Godfrey, "The Aesthetics of Laughter," 138.
78 Godfrey, "The Aesthetics of Laughter," 129.
79 Kant, *CPJ*, AA 5:334.
80 See John Zammito, *The Genesis of Kant's* Critique of Judgment (Chicago: University of Chicago Press, 1992), 299; and John Zammito, "The 'Sublime', the 'Supersensible Substrate', and 'Spirit'—Intuitions of the Ultimate in Kant's *Third Critique*, in *Kant on Intuition: Western and Asian Perspectives on Transcendental Idealism*, ed. Stephen Palmquist (London: Routledge, 2019), 139–58, esp. 146–7. For my response to the latter, see Robert R. Clewis, "Spirit and Sublimity, Pleasure and Freedom," in *Kant on Intuition*, 159–65, esp. 163.
81 Makkreel, *Imagination and Interpretation in Kant*, 88.

82 Michael J. Olson, "Kant on the Feeling of Health," in *Kant and the Feeling of Life*, ed. Jennifer Mensch (Albany: SUNY Press, forthcoming). Olson agrees with Makkreel that section §54 has a broader significance than many readers have acknowledged. I concur, even though I do not want to exaggerate the section's import either.

83 Wit, however, seems to be closest to what is of interest to contemporary philosophers of humor. They don't pay much attention to eighteenth-century notions of naiveté, including Kant's. Hounsokou appears to emphasize naiveté because it fits in best with her view of Kant's systematic aims.

84 Hounsokou, "Exposing the Rogue in Us," 318. "Laughter, because it is more than what Kant would call mere sense, and yet partakes of it insofar as it affects the whole body, could help elevate the body into Kant's project of integration of sense and freedom." Hounsokou, "Exposing the Rogue in Us," 330.

85 Hounsokou, "Exposing the Rogue in Us," 325.

86 Hounsokou, "Exposing the Rogue in Us," 332.

87 Recki, "So lachen wir," 185–6. For Kant, Recki claims (184), laughter involves a "communication" between the intelligible and the sensible.

88 For my interpretation of the sublime in terms of Kant's philosophical system, see Robert R. Clewis, "The Place of the Sublime in Kant's Project," *Studi Kantiani* 28 (2015): 149–68.

Chapter 3: Kant and the Ethics of Humor

1 Kant, *Anthropology*, AA 7:213; Menschenkunde anthropology lecture, AA 25:1043.

2 Kant, *Anthropology*, AA 7:249.

3 Kant, Friedländer anthropology lecture, AA 25:603. Goethe wrote a similar line: "There is nothing in which people more betray their character than in what they find to laugh at." Goethe, *Elective Affinities*, 184.

4 The phrase "moderate comic moralism" is used by Carroll, *Humour*, 110. To distinguish Kant's position from those recently discussed by Carroll and others, I will use the term "soft ethicism" (in a sense to be explained in a moment). As we will see, Kant does not directly examine the issues around which this recent debate revolves.

5 We can break down the jokes or anecdotes in this book along these lines. *Race/ethnicity*: Foam in a Bottle (No. 12), German Fools (No. 13), Two Moneylenders (in the commentary to No. 13).

Sex/gender/sexuality: Bearded Woman (No. 14), Samuel Johnson's Wife (No. 15), Hooped Skirts and Pruned Trees (No. 22), Heidegger as a Woman (No. 23), and Sex and Death (No. 29).
Age: Dying of Good Health (No. 4).
Disability: There Are No Ugly Noses (No. 24).
Not all of these are jokes; some are quips or anecdotes. Some are more offensive than others and touch more directly on the issue by which they are categorized; others seem quite light and innocent. For instance, No. 4 and No. 24 seem rather inoffensive since they don't make age or disability the target of ridicule or butt of the joke. While some of Kant's jokes or anecdotes touch on wealth, status, or power, I do not think any count as jokes about class as an identity-constituting feature.

6 Malcom Budd, *The Aesthetic Appreciation of Nature: Essays on the Aesthetics of Nature* (Oxford: Clarendon Press, 2002), 84. Budd is commenting on Kant's theory of the sublime.

7 Kant, *Groundwork of the Metaphysics of Morals*, AA 4:421.

8 Kant, *On a Supposed Right to Lie from Philanthropy*, AA 8:426.

9 Kant, *Groundwork of the Metaphysics of Morals*, AA 4:429.

10 Adapted from Michael Philips, "Racist Acts and Racist Humor," *Canadian Journal of Philosophy* 14, no. 1 (1984): 75–96, 77.

11 Quite persuasively, Gimbel maintains that whether or not a joke is funny is an *empirical* matter, and urges philosophers to hand over empirical investigation of it to the social scientists. Gimbel, *Isn't That Clever*, 4.

12 On moralism, see Carroll, *Humour*; Noël Carroll, "Moderate Moralism," *British Journal of Aesthetics* 36 (1996): 223–38; and Noël Carroll, "Moderate Moralism versus Moderate Autonomism," *British Journal of Aesthetics* 38 (1998): 419–24. Berys Gaut, "Just Joking: The Ethics and Aesthetics of Humor," *Philosophy and Literature* 22, no. 1 (1998): 51–68; and Berys Gaut, *Art, Emotion, and Ethics* (Oxford: Clarendon Press, 2007). Aaron Smuts, "Do Moral Flaws Enhance Amusement?" *American Philosophical Quarterly* 46, no. 2 (2009): 151–62; and Aaron Smuts, "The Ethics of Humor: Can Your Sense of Humor Be Wrong?" *Ethical Theory and Moral Practice* 13, no. 3 (2010): 333–47. On this debate with respect to Hume, see Reed Winegar, "Good Sense, Art, and Morality in Hume's 'Of the Standard of Taste'," *Journal of Scottish Philosophy* 9, no. 1 (2011): 17–35.

13 For a defense of immoralism in humor, see Scott Woodcock, "Comic Immoralism and Relatively Funny Jokes," *Journal of Applied Philosophy* 32, no. 2 (2015): 203–16. On immoralism in art more generally, see Daniel Jacobson, "In Praise of Immoral Art," *Philosophical Topics* 25, no. 1 (1997): 155–99.

14 Carroll, *Humour*, 107.

15 A defense of amoralism can be found in Oliver Conolly and Bashar Haydar, "The Good, the Bad, and the Funny," *The Monist* 88, no. 1 (2005): 121–34.

16 Ted Cohen, *Jokes*, 84. Cohen's book does not discuss Kant's theory of humor.

17 Gini, *Being Funny*, 61, 85. Gini holds that in some circumstances we should not tell an unethical joke, even if it is (or remains) funny. See also Al Gini, "Dirty Jokes, Tasteless Jokes, Ethnic Jokes," *Florida Philosophical Review* 15, no. 1 (2015): 50–65, 51. Gini follows Cohen, whom he cites several times.

18 Carroll, *Humour* 106.

19 Alix Cohen, "The Ultimate Kantian Experience," 329.

20 Kant, *Anthropology*, AA 7:279.

21 Godfrey, "The Aesthetics of Laughter," 138; spelling modified.

22 Alix Cohen, "The Ultimate Kantian Experience," 336 n. 61. She cites Kant, *Anthropology*, AA 7:278.

23 Kivy, "Joking Morality," 106. Construing the matter in terms of a moral "rule" or "precept," Kivy misses how to understand joking and humor in terms of Kantian ethics (or, as he puts it, "deontological ethics").

24 Kant, *Anthropology*, AA 7:199.

25 Kant, *Anthropology*, AA 7:199. Following Kant's handwritten manuscript, I am here reading "technical" as "theoretical."

26 Kant, *The Metaphysics of Morals*, AA 6:433 n. On counsels of prudence, see *Groundwork of the Metaphysics of Morals*, AA 4:416.

27 Kant, Mrongovius anthropology lecture, AA 25:1264.

28 Kant, *Anthropology*, AA 7:264.

29 Kant, *Anthropology*, AA 7:264; translation modified. There is a version of the Terrasson anecdote at Kant, Mrongovius anthropology lecture, AA 25:1350; a reference to the story (without naming Terrasson) at Kant, Friedländer anthropology lecture, AA 25:540; and a brief reference at Kant, "Remarks," AA 20:188.

30 Kant, "Remarks," AA 20:19; my translation.

31 Kant, *Observations*, AA 2:207.

32 A biographical aside: Kant seems to have lived up to this principle in real life, at least in his public role as a professor. Rink, a former student in the 1780s, wrote this about him. "Never did he belittle his colleagues, never did he want to impress by rodomontades, never did he seek approval by making questionable jokes and sexual innuendo." Quoted from Kuehn, *Kant*, 317. The source is Friedrich Theodor Rink, *Ansichten aus Immanuel Kant's Leben* (Königsberg: Göbbels and Unzer, 1805).

33 Kant, *Observations*, AA 2:234.

34 Kant, *Anthropology*, AA 7:278 n.

35 Kant, Friedländer anthropology lecture, AA 25:508.

36 Kant, Mrongovius anthropology lecture, AA 25:1256.

37 As Hutcheson had put it: "Another valuable purpose of ridicule is with relation to smaller vices, which are often more effectually corrected by ridicule, than by grave admonition." Hutcheson, in Townsend, *British Aesthetics*, 149. From the vast literature on satire, see Paul Provenza and Dan Dion, *Satiristas: Comedians, Contrarians, Raconteurs and Vulgarians* (New York: It Books, 2010).

38 While not discussing Kant on satire or the ethics of humor, Dadlez proposes that sarcasm and irony sometimes turn on an implicit ethical evaluation. E. M. Dadlez, "Truly Funny: Humor, Irony, and Satire as Moral Criticism," *Journal of Aesthetic Education* 45, no. 1 (2011): 1–17.

39 Kant, *CPJ*, AA 5:334.

40 Kant, *Anthropology*, AA 7:264; translation modified.

41 Kant, *Idea for a Universal History with a Cosmopolitan Aim*, AA 8:20.

42 Kant, *Lectures on Pedagogy*, AA 9:469; my translation.

43 Hutcheson identifies the social roots, and socializing effects, of comic merriment: "Our whole frame is so sociable, that one merry countenance may diffuse cheerfulness to many." Hutcheson, in Townsend, *British Aesthetics*, 146; see also 148.

44 Kant, *Anthropology*, AA 7:264. Recall this passage too: "Wit enlivens the social gathering; but the lack of the power of judgment makes the social gathering tasteless." Kant, Mrongovius anthropology lecture, AA 25:1264.

45 On wit and society, see Kant, *CPJ*, AA 5:334–5; *Anthropology*, AA 7:220ff., 7:263, 7:280–1; Reflection 763 (from 1772–75), AA 15:333; Reflection 1203 (from 1776–78), AA 15:529; and Kant, Parow anthropology lecture, AA 25:345ff.

46 Kant, *Anthropology*, AA 7:333 n.

47 Kant, Menschenkunde anthropology lecture, AA 25:858; on prudence, see Menschenkunde anthropology lecture, 25:855.

48 Eagleton, *Humour*, 136–7.

49 Many British writers, including Shaftesbury, Kames (Home), and Hume, recognized the import of sociability for aesthetics. For references to these authors, see Meredith, *Kant's Critique*, 272. The social aspects of laughter and humor were later elaborated by Bergson in *Laughter*. For laughter as social lubricant, see Robert R. Provine, *Laughter: A Scientific Investigation* (New York: Viking, 2000). On the fostering of community

through humor and on the reproduction of shared norms, see Ted Cohen, "Metaphor and the Cultivation of Intimacy," *Critical Inquiry* 5, no. 1 (1978): 3–12. He proposes that jokes create intimacy between teller and audience; Cohen, *Jokes*, 26–9. In his review essay of Cohen's *Jokes*, however, Carroll observes that humor can also be used to exclude people. Noël Carroll, "Intimate Laughter," *Philosophy and Literature* 24, no. 2 (2000): 435–50, 447.

50 Eagleton, *Humour*, 137. On humor's violation of norms, see also Kotzen, "The Normativity of Humor."

51 Kant, *Anthropology*, AA 7:282; translation modified.

52 Kant, Menschenkunde anthropology lecture, AA 25:930.

53 In arguing that for Kant dinner parties are part of the ultimate resolution of the conflict between our physical bodies and our moral powers, Alix Cohen provides an astute analysis of the "dress" metaphor, showing how beautiful illusion in social intercourse might indirectly promote virtue. Alix Cohen, "The Ultimate Kantian Experience," 318–22.

54 Kant, *Anthropology*, AA 7:151.

55 Kant, *Anthropology*, AA 7:153; translation modified. Alix Cohen shows in particular how the love of honor, though it has a negative side, can at the same time promote virtue and function as an aid to morality. While the love of honor's aim is to preserve the mere appearance of respect, it ends up fostering genuine respect. The natural function of the feeling of love of honor thus goes from being an inclination to fake virtue to being an inclination that aids virtue and morality. Alix Cohen, "From Faking It to Making It: The Feeling of Love of Honor as an Aid to Morality," in *Reading Kant's Lectures*, ed. Robert R. Clewis (Berlin: Walter de Gruyter, 2015), 243–56.

56 Kant, *The Metaphysics of Morals*, AA 6:473.

57 Kant, *The Metaphysics of Morals*, AA 6:473.

58 Kant, *The Metaphysics of Morals*, AA 6:473. On beautiful illusion, see also Kant, *Anthropology*, AA 7:152.

59 Kant, *The Metaphysics of Morals*, AA 6:473–4; translation modified.

60 Kant, *Anthropology*, AA 7:323.

61 On the concept of prudence in Kant's anthropology, see Nuria Sánchez Madrid, "Prudence and the Rules for Guiding Life. The Development of the Pragmatic Normativity in Kant's *Lectures on Anthropology* (Collins, Parow, Friedländer, Mesnchenkunde, Busolt)," in *Kant's Lectures / Kants Vorlesungen*, ed. Bernd Dörfinger, Claudio La Rocca, Robert B. Louden, and Ubirajara Marques Rancan de Azevedo (Berlin: Walter de Gruyter, 2015), 163–76, 168.

62 Kant, *Anthropology*, AA 7:244.

63 Holly Wilson, "Kant's *Anthropology* as *Klugheitslehre*," *Con-Textos Kantianos: International Journal of Philosophy* 3 (2016): 122–38, 134. Wilson aims to show that Kant intended his anthropology lectures and *Anthropology* to offer a theory of prudence (*Klugheitslehre*), that is, a theory of how to use other people for one's own ends in order to obtain personal happiness.

64 Wilson, "Kant's *Anthropology*," 133. Supporting this claim about taste, she cites Kant, *Anthropology*, AA 7:244.

65 Kant, *CPJ*, AA 5:294, 295.

66 Kant, *CPJ*, AA 5:296–8.

67 In 1764, Kant wrote that "strict moral judgment" does not belong in his analysis of potentially offensive jokes, "since in the sentiment of the beautiful I have to observe and explain only the appearances." Kant, *Observations*, AA 2:234.

68 Kant, Herder ethics lecture, AA 27:62; translation modified. This is not the place to scrutinize the development of Kant's ethics, but it is worth pointing out that already in the published work, *Inquiry Concerning the Distinctness of the Principles of Natural Theology and Morality*, completed by the end of 1762 and published in 1764 (thus, approximately when Herder attended Kant's course) Kant had already distinguished "problematic necessity" from the necessity of "law," a forerunner of the necessity of duty imposed by the moral law. Kant distinguishes "obligations" having "legal necessity" from the "problematic necessity" possessed by mere "recommendations." Kant, *Inquiry Concerning the Distinctness of the Principles of Natural Theology and Morality*, AA 2:298. Thus, while Kant certainly had not yet developed the idea that the principle of morality could *motivate* people (rather than just determine what was right or wrong, the content of morality), we should not easily dismiss the Herder notes merely on the grounds that it is from an early period in the development of Kant's ethics. On the content of the "supreme principle of morality" as already present in the Herder notes, see Oliver Sensen, "The Supreme Principle of Morality," in *Reading Kant's Lectures*, ed. Robert R. Clewis (Berlin: de Gruyter, 2015), 179–99, 185: "Kant's early views are already very close to the mature philosophy with regard to the content of the moral principle." Still, Sensen justly points out that "even in regard to lying Kant does not have his full mature view."

69 Kant refers to the beauty and dignity of human nature, and respect for the latter, at Kant, *Observations*, AA 2:217.

70 Kant, *Anthropology*, AA 7:281.

71 Carroll, *Humour*, 36.

72 Kant, *CPJ*, AA 5:305.

73 "When a joke transforms some subject-matter 'into nothing', the effect is to negate the theoretical and practical interests in the joke's subject-matter, thus rendering the pleasure in the laughter detached from such interests." Wicks, *Judgment*, 143.
74 Kant, *CPJ*, AA 5:331.
75 Carroll, *Humour*, 86.
76 Kant, *CPJ*, AA 5:333.
77 Kant, *CPJ*, AA 5:333–4; emphasis added.
78 Godfrey, "The Aesthetics of Laughter," 134.
79 Kant, Friedländer anthropology lecture, AA 25:601.
80 Mendelssohn, "Rhapsody," in *Philosophical Writings*, 150. For Hutcheson's view, see Townsend, *British Aesthetics*, 147.
81 Carroll, "Horror and Humor," *Journal of Aesthetics and Art Criticism* 57, no. 2, 145–60, 158.
82 John Morreall, "The Rejection of Humor in Western Thought," *Philosophy East and West* 39, no. 3 (1989): 243–65, 253.
83 Gimbel, *Isn't That Clever*, 39. A concept of a play frame in humor was presented by anthropologist Gregory Bateson in a number of papers in the 1950s and developed by a member of his team, William Fry. See Gregory Bateson, "A Theory of Play and Fantasy: A Report on Theoretical Aspects of *The Project for Study of the Role of the Paradoxes of Abstraction in Communication*," in *Approaches to the Study of Human Personality*: American Psychiatric Association Psychiatric Research Reports 2, 39–51 (Washington, D.C.: American Psychiatric Association, 1955). William Fry, *Sweet Madness: A Study of Humor* (Palo Alto: Pacific Books, 1963).
84 This list could of course be expanded: misogynistic jokes, ageist jokes, jokes about violence towards humans and animals, and so on.
85 Kant, *CPJ*, AA 5:305.
86 Kant, *CPJ*, AA 5:333.
87 Critchley, *On Humour*, 6.
88 Giamario, "Making Reason Think More," 165.
89 Kant, Pillau anthropology lecture, AA 25:775; and Kant, Menschenkunde anthropology lecture, AA 25:1043.
90 Kant, *Anthropology*, AA 7:281.
91 Steven Gimbel, *Take My Course, Please! The Philosophy of Humor* (Chantilly: The Teaching Company, 2018) 103. He also describes these positions (using different terms) at Gimbel, *Isn't That Clever*, 125.
92 Gimbel presents, then rejects, arguments defending each of these three positions. Gimbel, *Isn't That Clever*, 112–25.

93 Gimbel ascribes to Kant a "nihilistic version of neo-Shaftesburianism." (Neo-Shaftesburianism is Gimbel's term for the universal permissibility position: it is always acceptable to tell jokes about groups even when the jokes employ stock caricatures or "icons" of the group). Gimbel attributes to Kant the view that jokes lack content and meaning, or do not "mean" anything (hence Gimbel uses the term "nihilism"), and are not bona fide communications about the real world. Gimbel, *Isn't That Clever*, 118. As we saw in chapter one, however, the lack of meaning or the "nonsense" in a joke can be read as referring to a perceived incongruity, not to a total lack of content or meaning. Moreover, since it evokes in the judging audience a play with inexhaustible aesthetic ideas, a joke certainly has some kind of content and meaning, indeed it has a rich one. Finally, while it is true that many jokes are not bona fide communications (i.e., do not contain assertions about the real world that can be either true or false), Kant holds that jokes are still governed by ethical constraints, as I showed earlier in this chapter. Thus, we can't attribute the universal permissibility position to Kant.

94 Bergmann, "Sexist Humor," 70; emphasis added. Following her, I will for present purposes focus on sexism, but the remarks could be extended to racism, ageism, etc.

95 Bergmann, "Sexist Humor," 76.

96 Bergmann, "Sexist Humor," 79.

97 Kivy, "Joking Morality," 116. Kivy never explains what he means by "evidence," however, and simply follows his own intuitions.

98 Kivy, "Joking Morality," 115.

99 Bergmann proposes a distinction between perceiving and seeing a (sexist) incongruity. The distinction runs parallel to the one between endorsing and entertaining. To *perceive* the incongruity means that you think the thing or quality generating the incongruity actually exists (e.g., that women are irrational, unscientific, etc.). To *see* the incongruity, is just to entertain the thought imaginatively. Bergmann, "Sexist Humor," 70 n. 10.

100 In her article (published in 1986), Bermann uses the term "feminist," and I follow her, though the class could be expanded to refer to any person who opposes sexist attitudes, norms, and beliefs and discrimination based on gender and sexuality.

101 Bergmann, "Sexist Humor," 77. For similar arguments, see Ronald de Sousa, *The Rationality of Emotion* (Cambridge: MIT Press, 1987), 290; and Wilhelm Verwoerd and Melanie Verwoerd, "On the Injustice of (Un)Just Joking," *Agenda: Empowering Women for Gender Equity* 10, no. 23 (1994): 67–78. Verwoerd and Verwoerd reject the "just joking" argument put forward in defense of making and laughing at sexist jokes. They likewise imply that sexist jokes do actual harm, where

harm consists in the domination of one group (here, women) by another group (men) (73).

102 Carroll, *Humour*, 97.
103 Kant, Mrongovius anthropology lecture, AA, 25:1350; translation modified.
104 Kivy, "Joking Morality," 116.
105 Carroll, *Humour*, 89. Percival makes a similar point about the importance of *context* for morally evaluating an audience's response or amusement. "Whether it is morally wrong for an agent to respond in a certain way to an item [i.e., something potentially amusing] depends not just on the agent, and the agent's situation, but on the item's context too." Philip Percival, "Comic Normativity and the Ethics of Humour," *The Monist* 88, no. 1 (2005): 93–120, 111. The moral evaluation of *responses* to joking is so complex and multi-layered that it deserves more attention than I can offer here, but I can say that the moral evaluation of our responses to joking seems qualitatively different from our moral evaluation of joke *telling* since the latter is a more obviously voluntary act and thus, in my view, more easily subject to moral evaluation and appraisal. While we might be able to control laughter if or once we start to laugh, it is not so obvious that we can control or stop ourselves from finding something funny and from being amused in the first place.
106 While not connecting them to Kant, Gimbel examines punching up and group membership (calling it "political identity"). Gimbel, *Isn't That Clever*, 123. For the sake of space, I cannot here explore the interesting ways in which the guidelines may interact or possibly conflict with each other. Moreover, I am not suggesting that Kant would consider the Punching Up and Group Membership guidelines to be inviolable, and in this respect they differ from the Ethical Principles.
107 See Dave Chappelle's interview with Anderson Cooper, at "Inside Cable News," July 7, 2006. https://web.archive.org/web/20061029205225/http://insidecable.blogsome.com/2006/07/07/dave-chappelle-on-360-tonight/ [accessed October 19, 2019].
108 Kant, *Anthropology*, AA 7:265; translation modified.
109 Kant, Collins ethics lecture, AA 27:458. See also my foregoing discussion (ch. 1, sec. 2) of caustic mockery pertaining to Kant, *The Metaphysics of Morals*, AA 6:467. In a similar vein, Ronald de Sousa discusses when laughter is good (or bad) for the adequacy of our attitudes to the objective world. He maintains that unethical, malicious laughter involves "a wrong assessment of reality." Ronald de Sousa, "When Is It Wrong to Laugh?", in Morreall, *Laughter and Humor*, 226–49, 244.

110 Giving a proper defense of the claim that this guideline derives from Kant's body of writings would require delving into the details of Kant's philosophy of right and his views of socio-economic justice, which space does not allow here. But I hope that charitable readers will grant that the guideline is Kantian in spirit.

111 "Hannah Gadsby Decided to Quit Comedy, and Then Her Career Blew Up." June 19, 2018. https://www.vulture.com/2018/06/hannah-gadsby-on-her-netflix-stand-up-special-nanette.html [accessed July 17, 2019].

112 Gimbel, *Isn't That Clever*, 130. This potential objection gives me a chance to restate that I am not here evaluating these guidelines, but merely suggesting that they are Kantian in spirit.

113 Carroll, *Humour*, 88. Carroll hints at this principle when he suggests that we are unbothered by a riddle that pokes fun at lawyers, since that group is socio-economically advantaged (in other words, the riddle punches up). "What do you have if you have a lawyer buried up to his neck in sand? *Not enough sand*." Carroll, *Humour*, 87.

114 Ted Cohen, *Jokes*, 21.

115 Space does not allow me to enter into the various debates on Kant's complex views of race and race theory. This has been the source of a lively debate concerning what it means to count as "racial" (distinguishing the races) as opposed to "racist" (ranking them hierarchically), the extent to which Kant was racist, and whether and (if so) when he had "second thoughts" about racial hierarchies.

116 Kant, *Observations*, AA 2:253.

117 Kant, *Observations*, AA 2:253.

118 Jean-Baptiste Labat, *Voyage du père Labat aux îles de l'Amérique* (Haye, 1724), vol. 2, 54.

119 Kant, *Observations*, AA 2:254–5; emphasis added and translation modified.

120 Compare the possibly playful but ultimately ambiguous story related by Kant, according to which the short-sighted Caribbean sells his hammock in the morning—only to regret doing so at night. Kant, *Anthropology*, AA 7:186.

121 Kant, *Observations*, AA 2:243 n.

122 Kant, *Observations*, AA 2:254–5.

123 Kant, *Observations*, AA 2:254.

124 "The woman is not the more honored by all of this [i.e., fake attention]." Kant, *Observations*, AA 2:246 n.

125 Kant, *Observations*, AA 2:246 n.; translation modified.

126 It may here also be recalled that Kant *repudiates* the seemingly sexist Samuel Johnson quip (No. 15), on the grounds that it is not sufficiently substantial or interesting to reason.

127 Kant, *Anthropology*, AA 7:280–1; translation modified. On woman's ultimate governing of man, see Kant, *Anthropology*, AA 7:303.

128 There is a place for jest in marriage too. A wife can ridicule (*spotten*) her husband about his jealousy, for it is only a joke (*Scherz*). Kant, *Anthropology*, AA 7:310; Kant, Friedländer anthropology lecture, AA 25:715.

129 de Sousa, "When Is It Wrong to Laugh?", 243.

130 Kant, Mrongovius anthropology lecture, AA 25:1268, 1350; translation modified.

131 Kant, "Remarks," AA 20:95; my translation.

132 Kant, "Remarks," AA 20:95; my translation.

133 Pauline Kleingeld, "On Dealing with Kant's Sexism and Racism," *SGIR Review* 2, no. 2 (2019): 3–22, 5. Kleingeld (5) likewise sees Kant's qualification and admission that men, like women, *also* usually lack principles as a "gallant" flourish. She holds that it "does not diminish the gravity of his characterization of women as unreceptive to moral obligation and that of men as having to master the art of directing women toward the good." She is referring to Kant, *Observations*, 2:232.

134 Eagleton, *Humour*, 7.

135 Kant, *Anthropology*, AA 7:199.

136 Gimbel gives a useful (and not strictly Kantian) diagram on deliberating about telling a questionable joke. Gimbel, *Isn't That Clever*, 153.

137 Carroll ends *On Humour* with a similar conclusion.

Part Two Jokes

Incongruity Jokes

1 Kant, *CPJ*, AA 5:333.
2 Kant, *CPJ*, AA 5:211.
3 Kant, *CPJ*, AA 5:333.
4 Kant, *Anthropology*, AA 7:237. See also Kant, *CPJ*, AA 5:331.
5 Plato, *Ion*, 535e.
6 Kant, Mrongovius anthropology lecture, AA 25:1264–5.

7 Swift wrote in his *apologia*, "Verses on the Death of Dr. Swift": "Yet malice never was his aim; / He lashed the vice but spared the name. / No individual could resent, / Where thousands equally were meant. / His satire points at no defect, / But what all mortals may correct; / For he abhorred that senseless tribe, / Who call it humour when they jibe: / He spar'd a hump or crooked nose, / Whose owners set not up for beaux. / True genuine dullness moved his pity, / Unless it offered to be witty." Swift, quoted from Critchley, *On Humour*, 14–15.

8 Critchley, *On Humour*, 15.

9 Kant, *The Conflict of the Faculties* (1798), AA 7:93.

10 Kant, *Anthropology*, AA 7:333 n.

11 Letter of February 6, 1798 to Christoph Wilhelm Hufeland, in Kant, AA 12:232. Kant writes this after having asked Hufeland for advice concerning Kant's "sickliness" and then confessing that, anyway, he is not hopeful about the prognosis. For brief commentary, see Susan Meld Shell, *The Embodiment of Reason: Kant on Spirit, Generation, and Community* (Chicago: Chicago University Press, 1996), 290–1.

12 Kant, Mrongovius anthropology lecture, AA 25:1269.

13 The joke comes from Samuel Butler's *Hudibras*, part 3, canto 1, lines 277–80. "What makes all doctrine plain and clear? — / About two hundred pounds a year. / And that which was prov'd true before, / Prove false again? — Two hundred more." Samuel Butler, *Hudibras, In Three Parts* (London: Alex Murray and Son, 1869), 108.

14 Kant, Mrongovius anthropology lecture, AA 25:1268. A version is also found in Kant, Friedländer anthropology lecture, AA 25:518. Kant also wrote down a note: "*summum ius summa iniuria.*" See Kant, AA 15:203.

15 Cicero, *On Duties*, bk. 1, ch. 10, 33. Cicero, *The Treatise of Cicero, De Officiis; Or, His Essay on Moral Duty*, trans. William McCartney (Edinburgh: Bell and Bradfute, 1798), 25.

16 Kant, Mrongovius anthropology lecture, AA 25:1268.

17 Kant, Friedländer anthropology lecture, AA 25:506, 565.

18 Kant, *Anthropology*, 7:262 n.; translation modified and abridged. Kant mentions "Sagramoso" in a marginal note, Reflection 1515 (from the 1780s), AA 15:853.

19 *A Night at the Opera* (1935, USA, MGM), directed by Sam Wood, screenplay by George S. Kaufman and Morrie Ryskind. Rights owned by Turner Entertainment.

20 Quoted from John Pollack, *The Pun Also Rises: How the Humble Pun Revolutionized Language, Changed History, and Made Wordplay More Than Some Antics* (New York: Penguin, 2011), xxiii. Unable to resist a

pun, Pollack adds: "But of course, he could and did—and with good reason."

21 Kant, Mrongovius anthropology lecture, AA 25:1268. See also Kant, Collins anthropology lecture, AA 25:142.

22 Kant, Mrongovius anthropology lecture, AA 25:1349–50. Kant also makes a brief reference to "Busby" at Kant, Reflection 1515 (from the 1780s), AA 15:848. Richard Busby (1606–95) was an English headmaster; it is unclear how Kant came to learn of him. For another quip or joke involving Charles II, see Kant, *Anthropology*, AA 7:198–9.

23 Kant, Mrongovius anthropology lecture, AA 25:1381.

24 See Laurence Sterne, *Tristram Shandy*, vol. 2, ch. 7: "It is said in Aristotle's masterpiece, 'That when a man doth think of anything which is past he looketh down upon the ground; but that when he thinketh of something that is to come he looketh up towards the heavens.' My Uncle Toby, I suppose, thought of neither, for he looked horizontally." Laurence Sterne, *The Life and Opinions of Tristram Shandy, Gentleman* (New York: George Routledge and Sons, 1886), 54. *Tristram Shandy* was published in nine volumes, the first two appearing in 1759 and the last in 1767.

25 Kant cites an anecdote from Sterne's *Tristram Shandy* in Kant, *Lectures on Pedagogy*, AA 9:469. A June 1762 letter from Maria Charlotta Jacobi to Kant playfully alludes to Kant winding her clock; in *Tristram Shandy*, clock-winding is associated with sex. Kant, AA 10:39.

26 Kant, Mrongovius anthropology lecture, AA 25:1384. For Kant's conflicting views regarding physiognomy, see Kant, Menschenkunde anthropology lecture, 25:1177, 1179.

27 Kant, *Anthropology*, AA 7:309.

28 The final lines are: "Having thus seen the world, and all that is great, good, and admirable in it, I resolved to return to Candia, where, I married a little after my arrival, I was soon a cuckold, but plainly perceived it to be the most harmless, and tolerable situation in life." Voltaire, *The History of the Voyages of Scarmentado. A Satire* (London: Paul Vaillant, 1757), 18.

29 Ludwig Ernst Borowski, *Darstellung des Lebens und Charakters Immanuel Kant's* (Königsberg: Nicolovius, 1804), 146.

30 On the "postponement" and "finally the complete renunciation" of getting married, see Kant, *Observations*, AA 2:239.

31 Kant, Mrongovius anthropology lecture, AA 25:1265. A version is also found in Kant, Friedländer anthropology lecture, AA 25:506: "The English are very attentive to speech full of contradictions. They call it a *bull*, saying that someone has uttered a 'bull'. This technique helps them come up with witty inspirations." And in the Vienna lecture (1780s): "In our language some contradictions prevail. I go out alone with someone else. The English call that a *bull*." Kant, Vienna logic lecture, AA, 24:813.

On English and Irish bull, see also Kant, Menschenkunde anthropology lecture, AA 25:967.

32 Quoted from Gini, *Being Funny*, 85.
33 Salvatore Attardo and Victor Raskin, "Script Theory Revis(it)ed: Joke Similarity and Joke Representation Model," *Humor: International Journal of Humor Research* 4, nos. 3–4 (2009): 293–348, 333.
34 Quoted from Eagleton, *Humour*, 58. For a collection of Wilde's sayings and anecdotes, see Oscar Wilde, *The Wit and Wisdom of Oscar Wilde*, ed. Ralph Keyes (New York: Gramercy Books, 1999).
35 Steve Martin, *Born Standing Up* (New York: Scribner, 2007), 75. Martin called his act "unbridled nonsense" (144).
36 Schopenhauer, *The World as Will and Representation*, vol. 2, 96.
37 Quoted from Gini, *Being Funny*, xix.
38 Kant, *Anthropology*, AA 7:152.
39 Laertius reports: "He who has friends can have no true friend." Laertius, *Lives of Eminent Philosophers*, vol. 1, 465 (bk. 5, ch. 1, sec. 21). References to Laertius will be to volume and page in Hicks's translation of *Lives*, followed by the book, chapter, and section in parentheses.
40 Aristotle, *Eudemian Ethics*, bk. 7, ch. 12 (1245 b 20). See also Aristotle, *Nicomachean Ethics*, bk. 9, ch. 10, 6 (1171 a 15–17).
41 Kant repeats the (mis)quotation in *The Metaphysics of Morals* (1797), AA 6:470: "On the other hand Aristotle says: My dear friends, there is no such thing as a friend." Kant then goes on to describe the obstacles to a pure, perfect friendship. The misquotation appears in several versions of his anthropology lectures. See the Collins lecture, AA 25:106; the Parow lecture, AA 25:330; and the Menschenkunde lecture, AA 25:933. Kant also gives a version in his candid letter to Maria von Herbert (dated Spring 1792), at AA 11:332.
42 Kant, Friedländer anthropology lecture, AA 25:505; emphasis added. For brief commentary on this, "Aristotle's paradox," see Fenves, *Late Kant*, 139.

Ethnic and Sexist Jokes and Quips

1 Kant, *CPJ*, AA 5:333. He calls it a *bouteille* of champagne (not beer) at Kant, Reflection 1515 (from the 1780s), in AA 15:851.
2 Kant, *CPJ*, AA 5:332.
3 Critchley, *On Humour*, 9.
4 Critchley, *On Humour*, 6.

5   Kant, Mrongovius anthropology lecture, AA 25:1264. The "witty German philosopher and poet" (Kant says) who came up with this is Abraham Gotthelf Kästner (1719–1800), poet, satirist, and mathematician at Göttingen University. Kant's source is Abraham Kästner, *Einige Vorlesungen. In der Königlichen deutschen Gesellschaft zu Göttingen gehalten*, 2 vols. (Altenburg: in der Richterischen Buchhandlung, 1768), vol. 1, 102.
6   Quoted from Carroll, *Humour*, 88.
7   "The Germans travel to France to become gallant, but they only gain the look of a brazen dandy [*Gecken*]." Kant, "Remarks," AA 20:171; my translation. On *Laffe* and *Geck*, see also Kant, *Observations*, AA 2:214.
8   Kant, Mrongovius anthropology lecture, AA 25:1264.
9   Kant, Mrongovius anthropology lecture, AA 25:1306; there are two other (unamusing) miser jokes on 25:1306.
10 Kant, *Observations*, AA 2:229–30.
11 Bergmann, "Sexist Humor," 64.
12 See Meg Armstrong, "'The Effects of Blackness': Gender, Race, and the Sublime in Aesthetic Theories of Burke and Kant," *Journal of Aesthetics and Art Criticism* 54, no. 3 (1996): 213–36. Reprinted in *The Sublime Reader*, ed. Robert R. Clewis (London: Bloomsbury, 2019), 271–9.
13 See Mary Wollstonecraft, *A Vindication of the Rights of Men* (1790). Her criticism of Burke on sublimity and beauty is reprinted in Clewis, ed., *The Sublime Reader*, 118–21; see esp. 120.
14 Paul Guyer, "Translator's Introduction" to the *Observations*, in Kant, *Anthropology, History, Education*, 21. For a more critical response to such a conception, see Kleingeld, "On Dealing with Kant's Sexism and Racism," 5.
15 Kant, *Anthropology*, AA 7:222. Kant recounts a joke about Johnson's coarseness at *Anthropology*, AA 7:222 n. (translation modified):

>   Boswell says that a certain lord once expressed his regret that Johnson did not have a more refined education.
>   Baretti said: "No, no my lord. You could have done with him as you pleased, he would always have remained a bear."
>   "No doubt, but at least a *dancing* bear?" asked the lord.
>   A third person, his friend, thought to soften this by saying: "He has nothing of the bear but the *coat*."

16 Cited from John Zammito, *Kant, Herder, and the Birth of Anthropology* (University of Chicago Press, 2002), 121.
17 This line was used by American comedian George Carlin.
18 Cicero, bk. 2, ch. 65, in *On Oratory and Orators*, 160.

19 Addison, no. 62, May 11, 1711, in Addison and Steele, *The Spectator*, 75.
20 Francis Murray, ed., *World's Wildest Animal Jokes* (Sterling Publishing, NY, 1992), 11.
21 Murray, *Animal Jokes*, 58.
22 Murray, *Animal Jokes*, 39.

Jokes with a Point

1 Kant, Mrongovius anthropology lecture, AA 25:1272.
2 Kant, *Dreams of a Spirit-Seer*, AA 2:348; my translation.
3 Martin, *Born Standing Up*, 116.
4 Spelling and punctuation modified. Though often omitted (unsurprisingly) from collections of Franklin's writings, the piece is published in Benjamin Franklin, *Fart Proudly: Writings of Benjamin Franklin You Never Read in School*, ed. Carl Japikse (Berkeley: Frog Ltd, 2003).
5 Critchley, *On Humour*, 46, 48.
6 Kant, *Essay on the Maladies of the Head*, AA 2:271. Kant attributes the purification view about a "bad poem" to Jonathan Swift, though it is possible he meant to refer to Alexander Pope. More than three decades later, Kant referred to academics who can't get a joke (*Scherz*). Kant, *The Conflict of the Faculties*, AA 7:19.
7 Kant, *CPJ*, 5:332.
8 Nietzsche, *Basic Writings*, 422.
9 Paul Swift notices (plausibly) that even as Nietzsche radically transformed Kant's philosophy, certain strands of Nietzsche's theory of laughter grew "out of Kantian seeds." Swift, "Intestinal Laughter in Kant and Nietzsche," 102.
10 Kant, *Anthropology*, AA 7:211. See also the undated addition to Reflection 1485, AA 15:703: "Ein Narr in Prosa, ein anderer in Versen."
11 Kant's source may have been *Life of Voltaire*, translated into German from the French: Théophile Imarigeon Duvernet, *Lebensbeschreibung Voltaire's* (Nürnberg: J.G. Stiebner, 1787), 42. According to Auguste Gazier ("Le frère de Voltaire", *Revue des Deux Mondes* 32 [1906]: 614–46, 624), Voltaire senior said: "j'ai deux fils qui sont tous deux fous, l'un fou de dévotion, et l'autre fou pour les vers et pour le théâtre." (I have two sons who are both fools—one a fool for devotion, the other a fool for verse and the theater.)
12 Kant, *Anthropology*, AA 7:211. "Buffoon" translates *Narr*, and "fool" *Thor*.
13 Kant, Mrongovius anthropology lecture, AA 25:1269.

14 The saying comes from *Hudibras*, part 3, canto 3, lines 261–64. "If th' ancients crown'd their bravest men / That only sav'd a citizen, / What victory could e'er be won, / If every one would save but one?" Butler, *Hudibras*, 302. On *corona civica*, see Butler, *Hudibras*, 302 n. 3.

Part Three Sayings with a Message

1 Kant, Mrongovius anthropology lecture, AA 25:1256. See also Kant, Friedländer anthropology lecture, AA 25:491.

2 Kant's source is Dialogue XXII in George Lyttelton and Elizabeth Montagu, *Dialogues of the Dead* (London: W. Sandby, 1760), 238. Rabelais says to Lucian: "Good Sense is, like a Dish of plain Beef or Mutton, proper only for Peasants; but a Ragout of Folly, well dressed with a sharp Sauce of Wit, is fit to be served at an Emperor's Table."

A classic study of Rabelais is Mikhail Bakhtin, *Rabelais and His World* (Bloomington: Indiana University Press, 1984).

3 In *Julius Caesar,* Shakespeare reverses the metaphor: wit does not act as a sauce but is instead accompanied by one—bluntness. Cassius says of Casca: "This rudeness is a sauce to his good wit, which gives men stomach to digest his words with better appetite" (Act I, scene ii). William Shakespeare, *Julius Caesar*, ed. Burton Raffel (New Haven: Yale University Press, 2006), 24.

4 Kant, *Anthropology*, AA 7:280. For a discussion of these stages as contributing to the cognitive dimension of the dinner party experience, see Alix Cohen, "The Ultimate Kantian Experience," 322–3.

5 Kant, *Anthropology*, AA 7:281.

6 Kant, marginal note to *On the Philosopher's Medicine of the Body*, AA 15:945–6. Translated in Kant, *Anthropology, History, Education*, 187.

7 Kant, Mrongovius anthropology lecture, AA 25:1330.

8 Addison, no. 98, June 22, 1711, *The Spectator*. "There is not so variable a thing in nature as a lady's head-dress." Addison and Steele, *The Spectator*, 118. See also no. 127, Addison's entry of July 26, 1711. "What they have lost in height they make up in breadth, and, contrary to all rules of architecture, widen the foundations at the same time that they shorten the superstructure." Addison, in Addison and Steele, *The Spectator*, 150.

9 This version draws from both Kant, *Anthropology*, AA 7:300 n. and Kant, Mrongovius anthropology lecture, AA 25:1330. There are three additional versions: Kant, Collins anthropology lecture, AA 25:182–3; Kant, Parow anthropology lecture, AA 25:379; Kant, Friedländer anthropology lecture,

AA 25:665. (Thanks to Colin McQuillan and Matthew McAndrew for discussion of this joke.)

10 The relation between humor and taste/disgust merits further exploration. We often speak together of humor and taste, and think of an inappropriate joke as being in bad taste and tasteless. Morally inappropriate humor is often characterized as (morally) disgusting. Yet humor and disgust are more than simple contraries. In a comedic skit, Paul Simon and David Letterman once asked Steve Martin for advice about music and comedy. Martin replied, "Comedy is the ability to make people laugh without making them puke." Aristotle claims that the comic or laughable is merely a "species of the ugly" and "consists in some defect or ugliness which does not cause pain or disaster." Aristotle, *Poetics*, ch. 5 (1449 a 33–35); translation modified. Carroll explores the relation to some extent in Noël Carroll, "Horror and Humor." Menninghaus claims that every theorist of disgust is at the same time a theorist of laughter. Winfried Menninghaus, *Disgust: Theory and History of a Strong Sensation*, trans. Howard Eiland and Joel Golb (Albany: SUNY Press, 2003), 10.

11 Menninghaus, *Disgust*, 7.

12 Kant, Mrongovius anthropology lecture, AA 25:1378. See also Kant, Friedländer anthropology lecture, AA 25:666.

13 Kant, Mrongovius anthropology lecture, AA 25:1378.

14 Kant, *Anthropology*, AA 7:152.

15 The passage is from the Preface to Swift's *A Tale of a Tub* (1704): "Seamen have a custom when they meet a whale, to fling him out an empty tub by way of amusement, to divert him from laying violent hands upon the ship." Jonathan Swift, *Volume XX of the Author's Works, Containing, The Tale of A Tub* (Dublin: George Faulkner, 1771) xlv; spelling, italics, and punctuation modified.

16 Kant, *CPJ*, 5:331.

17 On gaming, see Kant, *CPJ*, 5:305–6 and 5:331.

18 Kant, *Anthropology*, AA 7:204.

19 See Laurence Sterne, *Tristram Shandy*, vol. 1, ch. 8. "*De gustibus non est disputandem*: that is, there is no disputing against hobby horses; and, for my part, I seldom do." Sterne, *Tristram Shandy*, 11; format and style modernized.

20 A hobby horse fast fact: In his 1951 essay "Meditations on a Hobby Horse or the Roots of Artistic Form," art historian Ernst Gombrich claimed that the eighteenth-century hobby horse acts as a *substitute* for the horse, rather than representing or portraying it. Ernst Gombrich, *Meditations on a Hobby Horse and other Essays on the Theory of Art* (London: Phaidon, 1985), 1.

21 Kant, *Anthropology*, AA 7:203; translation modified.

22 Kant, *Essay on the Maladies of the Head*, AA 2:262.
23 Laertius, *Lives of Eminent Philosophers*, vol. 2, 481 (bk. 9, ch. 11, sec. 68). "When his fellow-passengers on board a ship were all unnerved by a storm, he kept calm and confident, pointing to a little pig in the ship that went on eating, and telling them that such was the unperturbed state in which the wise man should keep himself."
24 Kant, *Anthropology*, AA 7:253; translation modified.
25 Modified from Kant, Collins anthropology lecture, AA 25:151. A version is also found at Kant, Parow anthropology lecture, AA 25:354. In the *Maladies of the Head*, Kant added: "Pyrrhus strictly followed the drive for ambition and was nothing more than what Cineas considered him to be: a fool [*Thor*]." Kant, *Essay on the Maladies of the Head*, AA 2:262. Kant also mentions Pyrrhus at Reflection 415 (from 1776–78), AA 15:168. The original source is Plutarch, *The Parallel Lives*, "The Life of Pyrrhus," section 14. See Plutarch, *Lives, Volume IX: Demetrius and Antony. Pyrrhus and Gaius Marius*, trans. Bernadotte Perrin (Cambridge, MA: Harvard University Press, 1920).
26 Kant, *Idea for a Universal History with a Cosmopolitan Aim*, AA 8:26. See also Kant, *Anthropology*, AA 7:326–7.
27 Kant, *Idea for a Universal History with a Cosmopolitan Aim*, AA 8:23.
28 Kant, Mrongovius anthropology lecture, AA 25:1254–5.
29 Steele, no. 509, October 14, 1712, in Addison and Steele, *The Spectator*, 611.
30 Henry Ford and Samuel Crowther, *My Life and Work* (Garden City: Garden City Publishing Company, 1922), 72.
31 Kant, *Critique of Practical Reason*, AA 5:97.
32 Kant, *Critique of Practical Reason*, AA 5:30.
33 Kant, *Critique of Practical Reason*, AA 5:156–7.
34 The joke is found in Sigmund Freud, *Der Witz und Seine Beziehung zum Unbewussten* (Leipzig and Wien: Franz Deuticke, 1905), 198; my translation. Freud analyzes the joke again in his 1927 essay, "Der Humor" ("Humor").

Bibliography

Addison, Joseph, and Richard Steele. *The Spectator; With Notes, and a General Index. The Eight Volumes Comprised in One*. Philadelphia: Hickman and Hazzard, 1822.

Arendt, Hannah. *Lectures on Kant's Political Philosophy*. Chicago: University of Chicago Press, 1992.

Aristotle. *The Complete Works of Aristotle*. 2 vols. Edited by Jonathan Barnes. Princeton: Princeton University Press, 1984.

Armstrong, Meg. "'The Effects of Blackness': Gender, Race, and the Sublime in Aesthetic Theories of Burke and Kant." *Journal of Aesthetics and Art Criticism* 54, no. 3 (1996): 213–36. Reprinted in *The Sublime Reader*, edited by Robert R. Clewis, 271–9. London: Bloomsbury, 2019.

Arnold, Jeremy. "Laughter, Judgment and Democratic Politics." *Culture, Theory, & Critique*, 50, no. 1 (2009): 7–21.

Attardo, Salvatore, and Victor Raskin. "Script Theory Revis(it)ed: Joke Similarity and Joke Representation Model." *Humor: International Journal of Humor Research* 4, nos. 3–4 (2009): 293–348.

Baeumler, Alfred. *Das Irrationalitätsproblem in der Ästhetik und Logik des 18. Jahrhunderts bis zur Kritik der Urteilskraft*. Darmstadt: Wissenschaftliche Buchgesellschaft, 1967.

Bakhtin, Mikhail. *Rabelais and His World*. Bloomington: Indiana University Press, 1984.

Banki, Peter. "Humor as the Inverted Sublime: Jean Paul's Laughter within Limitations." *Parrhesia* 21 (2014): 58–68.

Bateson, Gregory. "A Theory of Play and Fantasy: A Report on Theoretical Aspects of *The Project for Study of the Role of the Paradoxes of Abstraction in Communication*." *Approaches to the Study of Human Personality*: American Psychiatric Association Psychiatric Research Reports 2, 39–51. Washington, D.C.: American Psychiatric Association, 1955.

Baumgarten, Alexander. *Metaphysics*. Translated by Courtney Fugate and John Hymers. London: Bloomsbury, 2013.

Baumgarten, Alexander Gottlieb. *Metaphysica*. Halle: Hemmerde, 1739.

Baumgarten, Alexander Gottlieb. *Texte zur Grundlegung der Ästhetik*. Edited by Hans Rudolf Schweizer. Hamburg: Meiner, 1983.

Beard, Mary. *Laughter in Ancient Rome: On Joking, Tickling, and Cracking Up.* Berkeley: University of California Press, 2014.
Beattie, James. "An Essay on Laughter and Ludicrous Composition." In *Essays: On Poetry and Music, As They Affect the Mind*, 319–486. Edinburgh: William Creech, 1778.
Bennett, Jonathan. "Early Modern Texts." http://www.earlymoderntexts.com/ [accessed October 4, 2019]
Bergmann, Merrie. "How Many Feminists Does It Take to Make A Joke? Sexist Humor and What's Wrong with It." *Hypatia* 1, no. 1 (1986): 63–82.
Bergson, Henri. *Laughter: An Essay on the Meaning of the Comic.* Translated by Cloudesley Brereton and Fred Rothwell. Oxford: Macmillan, 1911.
Black, Lewis. *History of the Joke, with Lewis Black.* DVD, History Channel. Produced by Marc Etkind. May 9, 2008.
Borch-Jacobsen, Mikkel. "The Laughter of Being." *MLN* 102, no. 4 (1987): 737–60.
Borowski, Ludwig Ernst. *Darstellung des Lebens und Charakters Immanuel Kant's.* Königsberg: Nicolovius, 1804.
Botul, Jean-Baptiste. *La vie sexuelle d'Emmanuel Kant.* Edited by Frédéric Pagès. Paris: Éditions Mille et une nuits, 1999.
Brandt, Reinhard. *Kritischer Kommentar zu Kants* Anthropologie in pragmatischer Hinsicht *(1798).* Hamburg: Meiner, 1999.
Braun Annegret, and Siegfried Preiser. "The Impact of Disparaging Humor Content on the Funniness of Political Jokes." *Humor* 26, no. 2 (2013): 249–75.
Brommage, Tom, Michael Cundall, and Elizabeth Victor. *Florida Philosophical Review* 15, no. 1 (2015): i–viii.
Brown, Deborah. "What Part of 'Know' Don't You Understand?" *The Monist* 88, no. 1 (2005): 11–35.
Buckley, F. H. *The Morality of Laughter.* Ann Arbor: University of Michigan Press, 2005.
Budd, Malcolm. *The Aesthetic Appreciation of Nature: Essays on the Aesthetics of Nature.* Oxford: Clarendon Press, 2002.
Butler, Samuel. *Hudibras, In Three Parts.* London: Alex Murray and Son, 1869.
Canivet, Michel. "Le rire et le bon sens." *Revue Philosophique de Louvain* 86, no. 3 (1988): 354–77.
Cardelli, Mascia. "*Lachen e Piacere Estetico nella* Kritik der Urteilskraft." In Immanuel Kant, *Il piacere di ridere*, edited by Mascia Cardelli, 9–26. Firenze: Le Càriti, 2002.
Carroll, Noël. "Horror and Humor." *Journal of Aesthetics and Art Criticism* 57, no. 2 (1999): 145–60.
Carroll, Noël. *Humour: A Very Short Introduction.* Oxford: Oxford University Press, 2014.
Carroll, Noël. "Intimate Laughter." *Philosophy and Literature* 24, no. 2 (2000): 435–50.

Carroll, Noël. "Moderate Moralism." *British Journal of Aesthetics* 36, no. 3 (1996): 223–38.
Carroll, Noël. "Moderate Moralism versus Moderate Autonomism." *British Journal of Aesthetics* 38, no. 4 (1998): 419–24.
Carroll, Noël. "Two Comic Plot Structures." *The Monist* 88, no. 1 (2005): 154–83.
Cathcart, Thomas, and Daniel Klein. *Plato and a Platypus Walk into a Bar: Understanding Philosophy through Jokes*. New York: Abrams Image, 2006.
Cicero. *On Oratory and Orators*. Translated by J. S. Watson. New York: Harper and Brothers, 1860.
Cicero. *The Treatise of Cicero, De Officiis; Or, His Essay on Moral Duty*. Translated by William McCartney. Edinburgh: Bell and Bradfute, 1798.
Clark, Michael. "Humour and Incongruity." *Philosophy* 45, no. 171 (1970): 20–32.
Clark, Michael. "Humour, Laughter and the Structure of Thought." *British Journal of Aesthetics* 27 (3) (1987): 238–46.
Clewis, Robert R. "The Feeling of Enthusiasm." In *Kant and the Faculty of Feeling*, edited by Kelly Sorensen and Diane Williamson, 184–207. Cambridge: Cambridge University Press, 2018.
Clewis, Robert R. "Film Evaluation and the Enjoyment of Dated Films." *Projections: The Journal for Movies and Mind* 6 (2) (2012): 42–63.
Clewis, Robert R. "Imagination, Vital Forces, and Self-Consciousness in the Kantian Sublime." In *Kant and the Feeling of Life*, edited by Jennifer Mensch. Albany: SUNY Press, forthcoming.
Clewis, Robert R. *The Kantian Sublime and the Revelation of Freedom*. Cambridge: Cambridge University Press, 2009.
Clewis, Robert R. "The Place of the Sublime in Kant's Project." *Studi Kantiani* 28 (2015): 149–68.
Clewis, Robert R. "*Schwärmerei* and *Enthusiasmus* in Recent English Translations of Kant's Lectures and Writings on Anthropology." In *Kants Schriften in Übersetzungen*, edited by Gisela Schlüter and Hansmichael Hohenegger. Hamburg: Felix Meiner, forthcoming.
Clewis, Robert R. "Spirit and Sublimity, Pleasure and Freedom." In *Kant on Intuition: Western and Asian Perspectives on Transcendental Idealism*, edited by Stephen Palmquist, 159–65. London: Routledge, 2019.
Clewis, Robert R. "Towards a Theory of the Sublime and Aesthetic Awe." In *The Sublime Reader*, edited by Robert R. Clewis, 340–54. London: Bloomsbury, 2019.
Clewis, Robert R. "What Can Hume Teach Us About Film Evaluation?" *Aisthema* 1 (2) (2014): 1–22.
Clewis, Robert R. ed. *Reading Kant's Lectures*. Berlin: Walter de Gruyter, 2015.
Clewis, Robert R, ed. *The Sublime Reader*. London: Bloomsbury, 2019.

Cohen, Alix. "From Faking It to Making It: The Feeling of Love of Honor as an Aid to Morality." In *Reading Kant's Lectures*, edited by Robert R. Clewis, 243–56. Berlin: Walter de Gruyter, 2015.
Cohen, Alix. "The Ultimate Kantian Experience: Kant on Dinner Parties." *History of Philosophy Quarterly* 25, no. 4 (2008): 315–36.
Cohen, Ted. *Jokes: Philosophical Thoughts on Joking Matters*. Chicago: University of Chicago Press, 1999.
Cohen, Ted. "Metaphor and the Cultivation of Intimacy." *Critical Inquiry* 5, no. 1 (1978): 3–12.
Coleridge, Samuel Taylor. *The Complete Poetical Works of Samuel Taylor Coleridge, including Poems and Versions of Poems Now Published for the First Time*. Edited by Ernest Hartley Coleridge. Oxford: Clarendon, 1912.
Comte-Sponville, André. *A Small Treatise on the Great Virtues: The Uses of Philosophy in Everyday Life*. Translated by Catherine Temerson. New York: Metropolitan Books, 2001.
Conolly Oliver, and Bashar Haydar. "The Good, the Bad, and the Funny." *The Monist* 88, no. 1 (2005): 121–34.
Critchley, Simon. *On Humour*. New York: Routledge, 2002.
Dadlez, E. M. "Truly Funny: Humor, Irony, and Satire as Moral Criticism." *Journal of Aesthetic Education* 45, no. 1 (2011): 1–17.
de Sousa, Ronald. *The Rationality of Emotion*. Cambridge: MIT Press, 1987.
de Sousa, Ronald. "When Is It Wrong to Laugh?" In *The Philosophy of Laughter and Humor*, edited by John Morreall, 226–49. Albany: State University of New York Press, 1987.
Deimling, Wiebke. "Kant's Theory of Tragedy." *Southwest Philosophy Review*. 35, no. 1 (2019): 17–30.
Descartes, René. *The Passions of the Soul*. In *Philosophical Works of Descartes*, 2 vols., vol. 1. Translated by Elizabeth Haldane and George T. Ross. Cambridge: Cambridge University Press, 1984.
Dewey, John. "The Theory of Emotion." *Psychological Review* 1 (1894): 553–69.
Duvernet, Théophile Imarigeon. *Lebensbeschreibung Voltaire's*. Nürnberg: J.G. Stiebner, 1787.
Eagleton, Terry. *Humour*. New Haven: Yale University Press, 2019.
Eastman, Max. *The Enjoyment of Laughter*. New York: Simon and Schuster, 1936.
Elliott, Rob. *Laugh-out-loud Jokes for Kids*. Grand Rapids: Baker Publishing Group, 2010.
Fenves, Peter. *Late Kant: Towards Another Law of the Earth*. London: Routledge, 2003.
Figueroa-Dorrego, Jorge, and Cristina Larkin-Galiñanes, eds. *A Source Book of Literary and Philosophical Writings about Humour and Laughter: the Seventy-five Essential Texts from Antiquity to Modern Times*. Lewiston: Edwin Mellen, 2009.

Ford, Henry, and Samuel Crowther. *My Life and Work*. Garden City: Garden City Publishing Company, 1922.

Franklin, Benjamin. *Fart Proudly: Writings of Benjamin Franklin You Never Read in School*. Edited by Carl Japikse. Berkeley: Frog Ltd, 2003.

Freud, Sigmund. *Der Witz und Seine Beziehung zum Unbewussten*. Leipzig and Wien: Franz Deuticke, 1905.

Freud, Sigmund. "Humor." In *Standard Edition of the Complete Psychological Works of Sigmund Freud*, vol. 21, 161–6. London: Hogarth Press, 1961.

Freud, Sigmund. *The Interpretation of Dreams*. Translated by James Strachey. London: Penguin, 1976.

Freud, Sigmund. *Jokes and Their Relation to the Unconscious*. Translated by James Strachey. New York: W. W. Norton & Company, 1960.

Fry, William. *Sweet Madness: A Study of Humor*. Palo Alto: Pacific Books, 1963.

Gabriel, Gottfried. "Der 'Witz' der reflektierenden Urteilskraft." In *Urteilskraft und Heuristik in den Wissenschaften. Beiträge zur Entstehung des Neuen*, edited by Frithjof Rodi, 197–210. Weilerswist: Velbrück Wissenschaft, 2003.

Gadsby, Hannah. "Hannah Gadsby Decided to Quit Comedy, and Then Her Career Blew Up." June 19, 2018. https://www.vulture.com/2018/06/hannah-gadsby-on-her-netflix-stand-up-special-nanette.html [accessed July 17, 2019]

Gaut, Berys. *Art, Emotion, and Ethics*. Oxford: Clarendon Press, 2007.

Gaut, Berys. "Just Joking: The Ethics and Aesthetics of Humor." *Philosophy and Literature* 22, no. 1 (1998): 51–68.

Gazier, Auguste. "Le frère de Voltaire." *Revue des Deux Mondes* 32 (1906): 614–46.

Gerard, Alexander. *An Essay on Taste*. London: A. Millar, A. Kincaid, and J. Bell, 1759.

Gerhardt, Volker, ed. *Kant zum Vergnügen*. Stuttgart: Reclam, 2003.

Giamario, Patrick. "'Making Reason Think More': Laughter in Kant's Aesthetic Philosophy." *Angelaki* 22, no. 4 (2017): 161–76.

Gimbel, Steven. *Isn't That Clever: A Philosophical Account of Humor and Comedy*. New York: Routledge, 2018.

Gimbel, Steven. *Take My Course, Please! The Philosophy of Humor*. Chantilly: The Teaching Company, 2018.

Gini, Al. "Dirty Jokes, Tasteless Jokes, Ethnic Jokes." *Florida Philosophical Review* 15, no. 1 (2015): 50–65.

Gini, Al. *The Importance of Being Funny*. Lanham: Rowman & Littlefield, 2017.

Ginsborg, Hannah. "In Defence of the One-Act View: Reply to Guyer." *British Journal of Aesthetics* 57, no. 4 (2017): 421–35.

Godfrey, F. la T. "The Aesthetics of Laughter." *Hermathena* 25, no. 50 (1937): 126–38.

Goethe, Johann Wolfgang von. *Elective Affinities*. New York: Henry Holt, 1872.

Gombrich, Ernst. *Meditations on a Hobby Horse and other Essays on the Theory of Art*. London: Phaidon, 1985.

Gordon, Mordechai. "Exploring the Relationship between Humor and Aesthetic Experience." *Journal of Aesthetic Education* 46, no. 1 (2012): 111–21.

Gregory, J. C. *The Nature of Laughter.* London: Kegan Paul, Trubner & Co. 1924.

Grice, Paul. *Studies in the Way of Words*. Cambridge, MA: Harvard University Press, 1989.

Guyer, Paul. "Translator's Introduction." In Immanuel Kant, *Anthropology, History, Education*, edited by Günter Zöller and Robert B. Louden, 18–22. Cambridge: Cambridge University Press, 2007.

Guyer, Paul. "One Act or Two? Hannah Ginsborg on Aesthetic Judgement." *British Journal of Aesthetics* 57, no. 4 (2017): 407–19.

Hartley, David. "Of Wit and Humour." In *The Philosophy of Laughter and Humor*, edited by John Morreall, 41–4. Albany: State University of New York Press, 1987.

Heine, Heinrich. *On the History of Religion and Philosophy in Germany and Other Writings*. Edited by Terry Pinkard. Cambridge: Cambridge University Press, 2007.

Herder, Johann Gottfried. *Sämtliche Werke*, 33 vols. Edited by Bernhard Suphan. Berlin: Weidmann, 1877–1913.

Herder, Johann Gottfried. *Schriften zu Literatur und Philosophie, 1792–1800*, edited by Hans Dietrich Irmscher, 651–2. Frankfurt am Main: Deutscher Klassiker Verlag, 1998.

Herzog, Antje. *Lampe und Sein Meister Immanuel Kant*. Frankfurt am Main: Edition Buechergilde, 2017.

Herzog, Rudolph. *Dead Funny: Telling Jokes in Hitler's Germany*. Translated by Jefferson Chase. New York: Melville House, 2012.

Hobbes, Thomas. *The Treatise on Human Nature and That on Liberty and Necessity*. London: McCreery, 1812.

Holt, Jim. *Stop Me If You've Heard This: A History and Philosophy of Jokes*. New York: W. W. Norton, 2008.

Hounsokou, Annie. "Exposing the Rogue in Us." *Epoché: A Journal for the History of Philosophy* 16, no. 2 (2012): 317–36.

Huizinga, Johan. *Homo Ludens*. London: Routledge and Kegan Paul, 1949.

"Inside Cable News." Interview with Dave Chappelle. July 7, 2006. https://web.archive.org/web/20061029205225/http://insidecable.blogsome.com/2006/07/07/dave-chappelle-on-360-tonight/ [accessed October 19, 2019]

Jacobson, Daniel. "In Praise of Immoral Art." *Philosophical Topics* 25, no. 1 (1997): 155–99.

Kant, Immanuel. *Anthropology, History, Education*. Edited by Günter Zöller and Robert B. Louden. Cambridge: Cambridge University Press, 2007.

Kant, Immanuel. *The Cambridge Edition of the Works of Immanuel Kant*. Edited by Paul Guyer and Allen W. Wood. Cambridge: Cambridge University Press, 1992–

Kant, Immanuel. *Correspondence*. Translated and edited by Arnulf Zweig. Cambridge: Cambridge University Press.

Kant, Immanuel. *Critique of Judgment*. Translated by Werner S. Pluhar. Indianapolis: Hackett Publishing Company, 1987.

Kant, Immanuel. *Critique of the Power of Judgment*. Edited by Paul Guyer and translated by Paul Guyer and Eric Matthews. Cambridge: Cambridge University Press, 2000.

Kant, Immanuel. *Critique of Pure Reason*. Translated and edited by Paul Guyer and Allen W. Wood. Cambridge: Cambridge University Press, 1998.

Kant, Immanuel. *Il piacere di ridere*. Edited by Mascia Cardelli. Firenze: Le Càriti, 2002.

Kant, Immanuel. *Kant's Critique of Aesthetic Judgment*. Translated by James Creed Meredith. Oxford: Clarendon, 1911.

Kant, Immanuel. *Kant's gesammelte Schriften*. Edited by the Prussian Academy of Sciences (vols. 1–22), the Academy of Sciences of the GDR (vol. 23) and the Academy of Sciences of Göttingen (vols. 23–). Berlin: Reimer, later de Gruyter, 1900–

Kant, Immanuel. *Kant's Grosse Völkerschau: aus den Naturwissenschaftlichen Kollegs des Herrn Professor Immanuel Kant aus Königsberg*. Edited by Eugen Skasa-Weiss and illustrated by Wolfgang Felten. München: Heimeran, 1960.

Kant, Immanuel. *Kritik der Urteilskraft*. Edited by Museum Ludwig, Cologne. Hamburg: Felix Meiner, 2014.

Kant, Immanuel. *Lectures on Anthropology*. Edited by Robert B. Louden and Allen W. Wood. Translated by Robert R. Clewis, Robert B. Louden, G. Felicitas Munzel, and Allen W. Wood. Cambridge: Cambridge University Press, 2012.

Kant, Immanuel. *Practical Philosophy*. Translated and edited by Mary G. Gregor. Cambridge: Cambridge University Press, 1996.

Kant, Immanuel. *Vorlesungen über Anthropologie*, 2 vols. Berlin: Walter de Gruyter, 1997.

Kästner, Abraham. *Einige Vorlesungen. In der Königlichen deutschen Gesellschaft zu Göttingen gehalten*, 2 vols. Altenburg: in der Richterischen Buchhandlung, 1768.

Kierkegaard, Søren. *Concluding Unscientific Postscript*. Translated by David Swenson and Walter Lowrie. Princeton: Princeton University Press, 1941.

Kierkegaard, Søren. *The Humor of Kierkegaard: An Anthology*. Edited by Thomas C. Oden. Princeton: Princeton University Press, 2004.

Kivy, Peter. "Joking Morality." In *Once Upon a Time: Essays in the Philosophy of Literature*, edited by Aaron Meskin, 103–18. New York: Roman & Littlefield, 2019.

Kleingeld Pauline. "On Dealing with Kant's Sexism and Racism." *SGIR Review* 2, no. 2 (2019): 3–22.

Kotzen, Matthew. "The Normativity of Humor." *Philosophical Issues* 25, no. 1 (2015): 396–414.

Kuehn, Manfred. *Kant: A Biography*. Cambridge: Cambridge University Press, 2001.

La Rocca, Claudio. "Vorläufige Urteile und Urteilskraft. Zur heuristischen Logik des Erkenntnisprozesses." In *Kant und die Berliner Aufklärung: Akten des IX. Internationalen Kant-Kongresses*, vol. 2, edited by Volker Gerhardt, Rolf-Peter Horstmann, and Ralph Schumacher, 351–61. Berlin: Walter de Gruyter, 2001.

Labat, Jean-Baptiste. *Voyage du père Labat aux îles de l'Amérique*. Haye: Husson et al., 1724.

Laertius, Diogenes. *Lives of Eminent Philosophers*, 2 vols. Translated by Robert Drew Hicks. London: William Heinemann, 1925.

Larkin-Galiñanes, Cristina. "An Overview of Humor Theory." In *The Routledge Handbook of Language and Humor*, edited by Salvatore Attardo, 4–16. New York: Routledge, 2017.

Latta, Robert. *The Basic Humor Process: A Cognitive-Shift Theory and the Case against Incongruity*. Berlin: Mouton de Gruyter, 1999.

Lessing, Gotthold Ephraim. *Selected Prose Works*. Edited by Edward Bell. London: George Bell and Sons, 1889.

Lipman, Steve. *Laughter In Hell: The Use of Humor During the Holocaust*. London: Jason Aronson, 1991.

Locke, John. *An Essay concerning Human Understanding*, 2 vols., vol. 1. London: J. Buckingham, 1813.

Long, Debra L., and Arthur C. Graesser. "Wit and Humor in Discourse Processing." *Discourse Processes* 11, no.1 (1988): 35–60.

Lyttelton, George, and Elizabeth Montagu. *Dialogues of the Dead*. London: W. Sandby, 1760.

Makkreel, Rudolf. *Imagination and Interpretation in Kant: The Hermeneutical Import of the* Critique of Judgment. Chicago: The University of Chicago Press, 1990.

Malcolm, Norman. *Ludwig Wittgenstein: A Memoir*. New York: Oxford University Press, 1984.

Mankoff, Bob. *How about Never—Is Never Good for You? My Life in Cartoons*. New York: Henry Holt, 2014.

Marmysz, John. "Humor, Sublimity and Incongruity." *Consciousness, Literature and the Arts* 2, no. 3 (2001). www.dmd27.org/marm.html [accessed August 26, 2019]

Marmysz, John. *Laughing at Nothing: Humor as a Response to Nihilism*. Albany: SUNY Press, 2003.

Martin, Mike W. "Humour and Aesthetic Enjoyment of Incongruities." *British Journal of Aesthetics* 23, no. 1 (1983): 74–85.

Martin, Steve. *Born Standing Up*. New York: Scribner, 2007.

Meier, Georg Friedrich. *Thoughts on Jesting*. Edited by Joseph Jones. Austin: University of Texas Press, 1947.

Meo, Oscar. *Kantiana minora vel rariora*. Genova: Il Melangolo, 2000.

Mendelssohn, Moses. "Rhapsody or Additions to the Letters on Sentiments." In *Philosophical Writings*, edited by Daniel O. Dahlstrom, 131–68. Cambridge: Cambridge University Press, 1997.

Menninghaus, Winfried. *Disgust: Theory and History of a Strong Sensation*. Translated by Howard Eiland and Joel Golb. Albany: SUNY Press, 2003.
Menninghaus, Winfried. *In Praise of Nonsense: Kant and Bluebeard*. Translated by Henry Pickford. Stanford: Stanford University Press, 1999.
Menninghaus, Winfried. "Kant über ‚Unsinn', ‚Lachen' und ‚Laune.'" *Deutsche Vierteljahresschrift für Philosophie und Geistesgeschichte* 68 (1994): 263–86.
Menninghaus, Winfried. "Le mouvement du rire chez Kant." *Dix-huitième siècle* 32 (2000): 265–77.
Menninghaus, Winfried. *Lob des Unsinns: Über Kant, Tieck und Blaubart*. Frankfurt am Main: Suhrkamp, 1995.
Menninghaus, Winfried, Isabel Bohrn, Ulrike Altmann, Oliver Lubrich, and Arthur Jacobs. "Sounds Funny? Humor Effects of Phonological and Prosodic Figures of Speech." *Psychology of Aesthetics, Creativity, and the Arts* 8, no. 1 (2014): 71–6.
Meredith, James Creed, trans. *Kant's Critique of Aesthetic Judgment*. Oxford: Clarendon, 1911.
Morreall, John. "Humor and Aesthetic Education." *Journal of Aesthetic Education* 15, no. 1 (1981): 55–70.
Morreall, John. "Philosophy of Humor." *The Stanford Encyclopedia of Philosophy* (Winter 2016 Edition). Edited by Edward N. Zalta. https://plato.stanford.edu/archives/win2016/entries/humor/ [accessed October 20, 2019]
Morreall, John. "The Rejection of Humor in Western Thought." *Philosophy East and West* 39, no. 3 (1989): 243–65.
Morreall, John, ed. *The Philosophy of Laughter and Humor*. Albany: State University of New York Press, 1987.
Munro, D. H. *The Argument of Laughter*. South Bend: University of Notre Dame Press, 1963.
Murray, Francis, ed. *World's Wildest Animal Jokes*. New York: Sterling Publishing, 1992.
Naragon, Steve. "Kant in the Classroom." https://users.manchester.edu/Facstaff/SSNaragon/Kant/Lectures/lecturesIntro.htm [accessed August 19, 2019]
Nichols, Stephen G. "Laughter as Gesture: Hilarity and the Anti-Sublime." *Neohelicon* 32, no. 2 (2005): 375–89.
Nietzsche, Friedrich. *Basic Writings of Nietzsche*. Translated and edited by Walter Kaufmann. New York: Random House, 1992.
Nietzsche, Friedrich. *The Portable Nietzsche*. Translated and edited by Walter Kaufmann. New York: Penguin, 1982.
Olson, Michael J. "Kant on the Feeling of Health." In *Kant and the Feeling of Life*, edited by Jennifer Mensch. Albany: SUNY Press, forthcoming.
Otto, Beatrice K. *Fools are Everywhere: The Court Jester Around the World*. Chicago: University of Chicago Press, 2001.

Percival, Philip. "Comic Normativity and the Ethics of Humour." *The Monist* 88, no. 1 (2005): 93–120.

Philips, Michael. "Racist Acts and Racist Humor." *Canadian Journal of Philosophy* 14, no. 1 (1984): 75–96.

Plato. *Complete Works*. Edited by J. M. Cooper and D. S. Hutchinson. Indianapolis: Hackett, 1997.

Plutarch, *Lives, Volume IX: Demetrius and Antony. Pyrrhus and Gaius Marius*. Translated by Bernadotte Perrin. Cambridge, MA: Harvard University Press, 1920.

Pollack, John. *The Pun Also Rises: How the Humble Pun Revolutionized Language, Changed History, and Made Wordplay More Than Some Antics*. New York: Penguin, 2011.

Provenza, Paul, and Dan Dion. *Satiristas: Comedians, Contrarians, Raconteurs and Vulgarians*. New York: It Books, 2010.

Provine, Robert R. *Laughter: A Scientific Investigation*. New York: Viking, 2000.

Recki, Birgit. "So lachen wir. Wie Immanuel Kant Leib und Seele zusammenhält." In *Kants Schlüssel zur Kritik des Geschmacks. Ästhetische Erfahrung heute – Studien zur Aktualität von Kants "Kritik der Urteilskraft,"* edited by Ursula Francke, 177–87. Hamburg: Meiner, 2000.

Rink, Friedrich Theodor. *Ansichten aus Immanuel Kant's Leben*. Königsberg: Göbbels and Unzer, 1805.

Ritzel, Wolfgang. "Kant über den Witz und Kants Witz." *Kant-Studien* 82, no. 1 (1991): 102–9.

Sánchez Madrid, Nuria. "Prudence and the Rules for Guiding Life. The Development of the Pragmatic Normativity in Kant's *Lectures on Anthropology* (Collins, Parow, Friedländer, Mesnchenkunde, Busolt)." In *Kant's Lectures / Kants Vorlesungen*, edited by Bernd Dörfinger, Claudio La Rocca, Robert B. Louden, and Ubirajara Marques Rancan de Azevedo, 163–76. Berlin: Walter de Gruyter, 2015.

Sánchez Rodríguez, Manuel. "Ingenio, Uso Hipotético de la Razón y Juicio Reflexionante en la Filosofía de Kant." *Anales del Seminario de Historia de la Filosofía* 29, no. 2 (2012): 577–92.

Sánchez Rodríguez, Manuel. "Witz und reflektierende Urteilskraft in Kants Philosophie." In *Kant und die Philosophie in weltbürgerlicher Absicht*, vol. 4, edited by Stefano Bacin, Alfredo Ferrarin, Claudio La Rocca, and Margit Ruffing, 487–96. Berlin: Walter de Gruyter, 2013.

Schopenhauer, Arthur. *The World as Will and Representation*. 2 vols. Translated by E. F. J. Payne. New York: Dover, 1969.

Scruton, Roger. "Laughter." In *The Philosophy of Laughter and Humor*, edited by John Morreall, 156–71. Albany: State University of New York Press, 1987.

Sensen, Oliver. "The Supreme Principle of Morality." In *Reading Kant's Lectures*, edited by Robert R. Clewis, 179–99. Berlin: de Gruyter, 2015.

Shaftesbury, Third Earl of. *Sensus Communis: An Essay on the Freedom of Wit and Humour*. London: Egbert Sanger, 1709.

Shakespeare, William. *Julius Caesar*. Edited by Burton Raffel. New Haven: Yale University Press, 2006.
Sharpe, Robert. "Seven Reasons Why Amusement Is an Emotion." *Journal of Value Inquiry* 9, no. 3 (1975): 201–3.
Shaw, Joshua. "Philosophy of Humor." *Philosophy Compass* 5, no. 2 (2010): 112–26.
Shell, Susan Meld. *The Embodiment of Reason: Kant on Spirit, Generation, and Community*. Chicago: Chicago University Press, 1996.
Silva, Fernando M. F. "'Zum Erfinden wird Witz erfordert'. On the Evolution of the Concept of 'Witz' in Kant's Anthropology Lectures." In *Kant's Lectures / Kants Vorlesungen*, edited by Bernd Dörfinger, Claudio La Rocca, Robert B. Louden, and Ubirajara Marques Rancan de Azevedo, 121–32. Berlin: Walter de Gruyter, 2015.
Smuts, Aaron. "Do Moral Flaws Enhance Amusement?" *American Philosophical Quarterly* 46, no. 2 (2009): 151–62.
Smuts, Aaron. "The Ethics of Humor: Can Your Sense of Humor Be Wrong?" *Ethical Theory and Moral Practice* 13, no. 3 (2010): 333–47.
Spencer, Herbert. "On the Physiology of Laughter." In *Essays on Education and Kindred Subjects*, 298–309. London: J. M. Dent & Sons, 1911.
Spinoza, Benedict de. *Tractatus Theologico-Politicus*, in *The Chief Works of Benedict de Spinoza*, vol. 1. Translated by R. H. M. Elwes. London: George Bell & Sons, 1891.
Sterne, Laurence. *The Life and Opinions of Tristram Shandy, Gentleman*. New York: George Routledge and Sons, 1886.
Suzuki, Márcio. "Des Herrn Professors Kants Paradoxon des Comoedianten." *Kant-Studien* 109, no. 3 (2018): 395–418.
Swabey, Marie. "The Comic as Nonsense, Sadism, or Incongruity." *Journal of Philosophy* 55, no. 19 (1958): 819–33.
Swift, Jonathan. *Volume XX of the Author's Works, Containing, The Tale of A Tub*. Dublin: George Faulkner, 1771.
Swift, Paul. "In-jestion: Intestinal Laughter in Kant and Nietzsche." *International Studies in Philosophy* 27, no. 1 (1995): 97–103.
Townsend, Dabney, ed. *Eighteenth-Century British Aesthetics*. Amityville: Baywood Publishing, 1999.
Verwoerd, Wilhelm, and Melanie Verwoerd. "On the Injustice of (Un)Just Joking." *Agenda: Empowering Women for Gender Equity* 10, no. 23 (1994): 67–78.
Voltaire. *Candide and Other Stories*. Translated by Roger Pearson. Oxford: Oxford University Press, 2008.
Voltaire. *The History of the Voyages of Scarmentado. A Satire*. London: Paul Vaillant, 1757.
Warda, Arthur. *Immanuel Kants Bücher. Mit einer getreuen Nachbildung des bisher einzigen bekannten Abzuges des Versteigerungskataloges der Bibliothek Kants*. Berlin: Martin Breslauer, 1922.

Weems, Scott. *Ha! The Science of When We Laugh and Why*. New York: Basic Books, 2014.
Wicks, Robert. *Kant on Judgment*. London: Routledge, 2007.
Wiesenthal, Simon. *The Sunflower: On the Possibilities and Limits of Forgiveness*. Translated by H. A. Pichler. New York: Schocken Books, 1997.
Wilde, Oscar. *The Wit and Wisdom of Oscar Wilde*. Edited by Ralph Keyes. New York: Gramercy Books, 1999.
Wilson, Christopher P. *Jokes: Form, Content, Use and Function*. London and New York: Academic Press, 1979.
Wilson, Holly. "Kant's *Anthropology* as *Klugheitslehre*." *Con-Textos Kantianos: International Journal of Philosophy* 3 (2016): 122–38.
Wilson, Holly. *Kant's Pragmatic Anthropology: Its Origin, Meaning, and Critical Significance*. State University of New York Press, 2006.
Winegar, Reed. "Good Sense, Art, and Morality in Hume's 'Of the Standard of Taste'." *Journal of Scottish Philosophy* 9, no. 1 (2011): 17–35.
Wolff, Christian. *Psychologia empirica*. Frankfurt and Leipzig: officina libraria Rengeriana, 1732.
Wollstonecraft, Mary. *A Vindication of the Rights of Men*. In *The Sublime Reader*, edited by Robert R. Clewis, 118–21. London: Bloomsbury, 2019.
Woodcock, Scott. "Comic Immoralism and Relatively Funny Jokes." *Journal of Applied Philosophy* 32, no. 2 (2015): 203–16.
Young, Edward. *The Universal Passion, Satire 1*. London: J. Roberts, 1725.
Zammito, John. *The Genesis of Kant's* Critique of Judgment. Chicago: University of Chicago Press, 1992.
Zammito, John. *Kant, Herder, and the Birth of Anthropology*. University of Chicago Press, 2002.
Zammito, John. "The 'Sublime', the 'Supersensible Substrate', and 'Spirit'—Intuitions of the Ultimate in Kant's *Third Critique*." In *Kant on Intuition: Western and Asian Perspectives on Transcendental Idealism*, edited by Stephen Palmquist, 139–58. London: Routledge, 2019.
Žižek, Slavoj. *Žižek's Jokes (Did You Hear the One about Hegel and Negation?)*. Edited by Audun Mortensen. Cambridge: MIT Press, 2014.

Index

Abelard and the ox joke
    Kant's, 58, 75, 83, 147, 159
ableism, 68, 86
absurdity, 6, 11, 18, 23, 36, 63, 85, 90
    see also the incongruous
Addison, Joseph, 25, 28, 143, 161
aesthetic experience
    vs. aesthetic judgment, 46
    definition of, 45
    and Kant's system, 65
aesthetic ideas
    and caprice, 35
    definition of, 23–4
    and imagination, 50
    play with, 24–5, 45–8, 51–4, 57, 59
    and transcendental philosophy, 62, 64
aesthetic judgment
    as based on judging, 47–51
    of beauty and sublimity, 45, 51, 60
    as irreducible to concepts, 60, 102
    and laughter, 47–8, 50, 52, 54, 58
    and moral judgment, 71
    and necessity, 60
    pure, 38, 45
    agreeable vs. pure, 26, 47, 50, 62
affect
    definition of, 46
    laughter as, 15, 17, 46–8, 50–1, 62, 73
    in music, 167
    play of, 39
    Stoic control of, 171
    as in tension with judgment, 46
    and theater, 41
ageism, 68, 163
agreeable arts, 26–7, 167
    see also arts
agreeable
    vs. intellectual, 26, 50
    judgment of the, 46–8
    laughter as, 47–8, 59, 62, 135
    see also pleasure
ancient Greeks, 7, 38, 171
Anthropology from a Pragmatic Point of View
    on comedy, 40
    on release, 17
    on wit, 30
anthropology
    lectures on, 79, 155
    and transcendental philosophy, 62
Aristotle, 7–8, 12, 76, 123, 131
arts
    agreeable, 26, 167
    fine, 25–6, 82
    of laughter, 25–7
attitude endorsement theory, 90

Banki, Peter, 59
Baumgarten, Alexander Gottlieb, 27

bear joke, 6
Beattie, James, 11
beauty
　human, 165
　Kant's theory of, 51–2
　in poetry, 57–8
　relation to humor, 53–9
　as symbol of morality, 59, 65, 82
beer, 15, 87–8, 135
Bergmann, Merrie, 89–91, 98
Bergson, Henri, 9–10, 86
body
　interaction of the, with the mind, 123, 151
　movement of the, in comic amusement, 5, 15–19, 22, 56, 135, 159
Boleyn, Anne, 179
Borch-Jacobsen, Mikkel, 56, 210n.50
Brandt, Reinhard, 29
buffoon, 20, 77, 153
Burke, Edmund, 139
Butler, Samuel, 4, 31, 37, 58, 76
　jokes from, 115, 149, 155

Candide (Voltaire), 188n.6
caprice (*Laune*), description of, 34–7
　and the French, 41
　on translation of, 204n.186
Cardelli, Mascia, 62
Carroll, Noël, 12, 18, 84, 86, 92
categorical imperative, 67–8, 70, 72, 87
　see also moral law
causation (cause and effect)
　in laughter, 22–3, 197n.115
Chaplin, Charlie, 42
Châtelet, Marquise de, 139
Cicero, 12, 117, 143
clowning, 41
　see also pantomime
cognitions
　play of, 26, 39–40
Cohen, Alix, 61, 71

Cohen, Ted, 70, 95
comedy (literary genre) 4, 12, 37–43
comic amusement
　and morality, 69–70
　relation to humor, 5–7, 10, 12, 194n.69
comic
　amoralism, 69–70
　ethicism, 69–70
　immoralism, 69–70
concepts
　and humor, 9, 11, 23–5, 60, 102, 127
contradiction
　in humor, 11, 36, 127
contrast
　as antithesis, 32
　as incongruity, 11, 34, 36–7, 117
　see also the incongruous
conversion (antithesis), 143
　see also contrast
Critchley, Simon, 18, 48, 87, 149
Critique of the Power of Judgment
　as not discussing theatrical comedy, 38
　on the power of judgment, 28–30
　reasons for writing, 61
　structure of, 64
　on the three jokes in, 31, 76
Critique of Practical Reason, 3, 31, 175
Critique of Pure Reason, 3, 102, 151
　on causality, 197n.115

Dacier, Anne, 139
deduction
　of *a priori* validity of judgments of beauty, 53
Descartes, René, 8, 45, 61, 149
determinate
　jokes as not, 24
diaphragm, 16–18, 42, 56, 62, 89, 135, 159
　see also intestines
Diderot, Denis, 38

dignity, 68, 71–3, 84, 87, 94, 98, 102
dinner parties, 4, 61, 71, 167
   phases of, 79, 84, 99, 159
disgust, 31–3, 117, 159, 163
   and humor 230n.10
   moral, 74
   see also ugliness
disinterestedness
   as absorbed attention, 107
   as condition of comically amused response to joking, 15, 58–9, 62, 82, 84–5
   as criterion of pure aesthetic judgment, 46, 51
   and the play frame, 69, 92
dualism (mind/body), 45, 59, 61, 64, 123
duties
   to self, 20, 74, 80, 82, 93–4
   of virtue, 72

Eagleton, Terry, 12, 18, 61, 78
emotion, 40–1, 45–6, 85–6, 171
enthusiasm (*Enthusiasmus*), 211n.60
Epicureans, 171–2
ethical constraints, 66, 68–75, 89, 92, 99
Ethical Principle, 68, 92–4, 96, 98, 102
ethical theory
   review of Kant's, 67–9
ethicism
   as term for Kant's theory, 66, 69–83, 92
   see also soft ethicism
ethnic jokes
   Kant's, 135, 137

fashion, 20, 161
feeling
   as affect, 46, 167, 171
   of freedom, 52, 56, 65
   as ground of pure aesthetic judgment, 48
   of health, 24, 64
   of life, 39, 63–4
   moral, 20, 139–40
   for the ridiculous, 97
   for virtue, 81
Fielding, Henry, 4, 36, 76, 117
form
   of jokes, 5–6
   in jokes, 57–8
   in poetry, 57–8
found humor, 5, 9, 33–4
Franklin, Benjamin, 149
free judging
   distinguished from adherent judging, 195n.76
free play
   with aesthetic ideas, 23–5
   in beauty, 48, 52, 59
   in humor, 21–5, 62, 85
   of sensations, 47
   of thoughts, 22, 25, 53
   in wit, 27
freedom
   of imagination, 59, 82
   practical, 175, 177
French, the
   jokes involving, 121, 137
   as lighthearted, 32–3
   and tragedy, 41
Freud jokes
   fear and sex, 6
   gallows humor, 179–80
Freud, Sigmund, 13–14, 54–5, 86
Friedrich II (of Prussia), 77
   quip to Sulzer, 113
friendship, 131
   between the Indian and the Englishman, 87, 135

gallows humor, 179
games, 27, 39, 84, 159, 167, 169
gender, 66, 73, 101, 140
   in the Heidegger joke, 163
genius, 35
Gerard, Alexander, 11

German school philosophy
    and wit, 27, 30
Giamario, Patrick, 53–4, 87
Gimbel, Steven, 86, 89
Godfrey, F. la T., 23–4, 47–8, 55, 60, 63, 71, 85
Goethe, Johann, 11
Groundwork of the Metaphysics of Morals, 68, 92
group membership, 93–4, 137
Guyer, Paul
    two-act account of aesthetic judgment, 48, 208n.19

Hamann, Johann, 4, 39
harm
    by the buffoon, 153
    and ethics, 68
    of genuine lying, 68
    and joking, 73, 75, 77, 84, 88, 90, 92, 94, 96, 102
    and racism, 68, 87–8
harmless ridicule, 19–21, 43, 100
    see also ridicule
harmlessness
    as condition of humor, 13, 19, 69, 73, 84, 92, 100, 121
    of diversions, 169
    of joking lies, 83
    see also disinterestedness
harmony of imagination and understanding, 22–3, 48, 52, 57, 62
Hegel, G. W. F., 38
Heidegger, Johann Jacob, 163
Heine, Heinrich, 3
Herder, Johann, 83
Hippel, Theodore, 4, 39
history
    Kant's philosophy of, 113
Hobbes, Thomas, 8, 10, 78
honest man
    Abelard as, 147
    thought experiment involving an, 179

horses, 169, 175
Hounsokou, Annie, 25, 36, 53–4, 64–5
Hudibras (Samuel Butler), 37, 58, 115, 149, 155
Hume, David, 39–40, 97–8
humor
    and community, 65, 76–83
    and coping, 6
    definition of, 5
    function of, 6, 78
    judgment of, 46, 58
    and Kant's system, 38, 59–65
    physiological accounts of, 8, 13–14, 25–6, 42–3, 59
    theories of, 4–14
Hutcheson, Francis, 8, 10, 61, 77, 85

idea of reason, 24
illusion
    in jokes and poems, 57
    in mental play with humor, 16–17, 22, 24–5, 56, 63
    in social interactions, 79–81
imagination
    and aesthetic ideas, 24, 50, 59
    entertainment in, 91, 93
    freedom of, 59
    in harmony with understanding, 22–3, 48, 52, 57, 62
    in puns and word play, 57
    in sublime experiences, 52
imaginative resistance, 85
    in watching tragedy, 41
immediacy
    of beauty and humor, 59, 82
inclination, 79, 167, 172, 177
incongruity theory, 9–12
    Kant's, 15–16, 109
incongruous, the, 10–11, 18, 36, 63
indeterminate
    jokes as, 24–5
India
    jokes related to, 15, 87–8, 107, 135

infinite, the
    in humor, 192n.50, 198n.127
innocent joking
    as harmless ridicule, 19–21, 43,
        100
    Kant's, 53, 86, 102
intentions
    of joke teller, 88, 90, 92, 96, 101–2
intersubjectivity, 49, 51, 59–60, 82
    see also universality
intestines, 8, 16, 24, 42, 89
    see also diaphragm
invented humor, 5
irony, 11, 198n.127

Jean Paul (Richter), 192n.50
jest, see joke, jokes, and joking
Johnson, Samuel, 31, 33, 143–4
joke about Austrians, 127
joke
    and audience, 41–2, 67, 75, 82,
        92–3, 101–2, 109
    content, 16, 18, 24, 32, 43, 49,
        85, 102
    context, 67, 82–3, 86, 89, 92–3,
        95–6, 101–2, 139
    moral content of, 70, 75–6, 83,
        87, 92–3, 95–6, 155
    teller, 7, 67, 90, 92, 94–6, 101–2
    timing, 92, 101–2
jokes about Germans, 95, 137
jokes
    and aesthetic ideas, 24–5
    disagreements about, 58, 60
    kinds of, 5, 184n.12, 212n.69,
        213n.5
    with a point, 147, 149, 151, 153,
        155
    structure of, 5, 58
joking
    function of, 5–6, 78
    guidelines for appropriateness of,
        93–5, 101–2
    permissibility of, 20–1, 70, 73,
        89–96

judging
    vs. judgment, 48–50
judgment, the faculty of the power of
        (*Urteilskraft*)
    72, 82, 102
    as ability to compare and
        distinguish, 28–9
    reflecting vs. determining, 28–30
judgment
    aesthetic, 26, 38, 44–8, 50–4,
        60
    vs. experience, 46
    mistaken, 18, 23
    moral, 71
    synthetic *a priori*, 38, 62

Kant scholar joke, 6
Kant scholarship on humor
    typology of, 44
Kierkegaard, Søren, 11

La Rocca, Claudio, 29
Labat, Jean-Baptiste, 97–8
latitude (*Spielraum*), 32, 66, 72–3,
        83
laughter
    as affect, 15, 17, 46–8, 50–1, 62,
        73
    definition of, 5
    malicious vs. wholesome, 7,
        19–21, 66, 73
    as purgative, 18, 151
law
    empirical, 29
    moral, 61, 67–9, 75, 79, 81,
        177
    of nature, 64
Leibniz, Gottfried, 27
    Voltaire's joke about, 188n.6
Lessing, Gotthold, 11, 38–9
liar's paradox, 22, 25, 127
life
    feeling of, 39, 63–4
Locke, John, 28
logical paradoxes, 22, 25, 127

lying
    and ethics, 34, 68, 72, 79
    and joking, 75, 83, 91, 127, 147
    see also liar's paradox

Makkreel, Rudolf, 64
Marmysz, John, 18, 33, 53, 55–6
Martin, Steve, 127, 149
Marx Brothers, 118, 127
maxims, 3, 68, 82
Meier, Georg, 27
Mendelssohn, Moses, 11, 85
Menninghaus, Winfried, 45
mental play theory
    Kant's, 21–5
Meredith, James, 48, 53, 55, 63
metaphysics
    and humor, 63
Metaphysics of Morals
    and ridicule, 20
    and the social virtues, 80
misunderstanding
    as cause of amusement, 23, 25, 56–7, 63, 117
Molière, 38–9
moral education, 61, 179
moral feeling, 20
moral law, 61, 67–9, 75, 79, 81, 177
morality
    as symbolized by beauty, 59, 65, 82
Morreall, John, 86
music, 24, 26–7, 167, 199n.133

naiveté, 33–4, 37, 64, 88
nature and freedom
    reconciliation of, 53, 61, 64
Nichols, Stephen, 22–3, 53–4, 56
Nietzsche, Friedrich, 8, 13, 18, 151
nonsense, 15
norm, 9, 15, 69, 78, 90, 139
normativity, 48, 50–1, 58–9
nothing
    disappearance into, 15–17, 33–4, 55–6, 84, 88, 109, 121, 135, 149
    table of the, Kant's, 195n.74
    thought in a joke, 24

Observations on the Feeling of the Beautiful and Sublime
    on comedy and tragedy, 38–9
    on dignity, 84, 98
    on empty wit, 31, 33
    on the ethical limits to humor, 74
    joke from, 139
    racist claim in, 96–7
    on women, 99–101, 139
organisms, 62
originality, 35, 77, 111
oscillation
    in laughter, 16–17, 22, 56, 135
    in the sublime, 52, 56, 65

pantomime, 41–2
paradox, 22–3, 25, 37, 127
    see also contradiction
philosophy
    political, 77–8, 113, 172
physiognomy, 123
Plato, 7, 19, 39, 55, 75, 109
play (*Spiel*)
    of aesthetic ideas, 62
    with ideas, 32
    of representations, 14–15, 22
    of thoughts, 14, 17, 22, 47, 50–1, 53, 62, 167
play frame, 86, 96, 98, 101–2
    see also latitude
pleasure, 13, 17, 23, 26, 31–2, 40, 46–52, 55–6, 78, 151
    see also agreeable
Poetics (Aristotle), 7, 8
poetry
    as analogous to jokes, 57–8
    form in, 57–8
politics
    and humor, 77–8, 111, 113, 121

Pope, Alexander, 4, 31, 37
practical freedom, 52, 65, 175, 177
practical jokes, 92
　and April Fool's, 92
profound wit
　as garb for moral ideas, 31, 33
provisional judgment, 29, 201n.153
psychoanalysis, 13
　see also Freud
punch line, 15–16, 18, 24, 58, 87–8, 90, 135
punching up, 93–5, 121
puns, 9, 14, 25, 32, 57–8, 60, 117–18, 143
　see also word play
pure
　aesthetic judgment, 38, 45–8, 50–2, 54, 58–60, 62, 64–5
purposiveness (finality), 17, 46, 51, 64

Rabelais, François, 4, 75, 149, 159
race, 66, 101
racism, 7, 66, 68, 86–8, 92–4, 96–8, 101, 135
ragout of folly, 75, 159
reason
　combined with wit, 32, 42, 143, 159, 198n.128
　efficacy of, 45, 61, 63, 65
　ideas of, 24
　as taking an interest, 21, 42, 45, 62, 65
Recki, Birgit, 64
reflecting power of judgment, 28–30
reflection
　first-order vs. second-order, 49–51, 109
release theory, 12–14
　Kant's, 16–19
ridicule
　and disgust, 163
　of friends, 37
　harmful, 66, 92, 163
　harmless, 19–21, 43, 100
　as reforming, 36, 65, 76, 94, 151
　in superiority theory, 7–9
Rousseau, Jean-Jacques, 39, 99, 172

satire
　function of, 76, 78
　literary, 21, 31–2, 35–6, 65, 111, 115, 149, 153
　and women, 100
scatological humor, 149
schadenfreude, 8, 19
Schopenhauer, Arthur, 11, 14, 55
　joke by, 127
Scruton, Roger, 8
sensations
　and affect 46–7
　play of, 22, 26–7, 40, 47, 167
sex (sexuality), 13, 73–4, 99, 125
　Freud's joke about, 6
　Kant's anecdote about, 177
sexism, 33, 66, 68, 86, 90–101
　jokes with, 139, 143, 163
sexist jokes, 139, 143, 163
Shaftesbury, Earl of (Anthony Ashley Cooper), 12, 21, 78, 107
Silva, Fernando, 57
Skeptics (Greek), 171–2
sociability, 76–7, 79, 81–2
　as garment for morality, 79
soft ethicism
　as term for Kant's theory, 66, 83–6
Spencer, Herbert, 13–14
spirit, 35, 63–4
spirited, 24–5, 32
spouse jokes, 143, 223n.128
standup comedy, 25, 35, 86
Steele, Richard, 161, 175
Sterne, Lawrence, 4, 61, 77, 123, 169
Stoics, 171–2
Stuffed Aunt joke
　Kant's, 117

sublime, the
    Kant's theory of, 39, 52
Sulzer, Johann, 77, 113
superficial wit, 30–3
superiority theory, 7–9
    Kant's, 19–21, 37, 43, 56
supersensible, the, 45, 53, 64
Swift, Jonathan, 4, 77, 111, 167
symbol, 59, 65, 82
synthetic *a priori*, 38, 62
system
    humor and Kant's, 45, 53, 59, 61, 64

taste
    aftertaste, 40–1
    bad, 20, 73, 77, 94, 159
    for comedy, 40
    and disgust, 230n.10
    faculty of, 35, 107
    and laughter, 55, 63, 230n.10
    ordinary, 32
    social, 71, 82
    true, 161
teasing
    as having ethical limits, 73
    light, 19, 21, 37, 42–3, 86, 92
    as a skill, 72
    and women, 90, 99–100
    see also ridicule
teleology, 53, 62, 64
Terrasson joke
    Kant's, 73, 215n.29
The Texan and the graduate joke, 7
thing-in-itself, 63
tragedy, 12, 38–41
transcendental philosophy, 30, 48, 54
    and anthropology, 62
Tristram Shandy (Laurence Sterne), 4, 61, 77, 123, 169
Trublet, Nicolas, 31–3, 117
truth, 21, 33, 36, 71, 100, 115

Two Moneylenders joke
    Kant's, 95, 137

ugliness, 163, 165
understanding, the faculty of
    in beauty, 52
    in laughter, 15–16, 22–4, 45, 48, 50, 54, 56–7, 62–3
    maxims of, 82
    and play, 169
    and wit, 28, 32
    see also harmony of imagination and understanding
universality, 42, 48, 51

validity
    a priori, 53
    intersubjective, 51, 60
vice, 36, 76, 111, 172
viscera, 17, 56
    see also diaphragm
Voltaire, 4, 31–2, 38–9, 125, 139, 153
    "noses-exist-for-spectacles" joke, 188n.6
vulgarity, 74, 127

Wicks, Robert, 44, 84
Wilde, Oscar, 118, 127
wit (*Witz*)
    as ability to find similarities (*ingenium*), 27–30
    as ability to produce humor, 5
    as poeticizing, 57
    superficial vs. profound, 30–3
witticism, 5, 32, 57
Wolff, Christian, 11, 27
word play, 14, 25, 31, 57–8, 117
    see also puns

Young, Edward, 4, 31

Zammito, John, 63

www.ingramcontent.com/pod-product-compliance
Lightning Source LLC
Chambersburg PA
CBHW052105230426
43671CB00011B/1938